Dr. Laurence B.

MISGOD'ED
A Roadmap of Guidance and
Misguidance in the Abrahamic Religions

To
THE LOVERS OF TRUTH,
THE
FRIENDS OF FREE INQUIRY;
TO THOSE WHO DARE,
IN THE FACE OF CHURCH ESTABLISHMENTS,
OF
ORTHODOX DENUNCIATIONS,
AND OF
LUKEWARM, TIME-SERVINGCHRISTIANS,
TO OPENLY PROFESS
WHAT THEY BELIEVE TO BE TRUE:
THIS VOLUME IS INSCRIBED.

Dedication by the Editor of:

*An Enquiry into the Opinions of the
Christian Writers of the Three First
Centuries Concerning the Person of
Jesus Christ,*

by Gilbert Wakefield, B.A., 1824

– The Peace Prayer of St. Francis–

Lord, make me an instrument of your peace;
Where there is hatred, let me sow love;
Where there is injury, pardon;
Where there is doubt, faith;
Where there is despair, hope;
Where there is darkness, light;
And where there is sadness, joy.
Grant that I may not so much seek to be consoled as to console;
To be understood as to understand;
To be loved as to love;
For it is in giving that we receive;
It is in pardoning that we are pardoned;
And it is in dying that we are born to eternal life.

Table of Contents

– Notes on Scriptural Sources and Translations –

Biblical quotes in the following work, unless otherwise noted, are taken from the New King James Version. The reason for selecting this version of the Bible does not relate to the degree of scriptural fidelity, which is debatable, but rather to the popularity of the text. In English-speaking countries, the 1611 edition of the King James Version is the most widely read translation of the Bible. The *New* King James Version (NKJV) grew from an effort to render the 1611 translation more accessible to modern readers, tossing the *thees* and *thous* out the window. Unfortunately, little effort has been made to reconcile differences between the 1611 King James Version and the Sinaiticus and Vaticanus codices, which were discovered in the 1800's and contain the oldest and most authoritative New Testament manuscripts found to date. Furthermore, "most of the important copies of the Greek gospels have been 'unearthed' – mostly in museums, monasteries, and church archives – in the nineteenth and twentieth centuries."[1]Now that these texts are available, one can reasonably expect to see their influence upon more modern Bible translations.This is not the case in the New King James Version, which retains verses and passages in conflict with the most ancient and respected New Testament manuscripts. Therefore, while this book predominantly cites the New King James Version in the interest of satisfying the Protestant majority of Western Christianity, a complementary version is employed where greater scholastic accuracy is required.

7

The New Revised Standard Version (NRSV) fills this gap. Like its predecessor, the Revised Standard Version (RSV), the NRSV is an ecumenical collaboration, reflected in its three separate Protestant, Roman Catholic, and Eastern Orthodox editions. More importantly, the NRSV reflects modern biblical scholarship hitherto unavailable. Indeed, the dust had barely been blown off the Dead Sea Scrolls when the RSV translation of the Old Testament was first published in 1946. For these reasons, the NRSV has effectively replaced the Revised Standard Versionand enjoys the broadest acceptance of all Bible translations.

Quotations from the *World Bibliography of Translations of the Meanings of the Holy Qur'an* (hereafter TMQ), unless otherwise noted, are taken from Abdullah Yusuf Ali's *The Holy Qur'an: Translation and Commentary*. Where more exacting translation is required, those of Saheeh International or of Muhammad Al-Hilali and Muhammad Khan (i.e., *The Noble Qur'an*) are employed.

For those who question the use of multiple translations, it should be said that no language, and most especially one as complex as Arabic, can be translated with complete accuracy. As orientalist and translator Alfred Guillaume stated, "The Qur'an is one of the world's classics which cannot be translated without grave loss."[2] This opinion is echoed by A. J. Arberry, translator and author of *The Koran Interpreted:*"I have conceded the relevancy of the orthodox Muslim view . . . that the Koran is untranslatable."[3]

Hence the need for multiple translations of the Qur'an, for no single translation, and some would say no collection of translations, can adequately convey the meaning of the original.

8

– Introduction –

"Where shall I begin, please your Majesty?" he asked.

"Begin at the beginning," the King said, gravely, *"and go on till you come to the end: then stop."*

—Lewis Carroll, *Alice's Adventures in Wonderland*

Recent decades have witnessed a society-wide shift with regard to the values by which truth and quality are measured. In their homes and workplaces to community centers and town halls, our ancestors discussed subjects of depth and importance, vital issues such as political ethics, social mores and the practical limits of science, laws and religion. Jump forward to the modern world, and conversations typically focus on relationships, money, sports and entertainment. Whereas previous generations spent evenings in forums of discourse, analysis and intellectual exchange, most citizens of today subject themselves to vacuous hours of media brainwashing by that master of hypnosis, the television.

The results can be seen in every aspect of modern life. Salesmanship has come to rely less on factual analysis than on stylized presentation. Political offices are no longer won and lost on the basis of leadership qualities, social consciousness and moral example, but on photo ops and sound bites. News, both local and international, is "spun" to satisfy social and political agendas more than to convey events as they actually occurred.

Nowadays the general public is less reliant upon facts and more influenced by emotional ploys, even when false. Nowhere is this more evident than in religion, where the beliefs of billions have been swayed more by the media than by their own scripture. The image of Moses portrayed in the animated film, *The Prince of Egypt*, replaces previous generations' mental picture of Charlton Heston in Cecil B. DeMille's *The Ten Commandments*. Yet both movies present a Hollywoodized Moses with dynamic oratory skills, ignoring the prophet's own assessment on that score: "O my Lord, I *am* not eloquent, neither before nor since You have spoken to Your servant; but I *am* slow of speech and slow of tongue" (Exodus 4:10). Recent representations of Jesus Christ have similarly corrupted imaginations, with imagery that spans the spectrum from the rock opera *Jesus Christ Superstar* to accounts of this great messenger of God having married Mary Magdalene.

Spinning off from this swirl of generational trends, many religions have emerged with a new focus—that of style and emotional appeal. Rational analysis and theological discussion have been buried beneath an avalanche of popularized slogans and designer dogma. In this manner, hearts and souls are being seduced more by salesmanship than by truth.

But that is not what this book is about.

Throughout time, there have always been honorable individuals who refused to base religious beliefs upon such frail foundations as the whims of others, the fads of peers, the traditions of family, or even the convictions of seemingly sincere and pious clergy. These individuals, with a genuine hunger for the truth, boldly cross the currents of cultural convention. They demand answers to well-considered questions, and seek understanding of the history of revelation and man.

And *that* is what this book is about—the questions, the history, the revelation, and most of all, the answers.

This is the first of two books designed to analyze the scriptural foundation of the three Abrahamic faiths of Judaism, Christianity and Islam. In doing so, I hope to help readers identify the valid links in the chain of revelation and differentiate the truth of God's guidance from the falsehoods of human corruption.

The methodology and conclusions drawn herein are founded upon respected scholastic research—as well as common sense. With regard to methodology, there is no substitute for shaking the trees from which different faiths claim to harvest fruits of sacred knowledge, and seeing what falls out. Analysis of the foundation of Christian doctrines has become very popular recently, and many respected scholars have discovered that much of Christian canon derives from non-biblical sources. The real shock is that many of these non-biblical sources actually *contradict* the teachings of Jesus Christ. For example, nowhere in the foundational manuscripts of the New Testament does Jesus Christ refer to himself as a literalSon of God. He identifies himself as the Son of Man eighty-eight times, but not once as a Son of God in a literal, begotten and not made sense.

Nor does Jesus Christ espouse the Trinity. In fact, in three separate passages he teaches the exact opposite, defining God as One—never as a Trinity.

Here we have two critical elements of Christian belief. The first concerns the nature of Jesus, and the second the nature of the Creator. In both cases, Trinitarian dogma was derived not from the record of what Jesus said or taught, but from what others said or taught. Jesus was quoted as having called himself the Son of Man; others claimed he was the Son of God. Jesus

11

taught God is One; others proposed God is three-in-one. Could the teachings be more opposite? And should we care? After all, Jesus died for our sins. Or so someone said. Someone, that is, but once again, not Jesus. He said no such thing.

So is there a problem here? And should we investigate it?

Only if we consider the purpose of revelation being to *reveal,* to make clear. For if that is the purpose, we must assume that God revealed the truth, Jesus conveyed the revelation, but somewhere in the chain of transmission that message got garbled. How else can we explain the fact that many basic doctrines of modern Christianityeither fail to find support in Jesus' biblical teachings or, worse yet,actually contradict them?

Hmm. Perhaps the issue *is* worth investigating.

Perhaps Christians shouldn't be surprised to find that Moses and Jesus taught the same things. After all, Christians claim that both received revelation from the same source. Now, the idea that God changed overnight from the wrathful God of the Old Testament to the forgiving God of the New Testament conveniently dismisses inconsistencies between the two revelations. But not everybody accepts that explanation. Those Christians who consider God to be perfect and never-changing should be more surprised to find differences,rather than commonalities, in the teachings of Moses and Jesus. After all, Jesus was a rabbi who lived and taught the same Old Testament Law that Moses served to convey. "Do not think that I came to destroy the Law or the Prophets," Jesus says in Matthew 5:17. "I did not come to destroy but to fulfill."

And so, an important question arises. If scriptural teachings common to Moses and Jesus suggest continuity in revelation from the Old to New Testaments, then what should

12

we make of scriptural teachings common to Moses, Jesus and Muhammad, the prophet of Islam? If not by revelation, how did Muhammad so accurately convey the true teachings of Moses and Jesus?

Not surprisingly, Christians claim plagiarism. However, as discussed in the second book of this series, historical evidence seems to negate that possibility. The New Testament was not translated into Arabic until centuries after Muhammad's death, and the oral traditions that circulated among the Arab Christians during his lifetime were considered heretical by the Christian orthodoxy. And yet the Holy Qur'an doesn't convey early Arab Christians' heretical views of Jesus, but the truth as recorded in the Bible.

So the question remains: If not through revelation, how did Muhammad convey the true teachings of Moses and Jesus? This question demands analysis, and it is this analysis that forms the substance of the sequel to this book, *God'ed*.

The eleventh-century philosopher and theologian St Anselm of Canterbury proposed in his *Proslogium:* "I do not seek to understand that I may believe, but I believe in order to understand." The proposal of *this* author is that such a statement makes about as much sense as saying, "I had to taste the sandwich before I could pick it up." The true order of priorities should be the exact opposite. Belief logically follows understanding—not the other way around. Most people demand sufficient explanation to nurse the embryo of a proposal to a formed conclusion before embracing it.

Humankind is divided. Some people are slaves to their emotions, in line with Benjamin Franklin's wry comment, "The way to see by Faith is to shut the Eye of Reason." Others demand logical explanations and rational conclusions, and side with William Adams' comment, "Faith is the continuation of reason." Such individuals expect to find the truth of God in the union of common sense, scriptural analysis, and innate understanding of the Creator.

I count myself among the latter group, and such is my approach.

Lastly, the problem with heavily referenced works such as this is that the reader doesn't always know whether it's worth flipping pages to read the endnotes. To solve this problem, endnotes containing explanatory text are denoted by the endnote number followed by (EN), like this,[36(EN)] which means, "Endnote number 36: Explanatory Note." Endnote numbers lacking the ([EN]) denotation contain purely bibliographical information.

PART I: MONOTHEISM

Men despise religion. They hate it and are afraid it may be true.

—Blaise Pascal, *Pensées*

Judaism, Christianity and Islam constitute the three Abrahamic faiths. Although familiar by name, Judaism and Christianity prove surprisingly difficult to define. But define them we must, if we are to engage in any significant analysis. Islam is the least understood and the most maligned of the Abrahamic faiths in Western civilization, but is relatively easy to define once stripped of its mystique and negative image. The pages that follow lay the foundation for subsequentdiscussion by clarifying the essence of these three Abrahamic faiths.

1 — Judaism

*The Foundation of all foundations, the pillar
supporting all wisdoms, is the recognition of the reality
of God.*

—Maimonides

The term *Jew* originated as an ethnic definition of the
descendents of the tribe of Judah, with Judaism being a
contraction of *Judah-ism*. Orthodox Judaism defines a Jew as
one born of a Jewish mother or one, independent of bloodline,
converted to the Judaic faith. More liberal movements of
Judaism (e.g., Reform) deny the necessity of the maternal
bloodline, and propose that a child born of a Jewish father is
equally considered a Jew, if raised Jewish. Although modern
definitions vary, most include, implicitly or explicitly,
adherence to Mosaic Law as expressed in the Torah and
Talmud. Historically, however, even this was not agreed upon,
for the Sadducees believed only the written law and prophets to
be binding, and rejected the Talmud.
Ideological differences divide Orthodox from
Conservative, Reform, and Reconstructionist movements, all of
which possess smaller sectarian subdivisions. Geographic
origins distinguish the Sephardim (from Spain) from the
Ashkenazi (from Central and Eastern Europe); religious/political
differences divide Zionists from non-Zionists (such as the
Neturei Karta Jews); and Hasidic Jews are dissociated from

non-Hasidic (also known as *Misnagdim*, or "opponents") on the basis of their practices, extreme religious zeal, and devotion to a dynastic leader (known as a *rebbe*).

Although considering themselves a nation, present-day Jews are not united upon culture or ethnicity, are not a race in the genetic sense of the term, and do not unanimously agree upon a creed. Nonetheless, the most widely accepted tenets of Jewish faith are probably those defined by the twelfth-century rabbi Moshe ben Maimon (Maimonides), known as his Thirteen Principles of Jewish Faith:

1. God is the Creator and Ruler of all things.
2. God is One and unique.
3. God is incorporeal, and there is nothing like unto Him.
4. God is eternal.
5. Prayer is to be directed to God alone.
6. The words of the prophets are true.
7. Moses was the greatest of the prophets.
8. The Written Torah (i.e., the Pentateuch, the first five books of the Old Testament) and Oral Torah (teachings now codified in the Mishna and Talmud) were given to Moses.
9. The Torah will never be changed, and there will never be another given by God.
10. God knows the thoughts and deeds of men.
11. God will reward the good and punish the wicked.
12. The Messiah will come.
13. The dead will be resurrected.

Other definitions of Jewish creed exist, but in general the variations are minor, and for the purposes of this book the above list is considered the most representative model.

2 — Christianity

Even if you're on the right track, you'll get run over if you just sit there.

—Will Rogers

If the term *Jewish* is difficult to define, the term *Christian* is even more fraught with problems.

One stumbling block is that early Christians considered themselves Jews, as acknowledged in the following: "The Christians did not initially think of themselves as separate from the Jewish people, though Jesus had had severe things to say about Pharisees. (But then, so has the Talmud.)"[4] Initially, the Jews clashed over acceptance of Jesus Christ as a prophet. Subsequently, a steady flow of doctrinal evolution eroded a giant crevasse between the entrenched Jews and the new sect of Christian-Jews. Yet both groups considered themselves Jewish.

Notably, Jesus never identified himself as a Christian and never claimed to have established Christianity on Earth. In fact, while the word *Christian* is encountered three times in the Bible (Acts 11:26; Acts 26:28; Peter 4:16), none of these verses use the label *Christian* in a context which bears the authority of Jesus or of God.[5]

Most significantly, there is no record of the word *Christian* ever issuing from the lips of Jesus. We read in Acts 11:26 that "the disciples were called Christians first in

18

Antioch"—which means the term *Christian* was first applied to the disciples by non-believers around 43 CE.[6](EN—Explanatory Note, as opposed to a bibliographical reference.)

It was not a polite term.

Contrary to popular belief, the term *Christian* appears to have been conceived in contempt. *Christian* is what disbelievers called the followers of Christ—a distasteful name to believers who knew themselves as Jews, following the latest in the line of Jewish prophets. And yet, that very label is now worn with pride, despite the fact that, "It is not the usual designation of the NT, which more commonly uses such terms as brethren (Acts 1.16), believers (Acts 2.44), saints (Acts 9.32), and disciples (Acts 11.26)."[7] Furthermore, with regard to the term *Christian,* "It appears to have been more widely used by pagans, and according to Tacitus it was in common use by the time of the Neronian persecution (Annals, 15.44)."[8] In other words, the term *Christian* was a derogatory label imposed upon believers by their enemies. And yet, the term stuck and with typical Christian humility, was eventually accepted.

The second difficulty with the word *Christian* is that of definition. If we apply the term to those who affirm the prophethood of Jesus Christ, then Muslims demand inclusion, for the Islamic religion requires belief in Jesus Christ as an article of faith. Granted, the Islamic understanding of Jesus differs from that of the Trinitarian majority of those who would identify themselves as Christian. However, many Islamic beliefs are remarkably consistent with those of classic Unitarian[9](EN)Christianity.

If we apply the label *Christian* to those who follow the teachings of Jesus, we face a similar difficulty, for Muslims claim to follow the teachings of Jesus more faithfully than

19

Christians. That claim hurls a hefty gauntlet in the face of Christianity, but is made with sincerity and commitment, and deserves examination.

Should we associate the label of Christianity with the doctrines of original sin, the Deity of Jesus, the Trinity, crucifixion, and atonement? Makes sense, but here's the problem: Although these doctrines define creedal differences between Trinitarian Christianity and Islam, they also define creedal differences between various sects of Christianity. Not all Christians accept the Trinity, and many deny Jesus' alleged divinity. Not even the doctrines of original sin, the crucifixion, and atonement achieve universal acceptance within the fractured world of Christianity. Subgroups of Christianity have canonized widely variant creeds, but no single definition has ever gained unanimous acceptance.

Hence, the world of Christianity has been divided since the time of Jesus. History chronicles an initial two hundred years, during which the disciples and their followers split from Paul and his divergent theology. This early period is crucial to an understanding of Christianity, for one can reasonably expect the purity of Christology (doctrines of Christ) and Christian creed to have been best represented among those closest to the teachings of Jesus. However, our knowledge of this period is vague, with disappointingly little verifiable information surviving to the present day. What is clear is that opinions differed wildly. Some early Christians believed God manifested His message on Earth through inspiration, others through incarnation. Some believed the message was conveyed through direct transmission and interpretation by the prophet himself, others spoke of spiritual enlightenment, as claimed by Paul. Some followed the Old Testament Law taught by Jesus; others

20

negated the laws in favor of Paul's "Justification by Faith." Some (such as the disciples) believed God's law was to be interpreted literally. Others (such as Paul) felt the law was to be interpreted allegorically.

Whether the apostles ever agreed upon a creed is unclear. What is commonly known as the Apostles' Creed is *not*, in fact, the creed of the apostles, but rather a baptismal formula that evolved over an indefinite period. *Encyclopaedia Britannica* states that the Apostles' Creed "did not achieve its present form until quite late; just how late is a matter of controversy."[10] So how late is "quite late"? According to Ehrman, the Apostles' Creed was derived from credal formulas conceived in the fourth century.[11] That dates its origin, at the very earliest, three hundred years from the time of the apostles, and many would say considerably later.

Just as different understandings of Christology evolved over centuries, so too has the creed of Christianity remained in debate to the present day. Some seek answers in the New Testament and early Christian documents; others question the integrity of the New Testament in the first place—a discussion deferred to the final chapters of this book.

From these murky origins, the third century saw the many and varied Unitarian schools thrown into conflict with the newly conceived Trinitarian formula. This came to a head when Emperor Constantine sought to unify his empire under one Christian theology, and imperially summoned the Council of Nicaea, the First Ecumenical Council, in 325 CE. Convened to address the Unitarian theology of Arius, a prominent priest of Alexandria, seven ecumenical councils followed in well-spaced sequence over the next six centuries. A further thirteen councils (considered ecumenical by the Roman Catholic Church, but not

21

by the Orthodox) followed, the most recent being the Second Vatican Council of 1962–65, to make a total of twenty-one. And yet, debate continues to rage over issues which have failed to achieve unanimous acceptance.

Hence, Trinitarian theology has not only been at odds with Unitarian theology for the past two millennia, but has roused contentious debate among its *own* constituents. Historically, the greatest upheavals came in the form of gnostic theosophy, the schism between the Eastern Orthodox and Roman Catholic churches and, later still, the eruption of the Protestant Reformation in the sixteenth century. From the metaphysical seeds planted by Martin Luther, John Calvin, the Anabaptists and the Anglican reformers, myriad theologies grew, persisting to the present day in such a plethora of sects as to require religious encyclopedias to catalog the variants.

With such tremendous diversity, how should the term *Christianity* be defined? If used to identify those who claim to adhere to the teachings of Jesus Christ, then Muslims deserve inclusion. If used to define any specific system of beliefs to ideologically separate Christianity from Islam, these same tenets of faith divide the world of Christianity itself.

Hence, any attempt to define a term of such uncertain origin and meaning, and one that has defied definition by billions of people over two thousand years, would seem futile at this point. Consequently, for the purposes of this book, the term *Christian* is applied in the colloquial sense of the word, to all who identify with the label, whatever the beliefs of their particular Christian sect may be.

3 — Islam: Part 1

Man's mind, once stretched by a new idea, neverre-gains its original dimension.

—Oliver Wendell Holmes

As Margaret Nydell states in *Understanding Arabs,* "The God Muslims worship is the same God Jews and Christians worship (*Allah* is simply the Arabic word for God; Arab Christians pray to Allah)."[12]

The word *Islam* is the infinitive of the Arabic verb *aslama,* and is translated, "to submit totally to God."[13] Furthermore, "The participle of this verb is *muslim* (i.e., the one who submits completely to God) by which the followers of Islam are called."[14] The word *Islam* also connotes peace (being from the same root as the Arabic word *salaam*), with the understanding that peace comes through submission to God. Unlike the terms *Judaism* and *Christianity*, both of which aren't mentioned in their own bibles, *Islam* and *Muslim* are mentioned numerous times throughout the Holy Qur'an. Hence, those who consider the Holy Qur'an the revealed word of God find divine authority for the terms *Islam* and *Muslim* within their own scripture.

The above is the literal definition of *Muslim*—a person who submits to the will of God. What, then, is the definition in

23

accordance with Islamic ideology? The Islamic understanding is that true believers, since the creation of humankind, have always accepted belief in God as one God and in the teachings of the messenger of their time. For example, Muslims—meaning those who submitted to the will of God—during the time of Moses would have testified that there is no God but Allah, and Moses was the messenger of Allah. Muslims during the time of Jesus would have testified that there is no God but Allah, and Jesus was the prophet of Allah. For the last 1,400 years, Muslims have acknowledged Muhammad ibn (son of) Abdullah to be the last and final messenger of God. To this day, a person enters Islam and becomes Muslim by stating, "I testify that there is no god but Allah, and I testify that Muhammad is the Messenger of Allah."

Islam acknowledges the testimony of faith to be valid only if made by sincere and willing adults who understand the full meaning and implications of what they are saying. Despite the erroneous assumption that Islam was spread by the sword, the religion forbids coercion, as per the commandment "Let there be no compulsion in religion . . ." (TMQ 2:256). Furthermore, an entire chapter or the Holy Qur'an (TMQ, Chapter 109) teaches the following:

> In the name of Allah, Most Gracious, Most Merciful,
>
> Say: O you that reject faith!
>
> I worship not that which you worship,
>
> Nor will you worship that which I worship.
>
> And I will not worship that which you

have been wont to worship,

Nor will you worship that which I
worship.

To you be your way, and to me mine.

The seventeenth-century English philosopher John
Locke, though ranked in history as a Unitarian Christian,
provided a most beautiful argument, which might serve the
purpose of all (Muslims included) who seek to explain the
futility of forced conversion:

> No way whatsoever that I shall walk in
> against the dictates of my conscience, will
> ever bring me to the mansions of the
> blessed. I may grow rich by art that I take
> not delight in; I may be cured of some
> disease by remedies that I have not faith
> in; but I cannot be saved by a religion that
> I distrust, and by a worship that I
> abhor. . . . Faith only, and inward
> sincerity, are the things that procure
> acceptance with God. . . . In vain
> therefore do princes compel their subjects
> to come into their church-communion,
> under pretence of saving their souls. If
> they believe, they will come of their own
> accord; if they believe not, their coming
> will nothing avail them. . . .[15]

It is notable that the slander of Islam having been spread

by the sword was largely perpetuated by religious institutions that are themselves notorious for nearly two millennia of forced conversion, often by the most sadistic means. Clearly, testimony of faith cannot be coerced when a religion requires sincerity in the first place. Nearly three hundred years ago, the following comment was offered by George Sale, one of the first to translate the Qur'an into English, a self-professed antagonist of the man, Muhammad, and a hater of the Islamic religion:

> I shall not here enquire into the reasons why the law of Mohammed has met with so unexampled a reception in the world (for they are greatly deceived who imagine it to have been propagated by the sword alone), or by what means it came to be embraced by nations which never felt the force of the Mohammedan arms, and even by those which stripped the Arabians of their conquests, and put an end to the sovereignty and very being of their Khalifs: yet it seems as if there was something more than what is vulgarly imagined, in a religion which has made so surprising a progress.[16]

It is just such sentiments that have prompted modern scholars to cast aside the popularized slander of coercion. Hans Küng, believed by many Christian scholars to be, in the words of former Archbishop of Canterbury Lord George Carey, "our greatest living theologian,"[17] writes,

26

> Were whole villages, cities, regions and
> provinces forcibly converted to Islam?
> Muslim historiography knows nothing of
> this and would have had no reason to
> keep quiet about it. Western historical
> research, too, has understandably not been
> able to shed any light here either. In
> reality, everything happened quite
> differently. . . .[18]

And truthfully, how can claims of forced conversion be
seriously entertained when Indonesia, the country with the
largest Muslim population in the world, "never felt the force of
the Mohammedan arms,"[19] having assimilated the Islamic
religion from nothing more than the teachings and example of a
few merchants from Yemen? Such forces of Islamic progress are
witnessed to this day. Islam has grown within the borders of
countries and cultures that were not the conquered, but rather the
conquerors of many of the Muslim lands. In addition, Islam
continues to grow and prosper within populations that stand in
expressed contempt of the religion. No difficulty should be
encountered, then, in accepting the following comment:

> No other religion in history spread so
> rapidly as Islam. By the time of
> Muhammad's death (632 AD) Islam
> controlled a great part of Arabia. Soon it
> triumphed in Syria, Persia, Egypt, the
> lower borders of present Russia and
> across North Africa to the gates of Spain.
> In the next century, its progress was even

more spectacular.

The West has widely believed that this
surge of religion was made possible by
the sword. But no modern scholar accepts
that idea, and the Koran is explicit in
support of freedom of conscience.[20]

It is worth noting that Islam does not differentiate
between believers of different periods. The Islamic belief is that
all messengers since Adam conveyed God's revelation. The
faithful submitted and followed, the unfaithful didn't. Therefore,
ever since Cain and Abel, humankind has been divided between
the pious and impious, between good and evil.

Islam professes a consistency in creed from the time of
Adam, and asserts that the tenets of faith declared at each and
every stage in the chain of revelation were the same—without
evolution or alteration. As the Creator has remained perfect and
unchanged throughout time, so has His creed. The Christian
claim that God changed from the wrathful God of the Old
Testament to the benevolent God of the New Testament is not
honored by the Islamic religion, for it implies that God was
imperfect to begin with and required spiritual adjustment to a
higher, faultless state.

Because Islam's teachings have remained constant, there
are no creedal inconsistencies. Is it true that early man lived by
one creed and set of rules, the Jews by another, and the
Christians a third? That only Christians are saved by Jesus
Christ's atoning sacrifice? Islam answers "No" to both
questions. Islam teaches that from the creation of man until the
end of time, salvation depends on acceptance of the same eternal

28

creed, and adherence to the teachings of God's prophets.

Along this line of thought, a person might question how different religions view the fate of Abraham, as well as that of other early prophets. Was Abraham subject to the laws of Judaism? Apparently not. If Judaism refers to the descendants of Judah, then Abraham, being the great-grandfather of Judah, was most certainly not a descendant. Genesis 11:31 defines Abraham as being from an area in Lower Mesopotamia called Ur of Chaldees, in what is now present-day Iraq. Geographically speaking, and applying the terminology of today, Abraham was an Arab. Genesis 12:4–5 describes his move to Canaan (i.e., Palestine) at the age of seventy-five, and Genesis 17:8 confirms he was a stranger in that land. Genesis 14:13 identifies the man as "Abraham the Hebrew"—"Hebrew" meaning:

> Any member of an ancient northern
> Semitic people that were the ancestors of
> the Jews. Historians use the term Hebrews
> to designate the descendants of the
> patriarchs of the Old Testament (i.e.,
> Abraham, Isaac, and so on) from that
> period until their conquest of Canaan
> (Palestine) in the late 2nd millennium BC.
> Thenceforth these people are referred to
> as Israelites until their return from the
> Babylonian Exile in the late 6th-century
> BC, from which time on they became
> known as Jews.[21]

So Abraham was a Hebrew, in a time when the term *Jew* did not even exist. The descendants of Jacob were the Twelve

29

Tribes of the Israelites, and only Judah and his line came to be known as Jews. Even Moses, despite popular opinion, was not a Jew. Exodus 6:16–20 identifies Moses as a descendant of Levi and not of Judah, and therefore a Levite. He was a lawgiver to the Jews, certainly, but not a Jew by the definition of that time in history. This is not to diminish who he was and what he did, certainly, but just to state the case for the record.

So if Abraham was not a Jew—and most certainly he was not a Christian—what laws of salvation was he subject to? And what about the other prophets preceding Moses? While the Jewish and Christian clergy struggle over this point, Islam teaches that "Abraham was not a Jew nor yet a Christian; but he was true in Faith, and bowed his will to Allah's (which is Islam), and he did not join gods with Allah (God)" (TMQ 3:67). In addition to stating that the religion of Abraham was that of "submission to God" (i.e., Islam), this passage of the Holy Qur'an teaches that an individual's faith and submission is more important than the label by which that person is known.

4 — Islam: Part 2

Knowledge is the only instrument of production that is not subject to diminishing returns.

—J. M. Clark, *Journal of Political Economy*, Oct. 1927

We have already noted the Islamic belief that the world is peppered with those who are Muslim by literal but not by ideological definition. These individuals may call themselves agnostic, Jewish or Christian, but they submit to the will of the Creator as best they can, and if adequately exposed to the teachings of Islam will readily accept them. These are those who, when they learn the teachings of Islam, state, "We believe therein, for it is the Truth from our Lord: indeed we have been Muslims (bowing to Allah's Will) from before this" (TMQ 28:53), for prior to becoming Muslim, they submitted themselves to the evident truths of God, whether to their liking or not, and lived by His decree as they understood it. And that made them Muslim in everything but oath.

Ironically, the historical archetype of such individuals may very well be Thomas H. Huxley, the father of agnosticism. Huxley penned one of the most fluent statements of willingness, even desire, to submit his will to that of the Creator: "I protest that if some great Power would agree to make me always think what is true and do what is right, on condition of being turned into a sort of clock and wound up every morning before I got out

31

of bed, I should instantly close with the offer."[22]

Many profess a similar willingness or desire to live in submission to God, but the ultimate test is the embracing of divine truths when made evident. To leap backward from T. H. Huxley to the Bible, Muslims and Christians alike cite the story of Lazarus (John 11:1–44) by way of example. By the power of God, Jesus reportedly raised Lazarus from the dead "that they may believe that You sent me" (John 11:42). On the strength of this miracle, some Jews acknowledged Jesus' prophethood, while others condemned him.

The main lesson to be learned, from the Islamic viewpoint, is that when presented with clear evidence of prophethood, the sincere (Muslim by literal definition) follow (and become Muslim in the full meaning of the word). Meanwhile, the insincere favor worldly considerations over the direction of God.

The lessons don't end there. There is a moral to the story of Lazarus regarding the purpose behind revelation. A person may question, why else would God send messengers, if not to guide humankind to the straight path of His design? Who will reap the rewards of following God's directions if not those who submit to His evidence? And who is more deserving of punishment than those who deny the truth when made clear?

Muslims assert that all prophets bore revelation to correct the deviancies of their people. After all, why would God send a prophet to a people who were doing everything right? Just as Jesus was sent to the "lost sheep of the house of Israel" (Matthew 15:24) with divine evidence of prophethood and a corrective revelation, so was Muhammad presented to all people, from his time to the Day of Judgment, with evidence of prophethood and a final revelation. This final revelation

32

redresses the deviancies that had crept into the various world religions, Judaism and Christianity included. Muslims assert that those who live in submission to God and His evidence will recognize and accept Muhammad as a prophet, just as the pious Jews recognized and accepted Jesus. Conversely, those who live in submission to anything other than God—be it money, power, worldly enjoyment, cultural or family tradition, unfounded personal prejudices, or any religion more self- than God-centered—would be expected to reject Muhammad, just as the impious Jews rejected Jesus.

An interesting point is that Islam demands submission to God, whereas Judaism and Christianity demand submission to ecclesiastical doctrine. Muslims do not adhere to ecclesiastical doctrine for the simple reason that, in Islam, there *is* no ecclesiastical doctrine. In fact, there are no clergy to begin with. To quote the *Encyclopedic Dictionary of Religion*, "There is no centrally organized religious authority or magisterium in Islam and for this reason its character varies sometimes widely from traditional norms . . ."[23] and the *New Catholic Encyclopedia*, "Islam has no church, no priesthood, no sacramental system, and almost no liturgy."[24]

What Islam does have are scholars, who serve to answer religiously challenging questions. However, scholarship does not necessarily imply any greater closeness to God than that of a simple and pious, though uneducated, Muslim. Most notably, there is no papal equivalent, and there are no intercessors between man and God. Once a person accepts the Holy Qur'an as the word of God and Muhammad as His final prophet, all teachings follow from these foundational sources. Only in the deviant sects does one find what might be called clergy. The Shi'ites have their imams, the Sufis their saints, and the Nation of Islam their preachers. Not so in orthodox (i.e., Sunni) Islam, where *imam*means nothing more than "somebody who goes out in front." In other words, a leader of the prayer. The imam is not ordained and does not administer sacraments. His function is nothing more than to synchronize prayer by providing leadership. This position requiresno particular office or appointment, and can be fulfilled by any mature member of the congregation.

The Islamic religion is built upon the foundation of its faith. A person enters Islam professing belief in one God, in the Holy Qur'an as His final revelation, and in Muhammad as His final prophet. Subsequently, the answer to any particular question, whether regarding creed, laws, manners, spirituality, etc., must refer back to God's revelation and the teachings of the Prophet to be considered valid.

Not so with Judeo-Christian institutions, which, as we shall see later in this book, demand faith in doctrines that frequently supersede the commandments of God with the interpretations of men. The examples of Jesus never having called himself the Son of God or having taught the Trinity were discussed in the Introduction to this book. These are but two of a long list of creedal elements Jesus never taught. Hence, the Christian might enter the faith believing in one God (as Jesus taught), the Bible as revelation, and Jesus as a prophet of God. However, those who question the foundation of Christian creed find many creedal elements founded not on the teachings of God or Jesus, but on non-biblical sources, such as the writings of the apostolic fathers, Pauline theologians, or even contemporary clergy. That these sources are neither Jesus Christ nor God is obvious, although they typically claim to have spoken on behalf of Jesus Christ or God. Thus, Christians have reason to question their canon, for many of these non-biblical sources frankly contradict Jesus' teachings.

The situation is not much different in Judaism, where the majority of Jews are Reform Jews, following the teachings of those who "reformed" God's laws from harsh orthodoxy to a more flexible construct.

Much to the frustration of their Abrahamic neighbors, Muslims challenge the Jews and Christians to prove how the teachings of Moses or Jesus conflict with the Islamic understanding of God and revelation. After all, the Holy Qur'an commands Muslims to say, "We believe in Allah, and the revelation given to us, and to Abraham, Isma'il, Isaac, Jacob, and the Tribes, and that given to Moses and Jesus, and that given to (all) Prophets from their Lord: we make no difference between one and another of them, and we bow to Allah (in Islam)" (TMQ 2:136). By this *ayat* (i.e., verse), Muslims are duty-bound to follow the revelation given to Moses and Jesus. Therein lies the challenge. Had any of the prophets taught contrary to the creed[25(EN)] of Islam, Muslims would be duty-bound to face the significance of that contradiction. On the other hand, should Jews and Christians fail to prove a contradiction, they are duty-bound to face the striking agreement of these three prophets.

Fourteen hundred years have passed since the revelation of the Holy Qur'an, and to date this challenge hasn't been met. No one has ever proven the reality of God to differ from the Islamic understanding. Furthermore, no one has proven the teachings of Moses, Jesus, and Muhammad to conflict. In fact, many have suggested the exact opposite—that these three prophets firmly support one another.

As a result, many sincere nuns, priests, ministers and

rabbis—educated clergy who know their respective religions best—have embraced Islam.During the lifetime of Muhammad, a Christian monk of Syria named Bahira claimed to have recognized him as the final prophet when he was a small boy, decades prior to his first revelation.[26]WaraqahibnNawfal, the old, blind Christian cousin of Khadijah (Muhammad's first wife) swore, "By Him in whose hand is the soul of Waraqah, you (Muhammad) are the prophet of this nation and the great *Namus* (the angel of revelation—i.e., angel Gabriel) has come to you—the one who came to Moses. And you will be denied (by your people) and they will harm you, and they will expel you and they will fight you and if I were to live to see that day I would help Allah's religion with a great effort."[27]

In the early days of Islam, when the Muslims were weak and oppressed, the religion was embraced by such seekers of truth as Salman Farsi, a Persian Christian who was directed by his mentor, a Christian monk, to seek the arrival of the final prophet in the "country of the date-palms."[28] The Negus, the Christian ruler of Abyssinia, accepted Islam without ever having met Muhammad, and while the Muslims were still a small group, widely held in contempt and frequently fighting for their lives.[29]

One wonders, if Christian scholars and Christians of prominent position accepted Islam during a time when the Muslims were a persecuted minority lacking wealth, strength, and political position with which to attract, much less protect new Muslims, what drew these Christians to Islam, if not sincere belief? History records that even Heraclius, the Christian emperor of Rome, considered accepting Islam, only to renounce his resolve when he saw that conversion would cost him the support of his people as well as his empire.[30]

One of the most striking early conversions was that of Abdallahibn Salam, the rabbi whom the Jews of Medina called "our master and the son of our master."[31]*Encyclopedia Judaica* explains that when his co-religionists were invited to accept Islam as well, "The Jews refused, and only his immediate family, notably his aunt Khalida, embraced Islam. According to other versions, Abdallah's conversion occurred because of the strength of Muhammad's answers to his questions."[32]

So the conversions started, and so they have continued to the present day. Converts to Islam typically consider their conversion to be consistent with, if not dictated by, their own scripture. In other words, they discover that Islam is the fulfillment of, rather than in conflict with, teachings of the Bible. This naturally raises the question: Are Jews and Christians, in the face of the revelation of the Holy Qur'an, defying God and His chain of revelation? This issue cuts at the very root of the theological debate. Muslims believe that, as with those who denied Jesus Christ's prophethood, those who deny the same of Muhammad may continue to be accepted by their people and regarded highly by their peers—but at the cost of disfavor with God. If true, this claim deserves to be heard. If not, the error of this conviction demands exposure. In either case, there is no substitute for an examination of the evidence.

While there have always been significant numbers of educated and practicing Jewish and Christian converts to Islam, the reverse is not true, nor has it been true at any time in history. There are cases of those belonging to deviant sects of Islam who convert to different religions, but this is hardly surprising. Ignorant of the true teachings of the Islamic religion, they are often seduced by the worldly permissiveness of other religions. Examples of these deviant groups include the Baha'i, the Nation

37

of Islam, the Ahmadiyyah (also known as Qadianis), the Ansar, extreme Sufi orders, and many, if not most, of the Shi'ite sects. These groups may identify with the label of Islam, but like a man who calls himself a tree, lack sufficient roots in the religion to substantiate the claim. More importantly, the illegitimate doctrines of these misguided sects separate them from orthodox (Sunni) Islam, demanding rejection by all Muslims.

As for those born Muslim and raised in ignorance of their own religion, their conversion to other religions cannot fairly be viewed as turning away from Islam—since these individuals never truly embraced Islam in the first place. And, of course, not every person born into a religion is an example of piety, even if knowledgeable of their religion. Then there are those weak of faith, who find religious conviction pushed aside by worldly priorities or the allure of more permissive faiths. But the sum total of these apostates simply doesn't match 1,400 years of Jewish and Christian clergy converting in the opposite direction. Conspicuously absent from the equation is the conversion of sincere and committed, educated and practicing Sunni Muslims, much less scholars (the Islamic equivalent of the convert rabbis and priests).

The question remains: Why *do* some Jewish and Christian scholars embrace Sunni Islam? There is no pressure upon them to do so, and significant worldly reasons not to— things like losing their congregation, position and status, friends and family, jobs and retirement pension. And why don't Islamic scholars turn to something else? Other religions are much more permissive in matters of faith and morals, and there is no enforcement of a law against apostatizing from Islam in Western countries.

So why have Jewish and Christian scholars embraced

Islam, while educated Muslims remain firm in their faith? Muslims suggest the answer lies in the definition of Islam. The person who submits to God and not to a particular ecclesiastical body will recognize a divine sense to revelation. Islam represents a continuum from Judaism and Christianity which, once recognized, sweeps the sincere seeker down the smooth road of revelation. Once a person sees past Western prejudices and propaganda, the Muslim believes, doors of understanding open.

The Islamic viewpoint is that, between the missions of Jesus and Muhammad, those who recognized Jesus as the fulfillment of Old Testament prophesies bore witness to the one true God, and Jesus as his prophet. By Islamic definition, these early "Christians" were Muslims for all intents and purposes. Modern-day Muslims remind us that Jesus could not have taught things that did not exist in the period of his ministry, such as the label of "Christian" and Trinitarian doctrine, which was to evolve over the first few centuries in the post-apostolic age. What Jesus most certainly *did* teach was the simple truth of God being One, and of God having sent himself as a prophet. The Gospel of John says it best: "And this is eternal life, that they may know You, the only true God, and Jesus Christ whom You have sent" (John 17:3), and "Let not your heart be troubled; you believe in God, believe also in me" (John 14:1). Hence, the Islamic viewpoint is that whatever this group of early followers called themselves during the forty years following Jesus (before the word *Christian* was even invented), they lived in submission to the truth of God as conveyed in the teachings of Jesus. And despite whatever label they identified with back then, today their character would be defined by a word attributed to those who live in submission to God via the message of revelation—that is,

Muslim.

Similarly, "convert" Jewish and Christian scholars believed Muhammad fulfilled Old and New Testament prophecies of the final prophet. Some readers would object on the basis of never having found the name Muhammad in the Bible. On the other hand, how many times have they found the name Jesus in the Old Testament in reference to the promised messiah? The answer is *none.* The Old Testament contains numerous predictions of prophets to come, but none by their proper name. Some of these predictions are thought to describe John the Baptist, others allegedly speak of Jesus, and still others appear to be unfulfilled by any biblical personage. The Bible informs us that the Jews expected three prophets to follow, for the Pharisees are recorded as having questioned John the Baptist as follows:

> Now this is the testimony of John, when the Jews sent priests and Levites from Jerusalem to ask him, "Who are you?" He confessed, and did not deny, but confessed, "I am not the Christ." And they asked him, "What then? Are you Elijah?" He said, "I am not." "Are you the Prophet?" And he answered, "No." (John 1:19–21)

After John the Baptist identified himself in evasive terms, the Pharisees persisted by inquiring, "Why then do you baptize if you are not the Christ, nor Elijah, nor the Prophet?" (John 1:25).

So there we have it—"Elijah," "the Christ," and "the

Prophet." Not just once, but twice. That was the short list of prophets the Jews expected according to their scripture.

Now, despite the fact that John the Baptist denied being Elijah in the above quote, Jesus identified him as Elijah twice (Matthew 11:13–14, 17:11–13). Scriptural inconsistencies aside, let's chalk up Elijah on the word of Jesus, not think too deeply over who "the Christ" refers to, and concentrate on what remains. Who is the third and last on the Old Testament list of foretold prophets? Who is "the Prophet?"

Some Christians expect this final prophet to be Jesus returned, but others expect a different prophet entirely. Hence the reason why all Jews and many Christians are waiting for a final prophet, as predicted by their own scripture.

The Muslim believes this final prophet has already come, and his name was Muhammad. Through him the Holy Qur'an was revealed by Almighty God (Allah). Those who adhere to the Holy Qur'an as the revealed word of Allah, and to the teachings of the final prophet, Muhammad ibn Abdullah, are regarded to be Muslims both by literal definition *and* by ideology.

PART II: UNDERSTANDING AND APPROACHING GOD

We are all bound to the throne of the Supreme Being by a flexible chain that restrains without enslaving us. The most wonderful aspect of the universal scheme of things is the action of free beings under divine guidance.

—Joseph de Maistre,Considerations on France

While monotheistic faiths share a fundamental belief in one God, their understanding of His attributes differs greatly. Many of these differences, like individual strands of a spider web, may appear separate and divergent when viewed too closely. However, these individual threads knit together a larger design, the full significance of which is recognized only when viewed as a whole. Only from a distanced perspective does the complexity of design become known, and the fact that each strand points to a central truth becomes recognized.

1 — God's Name

The difference between the almost-right word & the right word is really a large matter—it's the difference between the lightning bug and the lightning.

—Mark Twain, Letter to George Bainton

A simple example of how several strands of evidence weave together a logical conclusion relates to the name of God. Evidence taken from Judaism, Christianity, and Islam tie together to support a conclusion that should be acceptable to all three religions. For example, recognition of God as "the Creator" and "the Almighty" are universal. Indeed, God is universally recognized by many beautiful names and glorious attributes. When a person calls upon the Creator by any of His many beautiful names or perfect attributes, He is sure to hear the call. So what more is needed?

Well, for some people, a name. A definitive name is needed.

That the name of God in Islam is *Allah* should be of no surprise to anybody. That a person might suggest that the name of God in Christianity is also *Allah* risks provoking consternation, if not violent protest, from the entrenched community of Western Christianity. But a visitor to the Holy Land quickly appreciates that *Allah* is the name by which God is known to all Arabs, Christians and Muslims alike. The Arab

43

Christians trace their heritage to the days of revelation—in fact, their distant ancestors walked the same land as the prophet Jesus—and they identify the Creator as *Allah*. Their lineage prospered for 2,000 years in a land renowned for religious tolerance up until the creation of the Zionist state of Israel (a little-known fact, and one hugely distorted by the Western media), freely practicing their beliefs up to the present day. And they identify the Creator as *Allah*.

The New International Dictionary of the Christian Church tells us "the name is used also by modern Arab Christians who say concerning future contingencies: 'In sha' Allah.'"[33] This phrase *In sha' Allah* is translated as "Allah willing" or "If Allah wills." The *Encyclopaedia Britannica* confirms the shared Arabic usage of the name "Allah": "Allah is the standard Arabic word for 'God' and is used by Arab Christians as well as by Muslims."[34]

In fact, from the Orthodox Christians of the land that was birthplace to Abraham (now modern-day Iraq), to the Coptic Christians of the Egypt of Moses, to the Palestinian Christians of the Holy Land trod by Jesus Christ, to the entire Middle Eastern epicenter from which the shockwaves of revelation radiated out to the entire world, *Allah* is recognized as the proper name for what Western religions call *God*. The Christian Arabs are known to call Jesus *Ibn Allah*—*ibn* meaning "son." Pick up any copy of an Arabic Bible and a person will find the Creator identified as *Allah*. So *Allah* is recognized as the name of God in the land of revelation of the Old and New Testaments, as well as of the Qur'an.

What is *not* recognized by Christian and Muslim purists in the Holy Land is the generic Westernized name, *God*. This word is completely foreign to the untranslated scriptures of the

Old and New Testaments, as well as the Qur'an—it simply doesn't exist in the foundational manuscripts of *any* of the three Abrahamic religions.

So while the *concept* of God is readily recognized, a little research reveals that the word *God* has an uncertain origin. It may have arisen from the Indo-European root, *ghut-*, it may have the underlying meaning of "that which is invoked," and may bear the prehistoric Germanic *guth-* as a distant ancestor (from which the modern German *Gott*, the Dutch *God*, and the Swedish and Danish *Gud* are derived).[35] Lots of maybes, but nothing definitive. No matter how the origin of the word is traced, the name *God* is of Western and non-biblical derivation, and its etymological origin and meaning are lost in history.

In short, we don't know where the word *God* came from, but we *do* know where it *didn't* come from—it didn't come from any of the biblical scriptures, whether Old or New Testament.

Nonetheless, the fact that Middle Eastern Christians equate *God* with *Allah* is an affront to the sensitivities of those who associate *Allah* with heathens. Be that as it may, the relevant question is whether *Allah* can be substantiated as the name of our Creator. Most people would like to be assured that their religious beliefs and practices have a basis in scripture and not just local custom, so one may reasonably question whether the Old and New Testaments support use of the name *Allah* in Judaism and/or Christianity.

The answer is *yes*.

In Judaic texts, God is referred to as *Yahweh, Elohim, Eloah,* and *El*. In Christian texts the terminology is little different, for the Greek *theos* is nothing more than the translation of *Elohim.Eloi* and *Eli* are also encountered.

In the Old Testament, *Yahweh* is used more than 6,000

times as God's name, and *Elohim* in excess of 2,500 times as a generic name for God; *Eloah* is encountered 57 times and *El* more that 200.[36],[37] How do these Old Testament names tie in with the name *Allah*? Simple. *Elohim* is the royal plural (a plural of majesty, not numbers) of *Eloah*.[38] The *Encyclopedia of Religion and Ethics* confirms that the Arabic word *ilah* (the generic Arabic word for "god") is "identical with the *eloah* of Job."[39] The linguistic explanation of the origin of the name "Allah" is that the contraction of the Arabic definite article *al* (the) and *ilah* (god), according to the rules of Arabic grammar, becomes *Allah* (The God). Consequently, the 2,500-plus entries of *Elohim* and the 57 entries of *Eloah* in the Old Testament bear direct relation to the name of God as Allah, for *Elohim* is the plural of *Eloah,* which itself is identical with the Arabic *ilah,* from which *Allah* appears to be linguistically derived.

Muslim scholars offer yet another tantalizing thought, for when calling upon their Creator, Muslims beseech Allah by the appellation of *Allahuma,* which means "Oh, Allah." The Siamese twin similarity of the Semitic cousins *Allahuma* and *Elohim* cannot escape easy recognition.

Unfortunately, such facts are not acknowledged by those who approach scriptural analysis more as a religious turf war than as an objective search for truth. An example of the extreme sensitivity over this issue concerns the *Scofield Reference Bible,* edited by the American theologian and minister, Cyrus I. Scofield, and published in 1909 by Oxford University Press. Its original publication incited Christian censure for invoking the name "Alah" *(sic).* Specifically, a footnote to Genesis 1:1 explained that the name *Elohim* is derived from the contraction of *El* and *Alah.* The fact that this explanation closely matches the aforementioned linguistic explanation that the origin of the name "Allah" may derive from the contraction of the Arabic definite article *al* (the) and *ilah*(god) to *Allah* (the God) did not escape the notice of certain Muslim apologists, the South African Ahmed Deedat in particular. However, the conclusions that can be drawn from the circumstance are speculative, for the *Scofield Reference Bible* did not identify "Alah" as the proper name of the Creator, but rather offered the definition: "*El*— strength, or the strong one, and *Alah,* to swear, to bind oneself by an oath, so implying faithfulness." Certainly the claim that the *Scofield Reference Bible* in any way implied that the proper name of the Creator is "Allah" would be inappropriate. However, their comment has relevance to what they meant to convey, and does not seem in any way improper, incorrect, or inflammatory. Yet the least suggestion that the name of God in the Old Testament matches that of the Holy Qur'an excited Christian sensitivities. As a result, this footnote was edited from all subsequent editions.

To move from the Old to New Testament, the Christian reader can fairly ask, "How does the New Testament fit into the above-described scheme?" Once again the answer is fairly simple, boiling down to a few concrete points. The first is that the most frequently used word for God (1,344 of the 1,356 entries) in the Greek New Testament is *theos*.[40] This word is found in the Septuagint (the ancient Greek translation of the Old Testament) primarily as the translation of *Elohim,* the Hebrew name for God.[41] The seventy-two Jewish scholars entrusted to translate the Septuagint (six from each of the twelve tribes of Israel) stuck to tradition by translating *Elohim* to *theos.* The New Testament is no different. The *theos* of the Greek New Testament is the same as the *theos* of the Greek Old Testament (i.e., the Septuagint), both derived from *Elohim.*

Recognizing that the basis of the *theos* of the New Testament is the *Elohim* of the Old Testament, a person is led back to the above-described link between *Elohim* and *Allah.*

And truly, a person should not be surprised. The *Eli* and *Eloi* allegedly found on the lips of Jesus in the New Testament (Mathew 27:46 and Mark 15:34) are immeasurably closer to "Allah" than to the word "God." As is the case with *Elohim* and *Eloah, Eloi* and *Eli* sound like "Allah" and linguistically match "Allah" in form and meaning. All four of these biblical names are Hebrew, a sister language to Arabic and Aramaic. The languages commonly acknowledged by scholars to have been spoken by Jesus are Hebrew and Aramaic. For example, in the phrase *"Eloi, Eloi, lama sabachthani"* (Mark 15:34), the words *Eloi* and *lama* are transliterated from Hebrew, while *sabachthani* is transliterated from Aramaic. Hence, being sister languages, it is not surprising that Hebrew, Aramaic and Arabic words having similar or the same meaning sound like phonetic cousins. All three are Semitic languages, with slight pronunciation differences for words of the same meaning, as in the Hebrew greeting, *shalom,* and the Arabic greeting, *salaam,* both meaning peace. Suspicion that the Hebrew *Elohim, Eloah, Eloi,* and *Eli* equate to the Arabic *Allah* in the same way that the Hebrew *shalom* equates to the Arabic *salaam* seems well founded.

Despite the above, there are still those who have been conditioned to propose that "Allah" is the name of a pagan god! They ignore the fact that pagans generically use the word "god" in the same way that Christians, Jews, and Muslims use it, and it does not change the fact that there is only one God. Similarly, the word *elohim* was used in the Septuagint to refer to pagan gods, as well as to the Greek and Roman gods, in addition to the one true God of the Old and New Testaments.[42]*EncyclopaediaJudaica* clarifies this point: "The plural form *elohim* is used not only of pagan 'gods' (e.g., Ex. 12:12; 18:11; 20:3) but also of an individual pagan 'god' (Judg. 11:24; 2 Kings 1:2ff.) and even of a 'goddess' (1 Kings 11:5). In reference to Israel's 'God' it is used extremely often—more than 2,000 times . . ."[43] Remembering that *Elohim* is the word from which the New Testament *theos* is primarily derived, one finds that use of this biblical term for God flowed from the lips and pens of the pagans, as well as from the Jews and Christians. Does this mean that *Elohim* is a pagan god, or even an exclusively Jewish or Christian God? Obviously, the fact that different religions, pagan religions included, have used "God," "Elohim," and "Allah" to identify their concept of the Supreme Being reflects nothing more than their adoption of a commonly recognized name for God.

"Commonly recognized? Sounds strange to me," some will say. Such is also likely to be the case with the names Shim'ownKipha, Yehowchanan, Iakobos, and Matthaios—but how strange are these names really? Unknown to some, maybe, but strange? No. These are transliterations of the Hebrew and Greek from which the biblical names Simon Peter, John, James, and Matthew are translated into English.

So which is really more strange—to invent and popularize new names in preference to those identified in scripture, or to remain faithful to what are held to be holy texts? To identify the Creator by the "God" label hatched from human creativity and incubated in Western culture, or by the name specified by the Almighty, as He declares Himself in scripture?

Undeniably, one who speaks of Yehowchanan, Iakobos, and Allah will be greeted with a certain reserve in the West, but the concern of true believers has never been one of popularity, but of truth of testimony in front of the Creator. A Creator whose proper name, according to Judaic, Christian, and Muslim sources, is "Allah."

2 — God's Name and the Royal Plural

You see things; and you say "Why?" But I dream things that never were; and I say "Why not?"

—George Bernard Shaw, *Back to Methuselah*

No discussion of God's name is complete without explaining the royal plural. This is a linguistic concept foreign to most native English speakers, but not to the English language. As recently as the seventeenth century, the word *thou* was applied to commoners while the word *you,* the Old English plural of respect, was reserved for royalty and the social elite. Hence "Your Highness" and "Your Lordship," rather than "Thou Highness" or "Thou Lordship." Hence also Queen Victoria's "*We* are not amused," and Margaret Thatcher's "*We* are a grandmother."

In sacred scripture (including the Old and New Testaments, as well as the Holy Qur'an), God is sometimes referred to as "We" or "Us." For example, Genesis 1:26 and 11:7 record God as having said, "Let Us make man . . ." and "Come, let Us go down . . ."

From the Muslim scripture, the name *Allah,* unlike the Hebrew *Elohim,* is singular and cannot be made plural.[44] Some Arabic terms (for example, pronouns and pronoun suffixes) do describe Allah in the plural, but in what is known as the royal plural. This is a plural not of numbers, but of respect. The royal

51

plural is a literary device of Oriental and Semitic languages that denotes majesty. In both Old and New Testaments, *Elohim* is the plural form of *Eloah* (the closest name to "Allah" in transliteration and meaning).[45] In the same way that expressions of the royal plural in the Qur'an denote the majesty of God, so *Elohim* in the Old and New Testaments conveys the plural of respect.[46],[47] The *Theological Dictionary of the New Testament* comments, "*Elohim* is clearly a numerical plural only in a very few instances (cf. Ex. 15:11). Even a single pagan god can be meant by the word (e.g., 1 Kgs. 11:5). In the main, then, we have a plural of majesty."[48]

People may lob opinions on this subject back and forth from the respectful distance of their individual faiths, but it is interesting to note the conclusion of at least one scholar who spent time on both sides of the theological fence. David Benjamin Keldani served for nineteen years as a Catholic priest of the Chaldean Rite in the diocese of Uramiah (in what was then called Persia), before converting to Islam at the beginning of the twentieth century. Known by the Islamic name of Abdul-AhadDawud, he authored one of the earliest scholarly works in the English language on the subject of biblical correlates with the prophet of Islam, Muhammad. In this work, he wrote,

> It would be a mere waste of time here to refute those who ignorantly or maliciously suppose the Allah of Islam to be different from the true God and only a fictitious deity of Muhammad's own creation. If the Christian priests and theologians knew their Scriptures in the original Hebrew instead of in translations

> as the Muslims read their Qur'an in its
> Arabic text, they would clearly see that
> Allah is the same ancient Semitic name of
> the Supreme Being who revealed and
> spoke to Adam and all the prophets.[49]

Just as Arab Christians identify God as "Allah," and just as the Bible employs the royal plural both in pronouns and in the proper name *Elohim,* Western Christians can adopt the same practice without compromising their creed. But faith need not depend on such issues, when there remains a more relevant point to ponder: Regardless of His name, how does God command humankind to understand Him?

3 — Understanding of God

Those who agree with us may not be right, but we admire their astuteness.

—Cullen Hightower

The Jewish understanding of God is relatively concrete, despite the vast differences between Orthodox, Conservative, Reform and Hasidic Judaism in other matters. Throughout Judaism, the One-ness of God remains the primary attribute of the Creator, followed by many others, including justice, love, mercy, omniscience, omnipresence, omnipotence, sovereignty, truth, wisdom, self-existence, goodness, holiness, eternity, and the even trickier concept of infinity. Furthermore, Jews consider God incomprehensible, for God's attributes transcend those of His creation.

The Jewish attributes of God carry over into Christian definitions as well, although God's One-ness suffered in the transformation from the strict monotheism of the apostolic age to the mysticism of the Trinity. Coming out of one corner is the Trinitarian understanding of three entities in One—a concept repudiated by Unitarian challenges. Indeed, how could substances with opposite polarities (i.e., mortality/immortality; with beginning/without beginning; mutable/immutable, etc.) possibly exist in one entity? Why did Jesus Christ ascribe his miraculous works exclusively to God and not to any divinity of

54

his own, if he was in fact a partner in divinity? And why did he testify to having received his gifts from God if he and the Creator are co-equal? (For relevant verses, see John 3:35, 5:19–23, 5:26–27, 10:25, 13:3, 14:10, Acts 2:33, 2 Peter 1:17, Rev 2:26–27.)

The doctrine of God being three, but One, that is to say three-in-One, lives up to its label of a religious mystery. Although many profess belief, none can explain it in terms a healthy skeptic can understand. The struggle to explain how "the created" can possibly equate to the Creator is ages-old, as are the other mysteries of Trinitarian belief. Cutting across such issues, the most common Christian image of God is the "big man in the sky," much like the aged, white-bearded and flowing-robed representation preserved in Michelangelo's ceiling fresco in the Sistine chapel. The fact that this image is not at all dissimilar to the ancient Greek representation of Zeus has not gone unnoticed, and many object, and not just on the basis of the second commandment (which forbids "any likeness *of anything* that is in heaven above, or that is in the earth beneath, or that is in the water under the earth . . ."(Exodus 20:4–5)

So, if not on the basis of the second commandment, why else should anyone object? Well, does the biblical passage stating that God created man "in Our image, according to Our likeness" mean that God created man to *look* like Him, or to have dominion over worldly creation, similar to how God has dominion over *all* Creation, ourselves included? The latter is the context in which this verse was revealed, for the full verse reads, "Then God said, 'Let Us make man in Our image, according to Our likeness; let them have dominion over the fish of the sea, over the birds of the air, and over the cattle, over all the earth and over every creeping thing that creeps on the earth" (Genesis 1:26). This verse doesn't read, "In Our image, according to Our likeness; let him have eyes and a nose, a mouth and ears . . ." No, it speaks of dominion, not of physical appearance. Not once, but twice, for in the following verses God said to humankind, "Be fruitful and multiply, fill the earth and subdue it, have dominion over the fish of the sea, over the birds of the air, and over every living thing that moves on the earth" (Genesis 1:28).

So how should we portray God? According to both the second commandment and the above verses, not at all. For not only does God command us not to, but we have no idea what He looks like in the first place.

Similarly, the Christian claim that the God of the Old Testament repented and changed from a harsh and wrathful God to the loving and forgiving God of the New Testament is not universally accepted. In fact, many consider this concept contradicted both by scripture—"God is not a man, that He should lie, nor a son of man, that He should repent. Has He said, and will He not do? Or has He spoken, and will He not make it good?" (Numbers 23:19)—and by common sense.

The Islamic understanding of God is simpler, and is similar to the Jewish understanding in many respects. The critical elements of Islamic creed rest upon the word *tawheed*, which defines the One-ness of Allah, affirms His many unique names and attributes, and directs people to speak and act in a manner pleasing to God.

According to the Islamic religion, Allah is One in essence, eternal and absolute. He is living, self-subsisting, all-knowing, all-powerful. He is in need of no one, but all are in need of Him. He does not beget, and is not begotten. He is "the First," without beginning, "the Last," without end, and He has no partners or co-sharers in divinity.

Allah is "the Predominant," above Whom there is no one. He is "the Omniscient," perfect in knowledge, comprehending all things large and small, open and concealed, and "All-Wise," free from errors in judgment. He is "the Compassionate," "the Merciful," whose mercy encompasses all creation. However, while Allah loves and rewards belief and piety, He hates impiety and punishes transgression. Being "the Omnipotent," His power is absolute, and none can frustrate His decree.

Many other characteristic names are given in the Holy Qur'an, such as Allah being the Lord and Master of creation: humankind having been created through His will and living, dying, and returning to Him on The Day of Judgment according to His decree. Muslims further recognize that Allah is beyond complete human understanding, as there is nothing in creation comparable to Him. Perhaps in the afterlife we will be gifted with greater understanding, but in this life, knowledge of our Creator is confined within the boundaries of revelation.

Similar to Judaism, but unlike Christianity, there are no physical representations of Allah in Islam. Consequently, the minds of the believers are not befuddled with anthropomorphic "big man in the sky" imagery. Furthermore, the Islamic religion does not assign gender to Allah, for Allah is understood to be transcendentally above all such characteristics. The attribution of sexual traits is considered especially offensive, blasphemous even, to Muslims. So, while referred to by the male pronoun in the Qur'an, this is nothing more than a linguistic necessity, for there is no gender-neutral pronoun in the Arabic language. Lord, God, Creator and Master though He may be, nowhere in Islam is Allah referred to as "Father."

The Islamic understanding of God meets a number of objections in the predominantly Christian West. The first is that Islam recognizes Jesus as a prophet but not as a "son of God," and especially not in a "begotten, not made" sense. The second is that Islam teaches the One-ness of God and condemns the concept of the Trinity. The third objection is that Muslims do not believe humankind inherited the burden of original sin, for this concept is not compatible with God's justice and mercy. The last is that Muslims believe Jesus was raised up and saved from crucifixion, which invalidates the doctrines of atonement and resurrection.

These differences in belief are significant, for they constitute the major fault-lines where the continental shelves of Christianity and Islam collide.

PART III: DOCTRINAL DIFFERENCES

The trouble with people is not that they don't know, but that they know so much that ain't so.

> —Josh Billings, *Josh Billings' Encyclopedia of Wit and Wisdom*

The differences between Judaism, Christianity, and Islam can be addressed on a number of levels, the most basic of which is that of common sense. Plain *Alice in Wonderland* kind of sense, exemplified by such sensible exchanges as:

> *"That's not a regular rule: you invented it just now."*
>
> *"It's the oldest rule in the book,"* said the King.
>
> *"Then it ought to be Number one,"* said Alice.[50]

When correctly applied, this form of logic leaves no room for further argument. However, a complementary avenue of analysis is to contrast Judaic, Christian, and Islamic teachings, and leave readers to weigh the evidence against their own beliefs.

Let us begin by taking an *Alice in Wonderland* peek at the history of the Unitarian/Trinitarian debate.

59

1—Unitarians vs. Trinitarians

*They decided that all liars should be whipped.And a
man came along and told them the truth.And they
hanged him.*

—T.W.H. Crosland, *Little Stories*

Many tenets of Trinitarian faith are regarded as the
"oldest rules in the book," but in fact are derived from non-
biblical sources. Rather than being "rule number one," as a
person might logically expect given their primacy, these tenets
of faith are not found in the Bible at all.

Alice would object.

And, in fact, many great thinkers *have* objected: thinkers
like Bishop Pothinus of Lyons (murdered in the late second
century along with *all* the dissenting Christians who petitioned
Pope Elutherus for an end to persecution); Leonidas (a follower
of Apostolic Christianity and expositor of Pauline innovations,
murdered in 208 CE); Origen (who died in prison in 254 CE
after prolonged torture for preaching the Unity of God and
rejection of the Trinity);Diodorus;Pamphilus (tortured and
murdered, 309 CE); Lucian (tortured for his views and killed in
312 CE);Donatus (chosen to be Bishop of Carthage in 313 CE,
and subsequently the leader and inspiration of a Unitarian
movement that grew to dominate Christianity in North Africa

right up until Emperor Constantine ordered their massacre. So complete was their obliteration that little of the sacred writings of this once huge sect remains); Arius (the presbyter of Alexandria, whose motto was "follow Jesus as he preached,"killed by poisoning in 336 CE); Eusebius of Nicomedia; and not to mention the million-plus Christians killed for refusing to accept official church doctrine in the immediate period following the Council of Nicaea.

Later examples include Lewis Hetzer (decapitated February 4, 1529); Michael Servetus (burned at the stake October 27, 1553, using green branches still in leaf to produce an agonizingly slow, smoldering fire);[51(EN)] Francis Davidis (died in prison in 1579); Faustus Socinus (died in 1604); John Biddle (who suffered banishment to Sicily and multiple imprisonments, the last of which hastened his death). Biddle, who considered the terminology employed by Trinitarians "fitter for conjurers than Christians,"[52] established a breastwork of arguments against the assault of Trinitarian theology of such effectiveness that, on at least one occasion, debate opponents arranged his arrest to avoid facing him in public forum.[53] He left a legacy of freethinkers affirming divine unity, including some of the leading intellectuals of the day, such as Sir Isaac Newton, John Locke, and John Milton. Biddle's days in banishment also gave rise to one of the most touching comments on religious persecution, penned by a sympathetic correspondent of *The Gospel Advocate*:

> The conclave met, the judge was set,
>
> Man mounted on God's throne;
>
> And they did judge a matter there,

> That rests with Him alone;
>
> A brother's faith they made a crime,
>
> And crushed thought's native right
> sublime.[54]

During his lifetime, Parliament attempted to kill (literally, that is) Biddle's movement by establishing the death penalty for those who denied the Trinity (May 2, 1648). The year of his death, Parliament passed the second Act of Uniformity and outlawed all non-Episcopal worship and clergy.[55] Under this act, 2,257 priests were ejected from the clergy and over 8,000 people died in prison out of refusal to accept the Trinity.

There is at least one case where, in the selective wisdom of the church, the population of an entire country was condemned:

> Early in the year, the most sublime sentence of death was promulgated which has ever been pronounced since the creation of the world. The Roman tyrant wished that his enemies' heads were all upon a single neck, that he might strike them off at a blow; the inquisition assisted Philip to place the heads of all his Netherlands subjects upon a single neck for the same fell purpose. Upon the 16th February 1568, a sentence of the Holy Office condemned all the inhabitants of the Netherlands to death as heretics. From

this universal doom only a few persons, especially named, were excepted. A proclamation of the King, dated ten days later, confirmed this decree of the Inquisition, and ordered it to be carried into instant execution, without regard to age, sex, or condition. This is probably the most concise death-warrant that was ever framed. Three millions of people, men, women, and children, were sentenced to the scaffold in three lines; and, as it was well known that these were not harmless thunders, like some bulls of the Vatican, but serious and practical measures, which were to be enforced, the horror which they produced may be easily imagined. It was hardly the purpose of government to compel the absolute completion of the wholesale plan in all its length and breadth, yet in the horrible times upon which they had fallen, the Netherlanders might be excused for believing that no measure was too monstrous to be fulfilled. At any rate, it was certain that when *all* were condemned, *any* might at a moment's warning be carried to the scaffold, and this was precisely the course adopted by the authorities. Under this universal decree the industry of the Blood-Council might now seem superfluous. Why should

63

not these mock prosecutions be dispensed with against individuals, now that a common sentence had swallowed the whole population in one vast grave? Yet it may be supposed that if the exertions of the commissioners and councilors served no other purpose, they at least furnished the government with valuable evidence as to the relative wealth and other circumstances of the individual victims. The leading thought of the government being, that persecution, judiciously managed, might fructify into a golden harvest, it was still desirable to persevere in the cause in which already such bloody progress had been made.

And under this new decree, the executions certainly did not slacken. Men in the highest and the humblest positions were daily and hourly dragged to the stake. Alva, in a single letter to Phillip, coolly estimated the number of executions which were to take place immediately after the expiration of holy week, at "eight hundred heads." Many a citizen, convicted of a hundred thousand florins and of no other crime, saw himself suddenly tied to a horse's tail, with his hands fastened behind him, and so dragged to the gallows. But although wealth was an unpardonable sin, poverty proved rarely a protection. Reasons sufficient could always be found for dooming the starveling labourer as well as the opulent burgher. To avoid the disturbances created in the streets by the frequent harangues or exhortations addressed to the bystanders by the victims on the way to the scaffold, a new gag was invented. The tongue of each prisoner was screwed into an iron ring, and then seared with a hot iron. The swelling and inflammation which were the immediate result, prevented the tongue from slipping through the ring, and of course effectually precluded all possibility of speech.[56]

Only a decade earlier Charles V, the Holy Roman Emperor and King of Spain, recommended that "all [Netherlanders] who remained obstinate in their errors were burned alive, and those who were admitted to penitence were beheaded."[57] So even the penitent were not to be spared.

The above list catalogs individuals once regarded by the Catholic Church as the most notorious of heretics and by Unitarian Christians as the greatest of martyrs to the revival of the teachings of Jesus Christ. Some of the Unitarians mentioned above were associated with movements of such significance as to have swept across countries, but in all cases the TrinitarianChurch eventually dominated through the combination of superior force, inferior tolerance, and willingness to sacrifice fellow men and women to the cause of religious purification.

Although they use the same book for guidance, Unitarian and Trinitarian Christianity could hardly differ more in their methodology. Trinitarian Christianity condemns anything that conflicts with derived doctrine, whereas Unitarian Christianity condemns anything that conflicts with scriptural evidence. The conflict between these two standards lies at the heart of the debate. The Catholic church succeeded in killing off dissenting individuals, but failed to suppress the thoughts and fierce passions they expressed. Far greater success would have been achieved had the church provided rational and conclusive rebuttal to the challenges, and established their authority through intellectual superiority rather than through tyranny. However, church history documents nearly two millennia of failure to overthrow the arguments of the Unitarians, much to the discredit of the Trinitarians.

Examples can be taken from the life of Arius, but with the caution that, with rare exception, few books about Arius remain, other than those written by his enemies. Consequently, most authors' opinions betray an unkind prejudice, and the only objective course is to examine his pure teachings.

Perhaps one of the earliest Arian arguments is that if Jesus was the "son of God," then there must have been a time when he did not exist. If Jesus was created of the Father, then there must have been a time when the Eternal Father preceded the later-created Jesus. Hence, the Creator and His creation are not the same, and Jesus cannot be considered a partner in Godhead.

Arius held that if Jesus truly did say, "My Father is greater than I" (John 14:28), then equating Jesus with God is to deny the Bible. Arius suggested that if anything is evident from the teachings of Jesus, it is that he affirmed his own humanity and the inviolability of divine unity.

When Trinitarian clergy claimed Jesus was "of the essence of God," Arius and Trinitarian Christians alike objected, for "from the essence" and "of one essence" are materialist expressions, Sabellian[58(EN)] in origin, not encountered in scripture, and are contrary to church authority (since the expression originated at a council at Antioch in 269 CE).[59] When the Catholic Church subsequently asserted that Jesus was "of God," the Arians responded that the Bible describes all people as being "of God" in the verse, "Now all things *are* of God . . ." (2 Corinthians 5:18—see also 1 Corinthians 8:6).[60] Forced to correct themselves, the church then asserted that Jesus Christ "is not a creature, but the power and eternal image of the Father and true God."[61] The Arian response that the Bible describes *all* men as "the image and glory of God" (1 Corinthians 11:7) left the church confounded.[62] In the words of British theologian Henry MelvillGwatkin, "The longer the debate went on, the clearer it became that the meaning of Scripture could not be defined without going outside Scripture for words to define it."[63] To adopt such a methodology is to propose that man can explain revelation better than The Source of revelation Himself.

So the arguments started and so they have continued to the present day. After failing to win through rational argument, the TrinitarianChurch violently suppressed dissension to the point where entire populations were terrorized into conformity. In the process, the church failed to address the issues. As Castillo, one of the followers of the sixteenth-century theologian Servetus, commented, "To burn a man is not to prove a doctrine." Meaning, the church can reduce a man to ashes but can only eliminate his arguments through intelligent rebuttal. Typical of those who lack the ability to substantiate their beliefs but who possess the power of oppression, violent response has been the historical reflex against those who challenged Trinitarian creed. That this oppression existed in the vacuum of reasonable justification weakens, rather than strengthens, the institution. As John Toland commented, "This conduct, on the contrary, will make them suspect all to be a cheat and imposture, because men will naturally cry out when they are touched in a tender part . . . no man will be angry at a question who's able to answer it. . . ."[64] In the words of H. G. Wells, "They were intolerant of questions or dissent, not because they were sure of their faith, but because they were not. They wanted conformity for reasons of policy. By the thirteenth century the church was evidently already morbidly anxious about the gnawing doubts that might presently lay the whole structure of its pretensions in ruins."[65]

Pythagoras summarized the risk of speaking one's mind in such a circumstance: "To tell of God among men of prejudicial opinion is not safe." Unitarians throughout history noted that Jesus himself predicted, "They will put you out of the synagogues; yes, the time is coming that whoever kills you will think that he offers God service. And these things they will do to you because they have not known the Father nor Me" (John 16:2–3).

The establishment of Trinitarian doctrine by the inquisitor's chamber, fire, sword, and the headman's axe does not threaten us today. Instead of the horrors of the past, we are now faced with a variety of emotionally provocative justifications, coupled with a systematic avoidance of relevant issues. Disarmed as they now are, much of the modern Christian world follows the example of Myser of Nicholas, a bishop at the Council of Nicaea who boxed his own ears whenever Arius spoke. Some would suggest the response of Trinitarians to Unitarian challenges is not much different today. Clergy tend to avoid debate and cloak their theology in a mantle of emotionally charged, manipulative oratory, embroidered with the glitter of self-righteousness.

Some are swayed by the sanctimonious presentation and parroted sectarian lines; others are not. More than a few God-fearing people tire of such psychological ploys and seek to reexamine the unfounded tenets of the past in the light of modern knowledge and open-minded analysis.

To this end, let us now consider the relevant issues one by one.

2 — Jesus Christ

But why do you call me "Lord, Lord," and not do the things which I say? Whoever comes to me, and hears my sayings and does them, I will show you whom he is like: He is like a man building a house, who dug deep and laid the foundation on the rock. And when the flood arose, the stream beat vehemently against that house, and could not shake it, for it was founded on the rock. But he who heard and did nothing is like a man who built a house on the earth without a foundation, against which the stream beat vehemently; and immediately it fell. And the ruin of that house was great.

—Jesus Christ (Luke 6:46–49)

Who was the historical Jesus? Throughout history, that question has haunted all who wished to know him. Jews have one concept, Unitarian Christians another, Trinitarians yet one more; and these viewpoints are well known. What is not so widely understood is the Islamic perspective.

Most Christians are pleasantly surprised to learn that Muslims recognize Jesus as Messiah and a Word of God. Most Jews are . . . well . . . not so positively impressed.

Translation of the Holy Qur'an, *surah* (Chapter) 3, *ayat* (verses) 45–47, reads,

> Behold! The angels said: "O Mary! Allah gives you glad tidings of a Word from Him: his name will be Christ Jesus, the son of Mary, held in honor in this world and the Hereafter and of (the company of) those nearest to Allah;
>
> "He shall speak to the people in childhood and in maturity. And he shall be (of the company) of the righteous."
>
> She said, "O my Lord! How shall I have a son when no man has touched me?"
>
> He said: "Even so: Allah creates what He wills: when He has decreed a Plan, He says to it, 'Be,' and it is!"

In a theological nutshell, Muslims believe Jesus to be *a* Word of Allah (unlike Christians, who regard him as *the*Word), a Messiah, born by virgin birth to Mary (Maryam) and strengthened by the Holy Spirit. Muslims believe he performed miracles from the cradle, conveyed revelation to humankind in fulfillment of previous scripture, healed lepers, cured the blind and raised the dead, all by the will of Allah. They also believe Allah raised Jesus up at the end of his ministry to spare him the persecution of the people, and substituted another to be crucified in his place. Muslims further believe a time will come when Jesus will be sent back to vanquish the Antichrist. Following this, he will eradicate deviant beliefs and practices in all religions, which will include correcting those who consider themselves to be following his teachings as Christians, but who

71

in fact are astray. He will then establish submission to God's will (again, the definition of Islam) throughout the world, live an exemplary life, die, and shortly thereafter will come the Day of Judgment.

Given the complexity of the issues, each point warrants separate discussion. No doubt, the reader hopes that once the picture of the scriptural Jesus is blown up for examination, detailed analysis will reveal a profile consistent with one's expectations. However, in seeking the truth, we must be prepared to encounter a Jesus at odds with two thousand years of false preconception and canonical corruption, the *real* Jesus in conflict with popularized notions, media profiles, and modern Christian teaching. Could Jesus be so contrary to personal and societal constructs that he will openly oppose the churches built around his existence? If so, then popes and priests, parsons and pastors, bishops and cardinals, evangelists and monks, ministers and messianic pretenders may all find Jesus condemning them just as he condemned the Pharisees in his homeland. In other words, a Jesus may surface who will disown those who claim to follow in his name, *just as he said he would*, as recorded in Matthew 7:21–23:

> Not everyone who says to me, "Lord,
> Lord," shall enter the kingdom of heaven,
> but he who does the will of my Father in
> heaven. *Many* will say to me in that day,
> "Lord, Lord, have we not prophesied in
> your name, cast out demons in your name,
> and done many wonders in your name?"
> And then I will declare to them, "I never
> knew you; depart from me, you who

practice lawlessness!"

This passage clearly predicts a time when Jesus will disown seemingly pious "followers," despite their impressive prophecies, wonders, and exorcisms. Why? Because, as Jesus said, they practiced "lawlessness." These are the followers who, despite their miracles of ministry, disregarded "the Law." What law? God's law, of course—the Old Testament Law Jesus upheld. The same Old Testament Law Paul negated. The same Paul from whom Trinitarian theology took root. The same Trinitarian theology founded largely upon non-biblical sources.

"Hey, wait a minute," the reader may say. "Who did Jesus say he would disown, and why?"

Let's take a closer look.

3— Word of God

It was then that I began to look into the seams of your doctrine. I wanted only to pick at a single knot; but when I had got that undone, the whole thing raveled out. And then I understood that it was all machine-sewn.

—Henrik Ibsen, *Ghosts*, Act II

Jesus is identified in the Holy Qur'an as a "Word" from Allah. *Surah* 3:45 reads,

> Behold! the angels said:

> "O Mary! Allah gives you glad tidings of
> a Word from Him: his name will be the
> Messiah, the son of Mary, held in honor
> in this world and the Hereafter and of (the
> company of) those nearest to Allah"
> (TMQ 3:45).

In biblical contrast, John 1:1 reads: "In the beginning was the Word, and the Word was with God, and the Word was God." Christian exegesis on this point is that Jesus is the Word of God, which means the *logos*—the Greek word for "word," or "saying." This redundant reasoning satisfies some, but not those who realize the explanation repeats the assertion. The question,

"What does it mean?" is left unanswered.

The point is that a statement must rest upon a foundation of axioms, or self-evident truths, if it is to be considered factual. Axioms establish a clear knowledge base from which valid conclusions can be derived. Should conclusions violate foundational axioms, these same conclusions are considered to fall outside the bounds of reason. In the field of mathematics, a simple axiom is that one plus one equals two. Anyone in the world can place an apple next to an apple and see that, by definition, there are now two apples. Add one more, and there are three. Should a scientist later derive some new and revolutionary concept, but one that violates the axiom that one plus one equals two, the whole theory is rendered invalid. In the case of the Christian concept of Jesus being "the Word," the doctrine unravels, for the simple reason that there *are* no axioms—there *are* no self-evident truths. All that exists is a reshuffling of words.

On the other hand, Islam teaches that the "Word of God" is the word by which Allah commands things into existence— the Arabic word *kun*, meaning "be." The foundational axiom in this regard is that God creates through willing things into existence. And just as He willed into existence every big, every little, every *thing*, He created Jesus through His divine command, "Be." *Surah* 3:47 points out: "Allah creates what He wills: when He has decreed a Plan, He but says to it, 'Be,' and it is!"

In the Bible we find the first example of the "Word of God," Islamically speaking, in Genesis 1:3, God said "Let there be . . ."—and it was! Returning to the Holy Qur'an, *surah* 3:59 reads, "The similitude of Jesus before God is as that of Adam; He created him from dust, then said to him: 'Be': and he was."

75

For those who claim the "Word" of John 1:1 ("In the beginning was the Word, and the Word was with God, and the Word was God") implies equality between Jesus and God, 1 Corinthians 3:23 muddies the doctrinal waters. This verse states, "And ye are Christ's; and Christ is God's." Now, in what way are "ye Christ's"? A follower of his teachings? But then, in what way is Christ God's? And if Jesus were God, why doesn't the passage read "Christ is God" rather than "Christ is God's"?

This verse emphasizes the fact that just as the disciples were subordinate to the prophet Jesus, so too was Jesus subordinate to God. Surely this distinction comes as no surprise to those who respect the authority of Isaiah 45:22 ("For I am God, and there is no other"), Isaiah 44:6 ("Thus says the Lord . . . 'I am the First and I am the Last; Besides Me there is no God'"), Deuteronomy 4:39 ("The Lord Himself is God in heaven above and on the earth beneath; there is no other"), and Deuteronomy 6:4 ("Hear, O Israel: The Lord our God, the Lord is one!"). Given the above, claiming the wording of John 1:1 to equate Jesus to God certainly is selective reasoning at best. All of which leaves a reasonable person to wonder if anything is wrong with the Islamic viewpoint on this issue, whether understood in the framework of Unitarian Christianity or Islam.

4 — Messiah (Christ)

*The Old Testament teems with prophecies of the
Messiah, but nowhere is it intimated that that Messiah
is to stand as a God to be worshipped. He is to bring
peace on earth, to build up the waste places, to comfort
the broken-hearted, but nowhere is he spoken of as a
deity.*

—Olympia Brown, first woman minister
ordainedin the U.S., Sermon of 13 January, 1895

The concept of Jesus being the predicted messiah is so
well known to the world of Christianity as to obviate need for
discussion. But Jesus,the messiah, in *Islam*? The fact that
Muslims recognize Jesus as the messiah has prompted Christian
evangelists to try to sway Muslims to Trinitarian beliefs.

"Was Jesus the Messiah?" questions the evangelist, to
which Muslims answer, "Yes." The evangelist asks, "Was
Muhammad the messiah?" Muslims answer, "No."

The evangelist then seeks to lead the Muslim to conclude
that Muhammad was not a messiah, and therefore not a prophet,
and that Jesus *was* the predicted messiah, and therefore is
partner in divinity.

It's a tortured argument, to which Muslims respond with
some questions of their own:

1. Other than Jesus, are there other biblical messiahs?

77

Answer: Yes, lots of them—no less than thirty-eight.[66](For specifics, see below.)

2. Were all biblical messiahs, such as the Davidic kings and high priests of ancient Palestine (now called Israel), prophets? Answer: no.
3. Conversely, were all biblical prophets, such as Abraham, Noah, Moses, etc., messiahs? Answer: no.
4. Therefore, if not all biblical prophets were messiahs, how can we disqualify any man's claim to prophethood on the basis of not being a messiah? For in that case, Abraham, Noah, Moses, and other biblical prophets would also be disqualified by the same standard.
5. Lastly, if there were biblical messiahs who were not even prophets, how can being a messiah equate to divinity when the label doesn't even equate to piety?

The fact is that the word *messiah* simply means "anointed one," and bears no connotation of divinity. So the Muslim has no difficulty recognizing Jesus as Messiah, or in the language of the English translations, Jesus as Christ, but without transgressing into the error of apotheosis (equating with divinity, i.e., deification). Where, then, do "messiah" and "Christ" come from in the first place?

The name "Christ" is derived from the Greek *christos*, which was subsequently Latinized to "Christ." The *Theological Dictionary of the New Testament* defines *christos* as "Christ, Messiah, Anointed One."[67] A second opinion is as follows: "The word Messiah (sometimes Messias, following the Hellenized transcription) represents the Hebrew *mashiah*, or *mashuah* 'anointed,' from the verb *mashah* 'anoint.' It is exactly rendered by the Greek *christos* 'anointed.'"[68] In plain English, if people read the Old Testament in ancient Hebrew they will read *mashiah*, *mashuah*, and *mashah*. Read it in ancient Greek, and the above three are "exactly rendered" as *christos*.

The subject becomes interesting at this point because Aramaic, Hebrew, and ancient Greek do not have capital letters, so how Bible translators got "Christ" with a capital C from *christos* with a small C is a mystery known only to them.Claims that context mandates capitalization in the case of Jesus Christ don't work, for *christos* is applied to a wide variety of subjects throughout the Bible. The verb *chrio*, meaning "to anoint," is found sixty-nine times in the Old Testament in reference to Saul, David, Solomon, Joash, and Jehoahaz, among others. The noun *christos* (the same *christos* translated to "Christ" in the case of Jesus) occurs thirty-eight times—thirty in reference to kings,[69(EN)]six in reference to the high priest, and twice in reference to patriarchs of the Old Testament.[70]

The argument can be made that "Christ" with a capital C was "anointed of God" in some special sense, different from all other "christs" with a small C. Either the difference needs to be defined or the argument abandoned. According to the *Theological Dictionary of the New Testament*, "Saul is most commonly called 'the Lord's anointed.' Apart from Saul, only Davidic kings bear the title (except in Is. 45:1)."[71] In reading this quote, few people are likely to take notice of the inconspicuous exception bracketed by parentheses—a literary cloaking device. The few readers who stop and overturn that little exception will find that what crawls out of Isaiah 45:1 is Cyrus the Persian— Cyrus the king of the fire-worshipping Zoroastrians, that is.

Graham Stanton, Lady Margaret's Professor of Divinity at the University of Cambridge, summarizes the above information as follows:

> The Hebrew word "messiah" means an
> anointed person or thing. It is translated
> by "christos" (hence Christ) in the Greek
> translation of the Old Testament, the
> Septuagint (LXX). In numerous passages
> in the Old Testament "anointed one" is
> applied to the divinely appointed King.
> (See, for example, I Sam. 12:3 (Saul) and
> 2 Sam. 19:22 (David)). In a few passages
> "anointed one" is used of prophets (most
> notably in Isa. 61:1) and of priests (Lev.
> 4:3,5,16), but without further designation
> the term normally refers to the king of
> Israel.[72]

Consequently, the "Lord's Christ" (i.e., the "Lord's
Christos"—the "Lord's anointed," or the "Lord's messiah") list
includes Saul the Christ, Cyrus the Christ, and the many Davidic
kings—all "Christs." Or at least, that's how the Bible would
read if everyone's title were translated the same.

But they aren't.

In the selective wisdom of the Bible translators, *christos*
is translated "anointed" in every case but that of Jesus Christ.
When the word "anointed" is found in any English translation of
the Bible, a person can safely assume that the underlying Greek
is the same *christos* from which Jesus gets his unique label of
"Christ." This exclusive title of "Christ" with a capital C, and
"Messiah" with a capital M, is singularly impressive. In fact, it
makes a person believe that the term implies some unique
spiritual link, distinct from the flock of lay "messiahs" with

small M's and no C at all—the *christos* hidden in the alternative translation of "anointed."

All this represents a point of embarrassment to educated Christians, for it suggests the questionable ethic of doctrinally driven Bible translation. Those who recognize the concern might also recognize that yet another fundamental difference between Unitarian/Islamic and Trinitarian beliefs exists in a vacuum of biblical support for the Trinitarian viewpoint.

The Islamic religion confirms that Jesus was *an* "anointed" one of God, but does not strain to elevate him beyond the station of prophethood, or to appear more unique than others bearing similar title or prophetic office. The most ancient biblical scriptures, as discussed above, support the Islamic belief that just as all prophets and Davidic kings were *christos*, so was Jesus. The conclusion that no particular king or prophet should bear unique labeling, separate and distinct from others possessing similar titles, is not unreasonable.

One intriguing directive of the Islamic religion is for humankind to be truthful and avoid extremes. In this instance, unjustified literary license is to be shunned. Honest translation should avoid the bias of doctrinal prejudice. A document perceived to be revelation from God should not be adjusted to suit personal or sectarian desires. Such a document should be held in due reverence, and translated faithfully. And the challenge to humankind has always been just this—for the faithful to mold their lives to the truth rather than the other way around. This concept, encompassing the recognition of Jesus and cautioning against extremes in religion, is succinctly expressed in *surah* 4:171 of the Holy Qur'an:

O People of the Book! Commit no

excesses in your religion: nor say of Allah
anything but the truth. Christ Jesus the
son of Mary was (no more than) a
Messenger of Allah, and His Word, which
He bestowed on Mary, and a Spirit
proceeding from Him [i.e., a soul, created
by His command]: so believe in Allah and
His messengers (TMQ 4:171).

5— Virgin Birth

A baby is God's opinion that life should go on.

—Carl Sandburg, *Remembrance Rock*

And in the case of Jesus, a baby was God's determination that revelation should go on.

The fact that Jews, as well as a few "progressive" Christian churches, deny the virgin birth is surprising, for the Old Testament foretells, "Therefore the Lord Himself will give you a sign. Behold, the virgin shall conceive and bear a son, and shall call his name Immanuel." (Isaiah 7:14) Whether this passage refers to Jesus Christ or to another of God's creation misses the point. The fact is that virgin birth is foretold, and in the context of a divine sign. Hence, to deny a prophet's legitimacy on this basis is purely capricious.

The mainstream Christian viewpoint is well-known, and the Islamic religion is entirely supportive. Islam teaches that just as God created Adam from nothing more than clay, He created Jesus without biological father as a sign to the people—a miraculous origin portending messianic status. *Surah* 19:17–22 (TMQ) describes Mary receiving the good news of her son as follows:

> She placed a screen (to screen herself)
> from them; then We sent to her Our angel,

83

and he appeared before her as a man in all respects.

She said: "I seek refuge from you to (Allah) Most Gracious: (come not near) if you fear Allah."

He said: "Nay, I am only a messenger from your Lord, (to announce) to you the gift of a holy son."

She said: "How shall I have a son, seeing that no man has touched me, and I am not unchaste?"

He said: "So (it will be): your Lord says, 'That is easy for Me: and (We wish) to appoint him as a Sign to men and a Mercy from Us': it is a matter (so) decreed."

So she conceived him, and she retired with him to a remote place.

Muslims believe that through the miraculous birth of Jesus, Allah demonstrates the completeness of His creative powers with regard to humankind, having created Adam without mother or father, Eve from man without mother, and Jesus from woman without father.

6 — Jesus Begotten?

To create is divine, to reproduce is human.

—Man Ray, *Originals Graphic Multiples*

Christian laity have accepted the doctrines of Jesus being of divine sonship and "begotten, not made" for so long that these doctrines have largely fallen from scrutiny. Until three centuries ago, dissenting views were suppressed by means sufficiently horrific to have driven intellectual challenges underground. Only in recent times have Western societies been freed from religious oppression, allowing a free exchange of opinions. Not so in Muslim lands, where these Christian doctrines have been freely opposed since the revelation of the Holy Qur'an, 1,400 years ago.

The Islamic understanding is that "begetting," which is defined in *Merriam Webster's Collegiate Dictionary* as "to procreate as the father," is a physical act implying the carnal element of sex—an animal trait light-years below the majesty of the Creator. So what does "begotten, not made" mean, anyway? Nearly 1,700 years of exegesis have failed to provide an explanation more sensible than the original statement, as expressed in the Nicene Creed. Which is not to say that the Nicene Creed is sensible, but that everything else seems even less so. The creed reads, "We believe in one Lord, Jesus Christ, the only Son of God, eternally begotten of the Father, God from

85

God, Light from Light, true God from true God, begotten, not made, one in Being with the Father . . ."

The question has been raised before, "What language is this?" If someone could explain the above in terms a child could understand, and not just be forced to blindly accept, then they will succeed where all others have failed. The oft-recited Athanasian Creed, which was composed roughly a hundred years following the Nicene Creed, bears such strikingly similar convolutions that Gennadius, the patriarch of Constantinople, "was so much amazed by this extraordinary composition, that he frankly pronounced it to be the work of a drunken man."[73]

More direct challenges arise. If Jesus is the "only begotten Son of God," who is David? Answer: Psalms 2:7—"The LORD has said to me, 'You are My Son, Today I have begotten you." Jesus the "only begotten son of God," with David "begotten" a scant forty generations earlier? The label of "religious mystery" may not satisfy all free-thinkers.

In the face of such conflicts, a reasonable person might question whether God is unreliable (an impossibility), or if the Bible contains errors (a serious possibility, and if so, how does a person know which elements are true and which false?).[74(EN)] However, let us consider a third possibility—that an incorrect creed has been constructed around a nucleus of scriptural colloquialisms.

One supremely disconcerting challenge revolves around the word, *monogenes*. This is the *only* word in the ancient Greek biblical texts that bears the translation "only begotten."[75] This term occurs nine times in the New Testament, and the translation of this term in the Gospel and First Epistle of John form the foundation of the "begotten, not made" doctrine. Of the nine occurrences of this term, *monogenes* occurs three times in

Brown / MisGod'ed

Luke (7:12, 8:42, and 9:38), but always in reference to individuals other than Jesus, and in *none* of these cases is it translated "only begotten." That alone is curious. A person would rationally expect an unbiased translation to render the same Greek word into equivalent English in all instances. Clearly that is not the case, but again, one would expect . . .

Only John applies *monogenes* to Jesus.[76] The term is found in five of the six remaining New Testament occurrences, namely John 1:14, 1:18, 3:16, 3:18, and the First Epistle of John 4:9. John 3:16 reads, "For God so loved the world that He gave His only begotten son . . ." Such a crucial element of church doctrine, and the other three gospel authors neglected to record it? The Gospel of John alone does not exactly exorcise the ghost of doubt when the other three gospels are conspicuously silent on this matter. By way of comparison, all four gospel authors agree that Jesus rode a donkey (Matthew 21:7, Mark 11:7, Luke 19:35, and John 12:14), which is relatively high on the "who cares?" list. But three of the gospel authors fail to support the critical "begotten, not made" tenet of faith? Hardly a sensible balance of priorities, one would think.

Should the doctrine be true, that is.

So three of the nine New Testament occurrences of the term *monogenes* are in the Gospel of Luke, refer to someone other than Jesus, and are selectively mistranslated. Occurrences four through eight are encountered in the Gospel and First Epistle of John, and are held to describe Jesus. But it's the ninth occurrence that's the troublemaker, for "Isaac is *monogenes* in Heb. 11:17."[77]

We are led to question biblical accuracy at this point, for Isaac was never the only begotten son of Abraham. How could he have been, when Ishmael was born fourteen years prior?

Comparison of Genesis 16:16—"Abram [i.e., Abraham] was eighty-six years old when Hagar bore him Ishmael"—with Genesis 21:5—"Abraham was a hundred years old when his son Isaac was born to him"—reveals the age difference. This is confirmed in Genesis 17:25, which tells us Ishmael was circumcised at the age of thirteen, one year prior to the birth of Isaac. Furthermore, Ishmael and Isaac both outlived their father, Abraham, as documented in Genesis 25:8–9. So how could Isaac ever, at any moment in time, have been Abraham's "only begotten son"?

A lay defense is the assertion that Ishmael was the product of illicit union between Abraham and Hagar, Sarah's maidservant. Therefore he was illegitimate and doesn't count.

No serious scholar agrees with this defense, and for good reason.To begin with, Ishmael was Abraham's begotten son regardless of the nature of his parentage. More concrete validation of his status as Abraham's legitimate son is simply that *God* recognized him as such, as encountered in Genesis 16:11, 16:15, 17:7, 17:23, 17:25, and 21:11. And if God recognized Ishmael as Abraham's son, who of humankind dares to disagree?

Yet man is inclined to argument, so by looking at all angles a person should recognize that polygamy was an accepted practice according to the laws of the Old Testament.[78] Examples include Rachel, Leah, and their handmaids (Gen 29 and 30), Lamech (Gen 4:19), Gideon (Judges 8:30), David (2 Samuel 5:13), and the archetype of marital plurality, Solomon (1 Kings 11:3). *The Oxford Dictionary of the Jewish Religion* notes that polygamy was permitted in the laws of the Old Testament, and was recognized as legally valid by the rabbis.[79]*Encyclopedia Judaica* acknowledges the common practice of polygamy among the upper classes in biblical times.[80] Polygamy was banned among Ashkenazi Jews in the tenth century, but the practice has persisted among Sephardi Jews.[81],[82] Even in Israel, the chief rabbis officially banned the practice only as recently as 1950, and considering the thousands of years it took to rewrite Mosaic Law, we have good reason to suspect the above rulings were motivated more by politics than by religion.[83]

So what should we understand when Genesis 16:3 relates, "Sarai, Abram's wife, took Hagar the Egyptian, her slave-girl, and gave her to her husband Abram as a *wife*" (italics mine)? Polygamy may offend Western sensitivities, be that as it may. The point is that according to the laws of Abraham's time, Ishmael was a legitimate child.

Purely for the sake of argument, let's just forget all that (as many do) and say that Hagar was Abraham's concubine. Even that claim has an answer. According to Old Testament Law, concubines were legally permitted, and their offspring had equal rights. According to Hasting's *Dictionary of the Bible*, "There does not seem to have been any inferiority in the position of the concubine as compared with that of the wife, nor was any idea of illegitimacy, in our sense of the word, connected with her children."[84] Jacob M. Myers, professor at Lutheran Theological Seminary and acknowledged Old Testament scholar, comments in his *Invitation to the Old Testament*:

> Archaeological discoveries help us to fill
> in the details of the biblical narrative and
> to explain many of the otherwise obscure
> references and strange customs that were
> commonplace in Abraham's world and
> time. For instance, the whole series of

89

> practices relating to the birth of Ishmael
> and the subsequent treatment of Hagar,
> his mother . . . all are now known to have
> been normal everyday occurrences
> regulated by law.
>
> A Nuzi marriage contract provides that
> a childless wife may take a woman of the
> country and marry her to her husband to
> obtain progeny. But she may not drive out
> the offspring even if she later has children
> of her own. The child born of the
> handmaid has the same status as the one
> born to the wife.[85]

Returning to the *Alice in Wonderland* perspective for a moment, what makes more sense, anyway? Would God design a prophet to violate the same commandments he bears from the Creator? Would God send a prophet with a "do as I say, not as I do" message? Doesn't it make more sense for Abraham to have acted within the laws of his time by engaging Hagar in a lawful relationship?

Given the above evidence, the union between Ishmael's parents was legal, God endorsed Ishmael as Abraham's son, and Ishmael was the first begotten. Look up *Ismael* in the *New Catholic Encyclopedia* (the reference of those who would be most likely to oppose, on ideological grounds, the piecing together of this puzzle), and there one finds the following agreement: "Ismael (Ishmael), son of Abraham, Abraham's firstborn . . ."[86]

So what should we make of the book of Hebrews using

monogenes to describe Isaac as the only begotten son of Abraham? A metaphor, mistranslation, or mistake? If a metaphor, then literal interpretation of *monogenes* in relation to Jesus is indefensible. If a mistranslation, then both the mistranslation and the doctrine deserve correction. And if a mistake, then a greater challenge surfaces—reconciling a biblical error with the infallibility of God.

This problem demands resolution, and the most respected modern translations of the Bible (i.e., the Revised Standard Version, New Revised Standard Version, New International Version, Good News Bible, New English Bible, Jerusalem Bible and many others) have recognized "begotten" as an interpolation and have unceremoniously expunged the word from the text. By so doing, they are narrowing the gap between Christian and Islamic theology, for as stated in the Holy Qur'an, "It is not consonant with the majesty of (Allah) Most Gracious that He should beget a son" (TMQ 19:92), and, "He (Allah) begets not, nor is He begotten" (TMQ 112:3).

7 — Jesus Christ: Son of God?

*One of the most striking differences between a cat and a
lie is that a cat has only nine lives.*

—Mark Twain, *Pudd'nhead Wilson's Calendar*

Son of God, son of David, or son of Man? Jesus is
identified as "son of David" fourteen times in the New
Testament, starting with the very first verse (Matthew 1:1). The
Gospel of Luke documents forty-one generations between Jesus
and David, while Matthew lists twenty-six. Jesus, a distant
descendant, can only wear the "son of David" title
metaphorically. But how then should we understand the title,
"Son of God?"

The "trilemma," a common proposal of Christian
missionaries, states that Jesus was either a lunatic, a liar, or the
Son of God—just as he claimed to be. For the sake of argument,
let's agree that Jesus was neither a lunatic nor a liar. Let's also
agree he was *precisely* what he claimed to be. But what, exactly,
was that? Jesus called himself "Son of Man" frequently,
consistently, perhaps even emphatically, but where did he call
himself "Son of God?"

Let's back up. What does "Son of God" mean in the first
place? No legitimate Christian sect suggests that God took a
wife and had a child, and most certainly none conceive that God
fathered a child through a human mother *outside* of marriage.

Furthermore, to suggest that God physically mated with an element of His creation is so far beyond the limits of religious tolerance as to plummet down the sheer cliff of blasphemy, chasing the mythology of the Greeks.

With no rational explanation available within the tenets of Christian doctrine, the only avenue for closure is to claim yet one more doctrinal mystery. Here is where the Muslim recalls the question posed in the Qur'an, "How can He have a son when He has no consort?" (TMQ 6:101)—while others shout, "But God can do anything!" The Islamic position, however, is that God doesn't do inappropriate things, only *Godly* things. In the Islamic viewpoint, God's character is integral with His being and consistent with His majesty.

So again, what does "Son of God" mean? And if Jesus Christ has exclusive rights to the term, why does the Bible record, "For I (God) am a father to Israel, and Ephraim (i.e., Israel) is my firstborn" (Jeremiah 31:9) and, "Israel is My son, even my firstborn" (Exodus 4:22)? Taken in the context of Romans 8:14, which reads, "For as many as are led by the Spirit of God, they are the sons of God," many scholars conclude that "Son of God" is metaphorical and, as with *christos,* doesn't imply exclusivity. After all, *The Oxford Dictionary of the Jewish Religion* confirms that in Jewish idiom "Son of God" is clearly metaphorical. To quote, "Son of God, term occasionally found in Jewish literature, biblical and post-biblical, but nowhere implying physical descent from the Godhead."[87] Hasting's *Bible Dictionary* comments:

> In Semitic usage "sonship" is a
> conception somewhat loosely employed
> to denote moral rather than physical or

> metaphysical relationship. Thus "sons of Belial" (Jg 19:22 etc.) are wicked men, not descendants of Belial; and in the NT the "children of the bridechamber" are wedding guests. So a "son of God" is a man, or even a people, who reflect the character of God. There is little evidence that the title was used in Jewish circles of the Messiah, and a sonship which implied more than a moral relationship would be contrary to Jewish monotheism.[88]

And in any case, the list of candidates for "son of God" begins with Adam, as per Luke 3:38: "Adam, which was the son of God."

Those who rebut by quoting Matthew 3:17 ("And suddenly a voice came from heaven, saying, 'This is My beloved son, in whom I am well pleased'") have overlooked the point that the Bible describes many people, Israel and Adam included, as "sons of God." Both 2 Samuel 7:13–14 and 1 Chronicles 22:10 read, "He (Solomon) shall build a house for My name, and I will establish the throne of his kingdom forever. I will be his Father, and he shall be My son."

Entire nations are referred to as sons, or children of God. Examples include:

1. Genesis 6:2, "That the *sons of God* saw the daughters of men . . ."
2. Genesis 6:4, "There were giants on the earth in those days, and also afterward, when the *sons of God* came in to the daughters of men . . ."
3. Deuteronomy 14:1, "Ye are the *children* of the Lord

94

your God."
4. Job 1:6, "Now there was a day when the *sons of God* came to present themselves before the LORD . . ."
5. Job 2:1, "Again there was a day when the *sons of God* came to present themselves before the LORD . . ."
6. Job 38:7, "When the morning stars sang together, and all the *sons of God* shouted for joy?"
7. Philippians 2:15, "that you may become blameless and harmless, *children of God* without fault in the midst of a crooked and perverse generation . . ."
8. 1 John 3:1–2, "Behold what manner of love the Father has bestowed on us, that we should be called *children of God*! . . . Beloved, now we are *children of God* . . ."

In Matthew 5:9 Jesus says, "Blessed are the peacemakers, for they shall be called sons of God." Later in Matthew 5:45, Jesus prescribed to his followers the attainment of noble attributes, "that you may be sons of your Father in heaven." Not exclusively *his* Father, but *their* Father. Furthermore, John 1:12 reads, "But as many as received Him, to them He gave the right to become children of God . . ." If the Bible is to be respected, any person of piety could aspire to the office of "child of God."

Graham Stanton comments, "In the Graeco-Roman world heroes, rulers, and philosophers were called sons of God. In the Old Testament 'son of God' is used of angels or heavenly beings (e.g., Gen. 6:2,4; Deut. 32:8; Job 1:6–12), Israel or Israelites (e.g., Ex. 4:22; Hosea 11:1), and also of the king (notably in 2 Sam. 7:14 and Psalm 2:7)."[89] And Joel Carmichael elaborates:

> The title "son of God" was of course
> entirely familiar to Jews in Jesus' lifetime
> and indeed for centuries before: *all* Jews
> were sons of God; this was in fact what
> distinguished them from other people . . .
>
> During the postexilic period in Jewish
> history the word was further applied to
> any particular pious man; ultimately it
> became common in reference to the
> Righteous Man and the Prince.
>
> In all these cases of Jewish usage, the
> phrase was plainly a mere metaphor to
> emphasize a particularly close connection
> between individual virtue and divine
> authority.[90]

So if the phrase "son of God" was "plainly a mere metaphor," why does Christianity elevate Jesus Christ to "son of God" in the literal sense of the phrase? The question echoes unanswered, "Where did Jesus get an exclusive on the title 'Son of God'?"

If this were not confusing enough, there is Hebrews 7:3, where Melchizedek, King of Salem, is described as being "without father, without mother, without genealogy, having neither beginning of days nor end of life, but made like the Son of God, remains a priest continually." An immortal, preexisting without origin and without parents? Fanciful thinking, or does Jesus have scriptural competition?

Strikingly, Jesus refers to himself as "Son of man" in the Bible, and not as "Son of God." *Harper's Bible Dictionary* suggests, "Jesus must have used 'Son of man' as a simple self-designation, perhaps as a self-effacing way of referring to himself simply as a human being."[91] The *New Catholic Encyclopedia* says of "Son of man," "This title is of special interest because it was the one employed by Jesus by preference to designate Himself and His mission."[92(EN)]

As a matter of detail, Jesus described himself as "son of man" eighty-eight times in the New Testament. "Son of God" occurs forty-seven times in the New Testament, but always on the lips of others. As *Harper's Bible Dictionary* states,

> Although the synoptic tradition contains two sayings in which Jesus refers to himself as "son" in relation to God as his Father (Mark 13:32; Matt. 11:27 [Q]), the authenticity of these sayings is widely questioned, and it remains uncertain whether Jesus actually called himself "son" in relation to God as Father. . . .
>
> It is noteworthy, however, that Jesus never claims for himself the title "Son of God." While he is represented as accepting it in Mark 14:61–62, both Matthew (26:64) and Luke (22:67) are at pains to tone down Jesus' acceptance of the title as though what he says to the High Priest is, "It—like the title 'messiah'—is your word, not mine."[93]

Hasting's Bible Dictionary concurs: "Whether Jesus

used it ["Son of God"] of himself is doubtful. . . ."[94]

Might the phrase "son of man" imply uniqueness? Apparently not—the book of Ezekiel contains ninety-three references to Ezekiel as "son of man."

All of which leaves an objective researcher with the following conclusions:

1. Jesus is assumed to be exactly what he called himself.
2. Jesus called himself "son of man." Eighty-eight times.
3. Nowhere in the Bible did Jesus call himself a literal "son of God." Not once. Anywhere.[95]
4. And in any case, in Jewish idiom the term "son of God" was either metaphorical or contrary to monotheism.

Christian clergy openly acknowledge the above, but claim that although Jesus never called himself "son of God," others did. This too has an answer.

Investigating the manuscripts that make up the New Testament, one finds that the alleged "sonship" of Jesus is based upon the mistranslation of two Greek words—*pais* and *huios*, both of which are translated as "son." However, this translation appears disingenuous. The Greek word *pais* derives from the Hebrew *ebed*, which bears the primary meaning of servant, or slave. Hence, the primary translation of *paistheou* is "servant of God," with "child" or "son of God" being an extravagant embellishment. According to the *Theological Dictionary of the New Testament,* "The Hebrew original of *pais* in the phrase *paistheou,* i.e., *ebed,* carries a stress on personal relationship and has first the sense of 'slave.'"[96] This is all the more interesting because it dovetails perfectly with the prophecy of Isaiah 42:1, upheld in Matthew 12:18: "Behold, My servant [i.e., from the Greek *pais*] whom I have chosen, My beloved in whom my soul is well pleased . . ."

Whether a person reads the King James Version, New King James Version, New Revised Standard Version, or New International Version, the word is "servant" in all cases. Considering that the purpose of revelation is to make the truth of God clear, one might think this passage an unsightly mole on the face of the doctrine of divine sonship. After all, what better place for God to have declared Jesus His son? What better place to have said, "Behold, My son whom I have begotten . . ."? But He *didn't* say that. For that matter, the doctrine lacks biblical support in the recorded words of both Jesus and God, and there is good reason to wonder why. Unless, that is, Jesus was nothing more than the servant of God this passage describes.

Regarding the religious use of the word *ebed*, "The term serves as an expression of humility used by the righteous before God."[97] Furthermore, "After 100 B.C. *paistheou* more often means 'servant of God,' as when applied to Moses, the prophets, or the three children (Bar. 1:20; 2:20; Dan. 9:35)."[98] A person can easily get into doctrinal quicksand over this point, for out of the eight mentions of *paistheou* in the New Testament, only five refer to Jesus (Matthew 12:18; Acts 3:13, 26; 4:27, 30)—the remaining three are divided between Israel (Lk. 1:54) and David (Lk. 1:69; Acts 4:25). So Jesus did not have exclusive rights to this term, and experts conclude, "In the few instances in which Jesus is called *paistheou* we obviously have early tradition."[99]

Furthermore the translation, if impartial, should be the same—all individuals labeled *paistheou* in the Greek should be identical in the translation. Such, however, has not been the case. Whereas *pais* has been translated "servant" in reference to Israel and David in the above-referenced verses, it is translated "Son" or "holy child" in reference to Jesus. Such preferential treatment is canonically consistent, but logically flawed.

Lastly, an interesting, if not key, religious parallel is uncovered: "Thus the Greek phrase *paistoutheou*, 'servant of God,' has exactly the same connotation as the Muslim name Abdallah—the 'servant of Allah.'"[100]

The symmetry is all the more shocking, for the Holy Qur'an relates Jesus as having identified himself as just this— Abdallah (*abd* being Arabic for slave or servant, Abd-Allah [also spelled "Abdullah"] meaning slave or servant of Allah). According to the story, when Mary returned to her family with the newborn Jesus, they accused her of being unchaste. Speaking from the cradle in a miracle that gave credence to his claims, baby Jesus defended his mother's virtue with the words, "*Inni Abdullah . . .*" which means, "I am indeed a servant of Allah . . ." (TMQ 19:30)

Translation of the New Testament Greek *huios* to "son" (in the literal meaning of the word) is similarly flawed. On page 1210 of Kittel and Friedrich's *Theological Dictionary of the New Testament*, the meaning of *huios* journeys from the literal (Jesus the son of Mary), to mildly metaphorical (believers as sons of the king [Matt. 17:25–26]), to politely metaphorical (God's elect being sons of Abraham [Luke 19:9]), to colloquially metaphorical (believers as God's sons [Matt. 7:9 and Heb 12:5]), to spiritually metaphorical (students as sons of the Pharisees [Matt. 12:27, Acts 23:6]), to biologically metaphorical (as in John 19:26, where Jesus describes his favorite disciple to Mary as "her son"), to blindingly metaphorical as "sons of the kingdom" (Matt. 8:12), "sons of peace" (Luke. 10:6), "sons of light" (Luke. 16:8), and of everything from "sons of this world" (Luke 16:8) to "sons of thunder" (Mark 3:17). It is as if this misunderstood word for "son" is waving a big sign on which is painted in bold letters: METAPHOR! Or, as Stanton eloquently puts it, "Most scholars agree that the Aramaic or Hebrew word behind 'son' is 'servant.' So as the Spirit descends on Jesus at his baptism, Jesus is addressed by the voice from heaven in terms of Isaiah 42:1: 'Behold my servant . . . my chosen . . . I have put my Spirit upon him.' So although Mark 1:11 and 9:7 affirm that Jesus is called by God to a special messianic task, the emphasis is on Jesus' role as the anointed servant, rather than as Son of God."[101]

The objective researcher now needs to expand the list of notes as follows:
1. Jesus is assumed to be exactly what he called himself.
2. Jesus called himself "son of man."
3. Nowhere in the Bible did Jesus ever lay claim to the literal title of "son of God."
4. And in any case, in Jewish idiom the term "son of God" was either metaphorical or contrary to monotheism.
5. The primary translation of the phrase *paistheou* is "servant of God," and not "son of God."
6. *Huios*, which is translated from New Testament Greek to the word "son," is used metaphorically with such frequency as to make literal translation indefensible.
7. Hence, when others spoke of Jesus as "son of God," the metaphorical sense can be assumed in consideration of Jewish idiom, in combination with the strictness of Jewish monotheism.

So, how does the world of Christianity justify the claim of divine sonship?

Some say Jesus was the son of God because he called

God "Father." But what do other people call God? For that matter, what is Jesus recorded as having taught in the Bible, if not, "In this manner, therefore, pray: Our Father . . ." (Matthew 6:9)? So not only did Jesus teach that any person can attain the title of "son of God," he taught his followers to identify God as "Father."

Some suggest that Jesus was human during life but became partner in divinity following crucifixion. But in Mark 14:62, when Jesus speaks of the Day of Judgment, he says that people will see him as "the Son of Man sitting at the right hand of the Power, and coming with the clouds of heaven." So if Jesus is the "Son of Man" come the Day of Judgment, what is he between now and then?

The question repeats itself, "Where did the concept of divine sonship come from?"

If we look to church scholars for an answer, we find "It was, however, at the Council of Nicaea that the church was constrained by circumstances to introduce non-biblical categories into its authentic description of the Son's relation to the Father. The Arian controversy occasioned this determination."[102]

Hmm . . . "constrained by circumstances" . . . "constrained by circumstances"—now what, exactly, does that mean? A person can't help but draw upon familiar parallels, such as, "I was constrained by circumstances—I didn't have enough money, so I stole," or, "The truth wasn't working, so I lied."

What, exactly, were the circumstances that constrained the church? Was it that Arius demonstrated that they couldn't justify their doctrine through scripture, and they responded in the only way they knew how to salvage their position? The

Bible was all fine and good right up until it failed to support their theology, and then they cast the sacred "rulebook" aside and came up with their own? Is that what happened? Because that's what they seem to say—that they couldn't get the Bible to work for them, so they turned to non-biblical sources for support.

Hey! Is that allowed?

Let's look at what happened.

Arius argued that the divine Triad was composed of three separate and distinct realities, and that Jesus Christ was of created, finite nature. In other words, a man. Arius' major work, *Thalia* (meaning "banquet"), was first publicized in 323 CE and created such a stir that the Council of Nicaea was convened in 325 to address the Arian challenges. For example, the Arian syllogism proposed that if Jesus was a man, then we shouldn't say he was God, and if Jesus was God, we shouldn't say he died. Arius proposed that the God-man concept doesn't stand up to critical analysis, and defies explanation.

Arian challenges to Trinitarian theology would swamp and sink below the surface of history if anyone could explain the God-man concept. But 1,700 years of sifting the sand of apologetics have failed to yield a jewel of Trinitarian reason sufficiently brilliant to satisfy the skeptics. Challenging questions periodically resurface and echo Arian arguments. For example, we can well ask, "When God reportedly became man, did He give up His divine powers?" For if He did, then He wasn't God anymore, and if He didn't, He wasn't man. "If the God-man died on the cross, does this mean God died?" No, of course not. So who died? Just the "man" part? But in that case, the sacrifice wasn't good enough, for the claim is that only a divine sacrifice could atone for the sins of humankind. The

103

problem is, the man-portion of the proposed tri-unity dying would contribute no more to the atonement of sins than would the death of a sinless man. Which leaves little option for explanation other than to revert to the claim that some element of divinity died. Strictly monotheistic Jews, Unitarian Christians, and Muslims would no doubt contend that, as for those who say it was God who died, well, they can just go to hell. (The expectation is that God, who is living and eternal, will agree.)

To continue the thought, Trinitarian doctrine claims that God not only became man, but remained God—a concept Unitarians consider the literary equivalent of an Escher "impossible construction"sketch. The statement satisfies the grammatical requirements of the English language for a sentence, but the impossible contortions can never a reality make. A tree can no more be converted to furniture and still be a tree than a cooked pot roast can be a cow. Once transformed, the qualities of the original are lost. And yet Catholicism made a religion out of transubstantiation, which claims the exact opposite—that two different substances are one.

The Unitarian declaration is that God is God and man is man. Those who confuse the two fail to recognize that God cannot give up His Godliness, because His entity is defined by His divine attributes. Neither does God need to experience human existence in order to understand the suffering of humankind. Nobody knows the plight of humankind better than the Creator, since He created humankind with knowledge of everything from thermoreceptors to thoughts, from cilia to subconscious. God *knows* the problems, plight, and suffering of humankind—He created a universe whose complexities transcend such superficial dimensions of human existence.

The "But God can do anything" defense prompts the question, "Well, if God can do anything, then why didn't He make sense of Trinitarian doctrine—assuming it's valid, that is?" If God can do anything, He could have provided a sensible explanation that would not require resorting to "non-biblical categories." But He didn't. Why? Did God leave humankind to figure it out for themselves, or can a person safely assume there's no basis in religious reality for something God didn't reveal?

The concept that God provided revelation without clarifying His Own nature grates painfully against our innate understanding of God as all-merciful, providing clear guidance to all humankind.

Standard Trinitarian response? That people would believe if only they understood. Standard Unitarian response? Nobody understands the Trinity—nobody. That's why it's a religious mystery. Talk with Trinitarian clergy long enough, bring up the above objections (and those that follow), and eventually the confirmed Trinitarian will admit, "It's a mystery." The you-just-have-to-have-faith defense is not far behind. The Unitarian typically points out, however, that moments earlier the Trinitarian proposed that people would believe, if only they understood. However, when a legitimate attempt is made to understand, by way of seeking answers to relevant questions, the claim transforms to one of a religious mystery (i.e., nobody understands!). A final defense is the suggestion that, "The only way a person can believe is to have faith" (i.e., the only way to believe is to believe). But if blind, unthinking faith is the methodology God bids us to follow, why does He command us to reason ("'Come now, and let us reason together,' says the Lord . . ." Isaiah 1:18)?[103(EN)]

So what is a non-biblical source? A person can safely assume that if it's not from scripture (that is, not from God), then it must be from the minds of men (and what does that equate to if not human imagination?). How much safer would it have been to have modified church doctrine to conform to rational argument and, more importantly, scripture?

No doubt adhering to Trinitarian notions cemented the job security of Trinitarian clergy, albeit upon questionable tenets of faith clothed in the mantle of church approval. Likewise, no doubt confidence in church teachings waned in the minds of thinkers like Arius—thinkers who continued to highlight the fact that Jesus never claimed sonship or partnership in divinity, and for that matter, neither did his disciples. Furthermore, evidence suggests neither did Paul.[104(EN)]

After admitting reliance upon "non-biblical categories" to define the church's view of Jesus Christ's relation to God, the *New Catholic Encyclopedia* outlines some of the constructed doctrines, such as consubstantiality, begotten and not made, etc. Next, they make the unbelievably straight-faced assertion that Augustine sought the ideology most compatible with inbred human understanding (i.e., "Augustine sought in man's psychology or way of knowing the natural analogate for understanding the eternal generation of the Son."[105]).

Nobody can be faulted for reading that statement and muttering, "They . . . are . . . joking. They must be." After all, isn't this the doctrine responsible for the Medieval and Spanish inquisitions, the eight waves of the Christian Crusades, and countless forced conversions of natives during the age of colonialism? The doctrine that makes so much sense that over twelve million died under torture in denial of the tenets of Trinitarian faith? *Twelve million!* The doctrine that makes so much sense that, to this day, African natives have to be coerced into conversion through baiting with food and medicine?

The average person on the street might conclude that if torture and coercion are required to refresh memories, someone needs to redefine the meaning of "innate understanding."

And why not? A lot of values have been redefined.

Pope Gregory IX instituted the Papal Inquisition in 1231, but couldn't stomach the sin of torture. It took twenty years for a pope to shoulder the responsibility and, in the height of irony, that pontiff took the name of Pope Innocent (cough, cough) IV. In 1252 he authorized torture with the papal bull *Ad extirpanda*.[106] However, some of the clergy must have wanted to get their hands dirty, up close and personal. To accommodate such lofty Christian sentiments, "in 1256 Pope Alexander IV gave them the right to mutually absolve one another and grant dispensations to their colleagues. With this legal and moral issue circumvented, one inquisitor could torture and his companion then absolve him."[107]

So innate understanding didn't exactly play a major role in the process.

Sympathizers might take a moment to imagine an ignorant, un-indoctrinated individual, isolated from civilization. Imagine this individual seeking the reality of God through a quiet life of contemplation. We can envision the foreign natives of distant lands, the illiterate masses, the lone individual on a tropical island. How many of them, do you imagine, snapped their fingers and slapped their foreheads in spiritual awakening and proclaimed the Father, Son and Holy Spirit?

The likelihood is slim to none that Augustine's judgment was based on a prospective, double-blind, controlled, and randomized study. Should the millions of "heretic" Unitarian

Christians who were executed in intolerant Trinitarian judgment be asked, they could be expected to have some very reasonable objections. In the modern day, some of them might even reference the Qur'an: "Let there be no compulsion in religion . . ." (TMQ 2:256)

But to return to the "son of God" issue, one more difficulty concerns the following quotes:

> In the Gospel of St. John, twice the title Son of God means nothing more than Messiah. Thus Nathanael's confession of faith, 'Rabbi, thou art the Son of God, thou art King of Israel!' (Jn 1:49) regards the two as equivalent.[108]

> It is not always clear what the term [Son of God] means when spoken by the demons; it may mean only man of God.[109(EN)]

> Used by the centurion at the Crucifixion, it (Son of God) seems to have meant only a just man.[110(EN)]

The above quotes suggest one of two possible scenarios. In the first, "son of God" can be understood to mean Messiah, King of Israel, "man of God," "holy one of God," or simply a righteous man, for parallel gospels relate these terms as if synonymous. For example, the demons identified Jesus as "the holy one of God" in one account and "Son of God" in another, and the centurion identified Jesus as the "Son of God" in Matthew and Mark, but as "a righteous man" in Luke. So maybe these terms mean the same thing.

In the second scenario, parallel accounts recording the same events in different words could represent biblical inaccuracy. In either case, there's a problem. If the differing terms are synonymous and a person can't trust the Bible enough to understand the meaning of "Son of God" in one instance, how can anybody interpret the same phrase with confidence elsewhere? And if the disagreements represent biblical inaccuracies, in which one gospel author got it right and the other(s) got it wrong, then to which account should we entrust our salvation?

A minor example is that two of the above-referenced gospels tell different stories, though witnessing the same event. Matthew 8:28–29 records two possessed men in the tombs and Luke 8:26–28 only one possessed man. Even if a person defends the Bible as being the inspired word of God—not the actual word, but the inspired word—would God inspire an error? Even a small one?

Some wonder why Christians smooth over biblical discrepancies. Others take a more jaundiced view. The Christian world would like to believe that church authorities are devoted to truth and not deception. But how many people would bend the truth to gain 10% of the gross income of an entire congregation? Suspicion can be fairly high that, in the words of George Bernard Shaw, "A government which robs Peter to pay Paul can always depend on the support of Paul."[111] In other words, a church that tithes the congregation to fund the salary and living expenses of the clergy can always depend on the support of the clergy.

A follow-up question is, "How many Bible-toting, Sunday school-teaching church leaders would bend the truth under pressure of wealth?" The person who conceives of none is either daft, naïve, or lying. Current affairs document countless priests and ministers who not only bend the truth, but the altar boys as well. Jesus warned about these false "men of God" in Matthew 7:15–16 when he said, "Beware of false prophets, who come to you in sheep's clothing, but inwardly they are ravenous wolves. You will know them by their fruits . . ."[112(EN)]

Nonetheless, we find ourselves returning once again to the unanswered question, namely, what does "Son of God" mean? Would the original Hebrew translate from *ebed* to "slave," "servant" or "son?" Even if the correct translation is "son," how is this different from all the other "sons of God" who were clearly nothing more than righteous individuals or, at most, prophets? Commenting on R. Bultmann's historical criticism of the New Testament, the *New Catholic Encyclopedia* states, "Son of God has recently been denied a place in theology on the grounds that, as found in NT writings, it is part of the mythological garb in which the primitive Church clothed its faith. . . . The problem confronting one constructing an adequate theological idea of Son of God is to determine the content that the idea expresses."[113]

Given non-conformity in understanding, one comes to grasp the survival-based need of the early church to define a belief system, whether true or not. And this is exactly what was done in 451 CE at the Council of Chalcedon, which declared the dogmatic definition that has dominated Christology ever since: "One and the same Christ, Son, Lord, only-begotten, known in two natures, without confusion, without change, without division, without separation."[114]

Anyone who embraces the evidence of this chapter recognizes the above quote as a statement, but not a truth. Even if the church fathers conceived the nature of Jesus to be "without confusion," the same cannot be said of his followers. Confusion, division and separation have plagued the seekers of truth in Christianity since the time of Jesus.

As Johannes Lehmann points out in *The Jesus Report*,

> So the concept of "the son of God" led to a misunderstanding which had undreamed-of consequences. Anyone with only a superficial knowledge of the East knows that the Orientals like picturesque speech . . . A simple liar is a son of lies, and anyone who can go one better becomes a father of lies. The phrase "son of God" is on the very same level of speech and thought.
>
> In Semitic linguistic usage this description says nothing more than that a bond exists between a man and God. A Jew would never even dream of thinking that the son of God meant a genuine relationship between a father and a son. A son of God is a blessed man, a chosen vessel, a man who does what God wants. Any attempt to take this image literally and so deduce the divinity of the son contradicts the facts.[115]

Understanding "son of God" to be metaphorical rather than literal permits resolution of a multitude of Christian doctrinal difficulties. In addition, recognizing "son of God" to mean a prophet or a righteous individual, and nothing more, challenges the Christian with the focused Qur'anic teachings. Allah specifically teaches, "The Christians call Christ the Son of Allah. That is a saying from their mouths; (in this) they but imitate what the Unbelievers of old used to say. Allah's curse be on them: how they are deluded away from the Truth!" (TMQ 9:30)

But lest a person misunderstand, the point is not that one book has it right and the others wrong. No, not at all. The point is that all three books—Old Testament, New Testament, and the Holy Qur'an—have it right. All three books teach the Oneness of God and the humanity of Jesus, thereby reinforcing one another. So all three have it right. What has it wrong is not the books of scripture, but the doctrines which have been of such illegitimate origin as to have been derived from "non-biblical categories."

8 — The Trinity

The Three in One, the One in Three? Not so!

To my own God I go.

It may be He shall give me greater ease

Than your cold Christ and tangled Trinities.

—Monotheistic rendition of Rudyard Kipling's
"Lispeth"

The Trinity: the foundation of faith for some, the focus of ridicule for others, but a mystery for all. And that should be no surprise. To quote the authorities, "The word does not occur in scripture . . ."[116] and, "The doctrine of the Trinity as such is not revealed in either the OT or the NT . . ."[117]

So where did it come from? Perhaps it is easier to answer where it *didn't* come from – it didn't come from Jesus or his companions, for the "Jews of Jesus' day knew nothing of a triune God. Such a concept would have been a radical and shocking, even a blasphemous innovation."[118] Hm. Back to where it *did* come from . . .

The Greek *trias* for "triad" was "a word first used of the Trinity in the Godhead by Theophilus of Antioch, who names as the Triad 'God and His Word and His Wisdom.'"[119] This, at the very least, is a triad that makes some sense once a person accepts that God's words are an expression of His wisdom. Why

Theophilus felt compelled to separate God from His attributes is a separate and largely irrelevant issue.

History indicates that the Latin word *trinitas* was first proposed in 220 CE by Tertullian, a third-century writer and early Christian apologist from Carthage, who theorized the co-sharing of divinity between God, Jesus, and the Holy Spirit. The fact that Tertullian was a lawyer tickles the fancy of those who have noticed that incomprehensible words and doubletalk frequently originate from lawyers and politicians (many of whom are lawyers anyway, but with the added political requirement of lacking even the minimal ethics of the legal profession). One wonders what was in Tertullian's fine print, and upon what evidence he based his theory. What spawned the theory that somehow escaped the minds of the gospel writers, the disciples, and even Jesus himself? A person should not expect to find definitive scriptural reference, for,"throughout the New Testament, whereas there is belief in God the Father, in Jesus the Son and in God's Holy Spirit, there is no doctrine of one God in three persons (modes of being), no doctrine of a 'tri-une God', a 'trinity'."[120] Bluntly put, "The formal doctrine of the Trinity as it was defined by the great church councils of the fourth and fifth centuries is not to be found in the NT."[121]

The best anyone can hope for, then, are passages that appear to suggest the Trinity, in concept if not in name.[122(EN)] Even so, we have to expect to be frustrated, because, "The trinitarian formula was shaped in a highly complex, sometimes contradictory and at all events wearisome process of thought."[123]

And this is precisely what we find.

The formal doctrines of the Trinity and divine sonship both sprang from the Council of Nicaea and were incorporated into the Nicene Creed—"A profession of faith agreed upon, although with *some misgivings* because of its *non-biblical* terminology, by the bishops at Nicaea I (325 CE) to defend the true faith against Arianism" (italics mine).[124] Now, stop. Rewind, and play again. The bishops of Nicaea derived the doctrine of the Trinity based on non-biblical terminology, pronounced theirs the "true" faith and then labeled Arius, whose Unitarian doctrines *were* taken from the Bible, a *heretic*? Normally, in religious discussion, we prefer to avoid the term "bass ackwards," but in this case . . .

Ahem. Where was I? Oh, yes . . .

So picture the church fathers, some three hundred years following the ministry of Jesus, being handed the Trinity—a mystical invention they simply could not recognize as the doctrinal child conceived through the teachings of Jesus. How did the church handle the dissenting bishops? It exiled them, along with Arius, after which none of the others dared to deny the doctrine.[125]

Only after overcoming Arius and other prominent Unitarians were the Trinity and the Nicene Creed formally ratified by the Council of Constantinople in 381 CE.[126]

Hmm. The Council of Nicaea in 325, then the Council of Constantinople in 381. How many years separate the two? Let's see, that's eighty-one minus twenty-five . . . take a one from the eight, subtract five from eleven, leaving seven minus two in the tens column . . . I get fifty-six years. Now, that might not seem like much in the span of human history, but that is a *verrry* long time for a church to make up its mind. Long enough for most, if not all, of the original council members to have died. By comparison, most biblical scholars agree that Jesus' mission was, what—three years long?

So why did it take fifty-six years for the church to

finalize the Trinitarian doctrine?

It didn't.

It was not so much a matter of the church needing *time* to pass as it was a matter of the church needing *people* to pass . . . away, that is.

What happened is this: During Emperor Constantine's reign, the Roman Empire was weakened by religious infighting while at the same time waging wars on multiple fronts. As a result, Constantine sought to strengthen the Roman Empire internally by uniting his realm under one Christian faith. For this purpose "The Emperor not only called the Council [of Nicaea] and took charge of its procedure, but he exercised considerable influence over its decisions. He was not yet a full member of the Church, for he did not receive baptism until he was on his deathbed, but in practice he acted as if he were the head of the Church, and in so doing set a precedent which was followed by his Byzantine successors."[127] And that is, after all, what every church wants, isn't it (cough, cough)—a politician who is not only uneducated in the faith, but not even fully a member, taking "charge of its procedure" and exerting "considerable influence over its decisions"?

As a result, "Controversy over doctrine ceased to be the private concern of the Church, but was affected by political needs and became an important element in political as well as in ecclesiastical life. Moreover, secular and ecclesiastical interests were by no means always identical, and co-operation between the two authorities was often replaced by conflict. All this was obvious even in Constantine's day which saw the intervention of the state in Church disputes."[128] Huh. And to think some people endorse separation of church and state (whoever those people are, they most certainly aren't Roman emperors). But the point is that as hard as Constantine tried, he never resolved the Unitarian-Trinitarian controversy.

For that matter, he even failed to unite his sons on the matter.

After his death one son, Constantius, "ruled the eastern half [of the Roman Empire] and declared for Arianism" while the other son, Constans, "controlled the West and acknowledged the Nicene Creed."[129] The two brothers called the Council of Sardica in 343 to reconcile these two views, but failed.

Constans was the more powerful, and so established the "orthodox" Trinitarian bishops on his authority, over Constantius' objections. However, Constans died first, whereupon Constantius reversed his brother's policy and proclaimed Arianism the religion of the realm at the synods of Sirmium and Rimini in 359.

The next Roman emperor, Julian (361–363), attempted to resurrect the pagan cults, which were still powerful, both in numbers and wealth. He was replaced in short order by Emperor Jovian (363–64), a Christian, who was replaced in even shorter order by the sons, Valentinian (364–75) and Valens (364–78). This brings us back to a divided realm, for as with Constantine's sons, Valentinian ruled the Western Roman Empire and acknowledged the Nicene Creed, while Valens ruled the East as an Arian. Their successor, Theodosius the Great (375–83), put an end to all that.

Emperor Theodosius penned a series of decrees that established Trinitarian Christianity as the only approved religion of the Roman Empire. The Council of Constantinople affirmed the Nicene Creed and established Trinitarian Christianity as orthodox. "It was during his [Theodosius'] reign that Christianity became the state religion, thus gaining a position of monopoly, while other religions and beliefs were denied the right to exist."[130]

So what happened between the Council of Nicaea in 325 and the Council of Constantinople in 381? A lot. The Nicene Creed was penned under Constantine, the realm was divided between Arianism and Trinitarian Christianity under Constantine's sons, confirmed upon Arianism by two synods under Constantius, reverted to paganism under Julian, restored to Christianity under Jovian, divided once again between Arianism and Trinitarianism under Valentinian and Valeus, and then confirmed upon Trinitarianism during Theodosius' reign.

The Nicene Creed was subsequently made authoritative at the Council of Chalcedon in 451. The rest, alas, is history.

The process of deriving the Trinitarian formula was so belated, convoluted and questionable that, "It is difficult, in the second half of the 20th century, to offer a clear, objective, and straightforward account of the revelation, doctrinal evolution, and theological elaboration of the mystery of the Trinity. Trinitarian discussion, Roman Catholic as well as other, presents a somewhat unsteady silhouette."[131]

"Unsteady," indeed: "The formula itself does *not* reflect the immediate consciousness of the period of origins; it was the product of 3 centuries of doctrinal development . . . *It is this contemporary return to the sources that is ultimately responsible for the unsteady silhouette*" (italics mine).[132]

In other words, from the church's point of view the problem is that educated laity are beginning to trust scripture more than the imaginative minds and non-biblical sources from which the church derived its dogma. We can understand their concern. After all, it's much easier to tell people what to believe (and how much to tithe) than to have to deal with the

problematic issues that result from objective analysis. Issues
like, like, like . . . well, like these.

In any case, as if the above quote were not enough, the
NCE continues:

> The formulation "one God in three
> Persons" was not solidly established,
> certainly not fully assimilated into
> Christian life and its profession of faith,
> prior to the end of the 4th century. But it is
> precisely this formulation that has first
> claim to the title *the Trinitarian dogma.*
>
> Among the Apostolic Fathers, there
> had been nothing even remotely
> approaching such a mentality or
> perspective.[133]

Okay, let's all sit back, scratch our heads, and say a
collective "Hunh?"

The church admits that the Trinity was unknown to the
Apostolic Fathers,[134] and the doctrine was derived from non-
biblical sources, but insists we believe it anyway? No wonder it
took so long to catch on.

Once approved by the church councils, another several
centuries passed before this foreign concept gained acceptance.
The *New Catholic Encyclopedia* observes that devotion to the
Trinity wasn't realized until the eighth century, at which time it
began to take hold in monasteries at Aniane and Tours.[135]

In the midst of the growing awareness of the differences
between Trinitarian doctrine and the period of origins, one

might be surprised to find one group claiming to be followers of Jesus Christ (i.e., Muslims!) reading the following in their book of guidance (i.e., the Holy Qur'an):

> O People of the Book! Commit no excesses in your religion: nor say of Allah anything but the truth. Christ Jesus the son of Mary was (no more than) a Messenger of Allah, and His Word, which He bestowed on Mary, and a Spirit proceeding from Him: so believe in Allah and His Messengers. Do not say "Trinity": desist: it will be better for you: for Allah is One God: glory be to Him: (far Exalted is He) above having a son. To Him belong all things in the heavens and on earth. And enough is Allah as a Disposer of affairs (TMQ 4:171).

And warning:

> O People of the Book! Exceed not in your religion the bounds (of what is proper), trespassing beyond the truth, nor follow the vain desires of people who went wrong in times gone by—who misled many, and strayed (themselves) from the even Way (TMQ 5:77).

One may wonder what, from the New Testament,

separates these two groups by such a vast expanse of understanding. Trinitarians, Unitarians and Muslims all claim to follow the teachings of Jesus. But who really does, and who doesn't?

For centuries, the argument has been advanced that Trinitarians follow Pauline theology in preference to that of Jesus. This charge is difficult to deny, for Jesus taught Old Testament Law whereas Paul negated it. Jesus preached orthodox Jewish creed; Paul preached mysteries of faith. Jesus spoke of accountability; Paul proposed justification by faith. Jesus described himself as an ethnic prophet; Paul defined him as a universal prophet.[136(EN)] In disrespect to thousands of years of revelation conveyed through a long chain of esteemed prophets, and contrary to the teachings of Rabbi Jesus, Paul focused not on the life and teachings of Jesus, but upon his death. As Lehmann writes, "The only thing which Paul considers important is the Jew Jesus' death, which destroyed all hopes of liberation by a Messiah. He makes the victorious Christ out of the failed Jewish Messiah, the living out of the dead, the son of God out of the son of man."[137]

More than a few scholars consider Paul the main corrupter of Apostolic Christianity and the teachings of Jesus, and they are not alone. Many early Christian sects also held this view, including the second-century Christian sect known as Adoptionists. According to Bart D. Ehrman, "In particular, [the Adoptionists] considered Paul, one of the most prominent authors of our New Testament, to be an arch-heretic rather than an apostle."[138]

Perhaps the most conclusive contribution to this argument is encountered in the Dead Sea Scrolls, which many scholars believe condemn Paul for his abandonment of Old

Testament Law and rebellion against Jesus' teachings and early Christian leadership. The end of the Damascus Document, in particular, appears to document the early Christian community's cursing and excommunication of Paul.[139]

Eisenman informs us that the Ebionites—the descendants from James' Christian Community in Jerusalem—considered Paul "an apostate from the Law."[140] Of the Ebionites, he writes:

> They are certainly the community that held the memory of James in the highest regard, whereas Paul they considered "the Enemy" or Anti-Christ. . . . Such a stance is not unparalleled in crucial passages from the letter in James' name in the New Testament. We have already shown that this letter, in responding to some adversary who believes that Abraham was justified only by faith, states that by making himself "a friend of man," this adversary has turned himself into "the Enemy of God." This "Enemy" terminology is also known in Matt. 13:25–40's "parable of the tares," perhaps the only anti-Pauline parable in the Gospels, where an "Enemy" sows the "tares" among the good seed. At the "harvest" these will be uprooted and thrown into "the burning."[141]

Johannes Lehmann writes, "What Paul proclaimed as

'Christianity' was sheer heresy which could not be based on the Jewish or Essene faith, or on the teaching of Rabbi Jesus. But, as Schonfield says, 'The Pauline heresy became the foundation of Christian orthodoxy and the legitimate church was disowned as heretical.'"[142]

He continues, "Paul did something that Rabbi Jesus never did and refused to do. He extended God's promise of salvation to the Gentiles; he abolished the law of Moses, and he prevented direct access to God by introducing an intermediary."[143]

Bart D. Ehrman, author of *The New Testment: A Historical Introduction to the Early Christian Writings* and perhaps the most authoritative contemporary voice reminds us that "Paul's view was not universally accepted or, one might argue, even widely accepted," and that there were prominent Christian leaders, including Jesus' closest disciple, Peter, "who vehemently disagreed with him on this score and considered Paul's views to be a corruption of the true message of Christ."[144]

Commenting on the views of some early Christians in the Pseudo-Clementine literature, Ehrman writes, "Peter, not Paul, is the true authority for understanding the message of Jesus. Paul has corrupted the true faith based on a brief vision, which he has doubtless misconstrued. Paul is thus the enemy of the apostles, not the chief of them. He is outside the true faith, a heretic to be banned, not an apostle to be followed."[145]

Others elevate Paul to sainthood. Joel Carmichael very clearly is not one of them:

> We are a universe away from Jesus. If Jesus came "only to fulfill" the Law and the Prophets; If he thought that "not an

> iota, not a dot" would "pass from the
> Law," that the cardinal commandment
> was "Hear, O Israel, the Lord Our God,
> the Lord is one," and that "no one was
> good but God." . . . What would he have
> thought of Paul's handiwork!

> Paul's triumph meant the final
> obliteration of the historic Jesus; he
> comes to us embalmed in Christianity like
> a fly in amber.[146]

While many authors have pointed out the disparity in the teachings of Paul and Jesus, the best of them avoided opinionated commentary and concentrated on simply exposing differences. Dr. Wrede comments,

> In Paul the central point is a divine act, in
> history but transcending history, or a
> complex of such acts, which impart to all
> mankind a ready-made salvation.
> Whoever believes in these divine acts—
> the incarnation, death, and resurrection of
> a celestial being, receives salvation.

> And this, which to Paul is the sum of
> religion—the skeleton of the fabric of his
> piety, without which it would collapse—
> can this be a continuation or a remoulding
> of the gospel of Jesus? Where, in all this,
> is that gospel to be found, which Paul is
> said to have understood?

> Of that which is to Paul all and
> everything, how much does Jesus know?
> Nothing whatever.[147]

And Dr. Johannes Weiss contributes, "Hence the faith in Christ as held by the primitive churches and by Paul was something new in comparison with the preaching of Jesus; it was a new type of religion."[148]

Baigent and Leigh neatly summarize the situation as follows:

> In all the vicissitudes that follow, it must
> be emphasized that Paul is, in effect, the
> first "Christian" heretic, and that his
> teachings—which become the foundation
> of later Christianity—are a flagrant
> deviation from the "original" or "pure"
> form extolled by the leadership. . . .
> Eisenman has demonstrated that James
> emerges as the custodian of the original
> body of teachings, the exponent of
> doctrinal purity and rigorous adherence to
> the Law. The last thing he would have
> had in mind was founding a "new
> religion." Paul is doing precisely that. . . .
> As things transpired, however, the
> mainstream of the new movement
> gradually coalesced, during the next three
> centuries, around Paul and his teachings.
> Thus, to the undoubted posthumous
> horror of James and his associates, an

> entirely new religion was indeed born—a
> religion which came to have less and less
> to do with its supposed founder.[149]

Which theology won the day—why and how—is a question best left to the analyses of the above authors. Should we recognize that Paul's and Jesus' teachings contradict one another, we are forced to take sides. Michael Hart had the following to say in his scholastic tome, *The 100, a Ranking of the Most Influential Persons in History:* "Although Jesus was responsible for the main ethical and moral precepts of Christianity (insofar as these differed from Judaism), St. Paul was the main developer of Christian theology, its principal proselytizer, and the author of a large portion of the New Testament."[150]

"A large portion" of the New Testament? Out of 27 books and epistles Paul wrote 14—more than half. That represents ample literary moment arm with which to leverage his theology to the top. In regard to Paul's perspective, "He does not ask what led to Jesus' death, he only sees what it means to him personally. He turns a man who summoned people to reconciliation with God into the savior. He turns an orthodox Jewish movement into a universal religion which ultimately clashed with Judaism."[151]

In fact, Paul's teachings split Trinitarian Christianity from the trunk of revealed monotheism. Whereas the monotheistic teachings conveyed by Moses, Jesus and Muhammad are all aligned in smooth continuity, Paul's teachings stand distinctly out of joint.

To begin with, Jesus taught the oneness of God: "Jesus answered him, 'The first of all the commandments is: "Hear, O

Israel, the Lord our God, the Lord is One. And you shall love the Lord your God with all your heart, with all your soul, with all your mind, and with all your strength." This is the first commandment.'" (Mark 12:29–30). Not only did Jesus stress importance by sandwiching his words between the repeated "This is the first [some translations say 'greatest'] commandment," but the importance of this teaching is equally stressed in Matthew 22:37 and Luke 10:27. Recognizing the continuity from Judaism, Jesus conveyed his teaching from Deuteronomy 6:4–5 (as acknowledged in all reputable Bible commentaries).

Hans Küng contributes, "As a pious Jew, Jesus himself preached a strict monotheism. He never called himself God, on the contrary: 'Why do you call me good? No one is good save God alone.' [Mark 10:18]. . . . There is no indication in the New Testament that Jesus understood himself as the second person in God and was present at the creation of the world. In the New Testament, God himself (ho theos', 'the God,' 'God') is always the one God and Father—not the Son."[152]

And yet, Pauline theology somehow arrived at the Trinity. But how? Jesus referred to the Old Testament. What did the Pauline theologians refer to?

Significantly absent from Jesus' teaching is the association of himself with God. There never was a better time or place, throughout the New Testament, for Jesus to have claimed partnership in divinity, were it true. But he didn't. He didn't say, "Hear, O Israel, the Lord our God, the Lord is one—but it's not quite that simple, so let me explain . . ."

To review the relevant issues in this discussion:

1. The Trinitarian formula was conceived in the third century and codified in the fourth, distant both in time

and theology from the period of revelation.

2. The Trinitarian formula was completely unknown to the Apostolic Fathers.
3. The Trinity is not found in the Old or New Testaments, either in name or in concept.
4. The "achievement" of Pauline theology—the Trinitarian formula—was conceived by men, relying upon the mysticisms of Paul, and is in direct conflict with the strict monotheism conveyed both in the Old Testament and in the teachings of Jesus Christ.

So with all this evidence against the Trinity, what's the evidence *for* it?

Depends on whom you ask.

Christian laity are fond of quoting the Johannine Comma (First Epistle of John, verses 5:7–8), although no true biblical scholar ever would. And there's good reason not to. The verses read, "For there are three who bear witness in heaven: the Father, the Word, and the Holy Spirit; and these three are one, And there are three that bear witness on earth: the Spirit, the water, and the blood; and these three agree as one." One problem—the phrase "the Father, the Word, and the Holy Spirit; and these three are one" has long been recognized as an interpolation (a misleading insertion).

The *Interpreter's Bible* comments:

> This verse in the KJV is to be rejected
> (with RSV). It appears in no ancient
> Greek MS nor is it cited by any Greek
> father; of all the versions only the Latin
> contained it, and even this in none of its

most ancient sources. The earliest MSS of
the Vulg. do not have it. As Dodd
(*Johannine Epistles*, p. 127n) reminds us,
"It is first quoted as a part of 1 John by
Priscillian, the Spanish heretic, who died
in 385, and it gradually made its way into
MSS of the Latin Vulgate until it was
accepted as part of the authorized Latin
text."[153]

Dr. C.J. Scofield, D.D., backed by eight other Doctorates
of Divinity, asserts the above even more clearly in his footnote
to this verse: "It is generally agreed that this verse has no
manuscript authority and has been inserted."[154]

"Generally agreed"? In the words of Professors Kurt and
Barbara Aland, "A glance at the data in the critical apparatus of
Nestle-Aland (which is exhaustive for this passage) should make
any further comment unnecessary to demonstrate the secondary
nature of this addition and the impossibility of its being at all
related to the original form of the text of 1 John."[155]

Professor Metzger, who also attributes this passage
either to Priscillian or to his follower, Bishop Instantius, states,
"That these words are spurious and have no right to stand in the
New Testament is certain . . ."[156] In another work, he adds,
"Modern Roman Catholic scholars, however, recognize that the
words do not belong in the Greek Testament. . . ."[157]

How, then, did 1 John 5:7 invade the scripture? This is
no mystery to students of divinity. It appears to have been
originally written into the margin of scripture by a late
manuscript copier. Those who sought support for Trinitarian
ideology transported the marginal note into the text and

incorporated it into the Old Latin Bible sometime during the fifth century.[158] In this manner, they adopted the verse not because it was valid, but because it was useful. In the words of E. Gibbon:

> The memorable text, which asserts the unity of the *Three* who bear witness in heaven, is condemned by the universal silence of the orthodox fathers, ancient versions, and authentic manuscripts. . . . An allegorical interpretation, in the form, perhaps, of a marginal note, invaded the text of the Latin bibles, which were renewed and corrected in a dark period of ten centuries. After the invention of printing, the editors of the Greek Testament yielded to their own prejudices, or to those of the times, and the pious fraud, which was embraced with equal zeal at Rome and at Geneva, has been infinitely multiplied in every country and every language of modern Europe.[159]

Ehrman, in his *Misquoting Jesus,* brilliantly exposes how these verses infiltrated the Greek in the form of a sixteenth-century forgery.[160]

All of which explains why laity love 1 John 5:7, and scholars don't.

Although the King Jamesand Catholic Douay-Rheimsversions retain the verse, scholars have unceremoniously expunged 1 John 5:7 from more modern and reputable translations, to include the Revised Standard Version of 1952 and 1971, New Revised Standard Version of 1989, New American Standard Bible, New International Version, The Good News Bible, The New English Bible, The Jerusalem Bible, Darby's New Translation, and others. Most striking, however, is not the number of translations that have removed this verse, but the number that have retained it despite its lack of manuscript authority. What should we conclude—that such devotion is to truth, or to doctrinal convention? The New King James Version, seemingly reluctant to correct the 1611 version at risk of losing the paying audience, appears to fall into the doctrinal convention category.

Even the New Scofield Reference Bible retains the verse. And here is a prime example of disingenuousness in Bible translation. The Scofield Reference Bible is designed to meet the needs of scholars and students of divinity, and as such, acknowledges the illegitimacy of 1 John 5:7 through the above-quoted footnote. *The ScofieldStudy Bible,* however, is designed for the less critical eye of Christian laity, and retains the verse without even hinting at its illegitimacy. Truth in translation, it would seem, is audience-adjusted.

So what *do* scholars cite as scriptural evidence for the Trinity?

Very little. The *New Catholic Encyclopedia* states, "In the Gospels evidence of the Trinity is found explicitly only in the baptismal formula of Mt 28:19."[161] And what is the baptismal formula of Matthew 28:19? In this verse, Jesus allegedly commanded his disciples, "Go, therefore, and make disciples of all the nations, baptizing them in the name of the Father and of the Son and of the Holy Spirit." This being the only gospel verse that explicitly mentions the Father, son and holy spirit together,[162] we should not be surprised to find it echoed in Paul's teachings—"The grace of the Lord Jesus Christ, and the love of God, and the communion of the Holy Spirit be with you all" (2 Corinthians 13:14).

Nonetheless, we can repeat this benediction a thousand times, and a gaping chasm will still remain between Matthew 28:19 and the unyielding wall of Trinitarian doctrine—a chasm that requires a leap of faith unprotected by a net of solid evidence. Nobody reads, "Lions and tigers and bears, oh my," and imagines a triune beast. Why, then, are we asked to read the above benediction and imagine a triune God?

Mark 16:15–16 relates the exact same "Great Commission" as does Matthew 28:19, and yet the "Father, Son, and Holy Spirit" formula is conspicuously absent. Why? Both gospels describe Jesus' last command to his disciples, but while Trinitarian theologians have bent Matthew 28:19 (again, the *only* gospel verse that explicitly mentions the Father, son and holy spirit together) into service, Mark 16:15–16 provides no such support. So which gospel author got it right, which got it wrong, and how can we tell?

One way we can decide which of these two passages is correct is to examine what Jesus' disciples actually did. Paul's letters reveal that baptism in the early church was only done in Jesus' name (examples include Acts 2:38, 8:16, 10:48, 19:5, and Romans 6:3.), and not "in the name of the Father and of the Son and of the Holy Spirit." Assuming the disciples actually did as they were told, their actions endorse Mark 16:15–16 and condemn both Matthew 28:19 and 2 Corinthians 13:14. On the other hand, if the disciples didn't do as they were told, then we have no reason to trust anything they are recorded as having said or done. And if the *disciples* are not to be trusted, how much less should Paul, who never even met Jesus, be trusted?

There is an even bigger elephant in the room of this frail Trinitarian argument, and most theologians prefer not to discuss it. The issue is this: Although the Bible attributes the "Great Commission" in Mark 16:15–16 and Matthew 28:19 to Jesus Christ, the two hundred scholars of the Jesus Seminar opine that he didn't say either one.[163] How, then, can we reasonably consider either of these verses as evidence for the Trinity?

When the above justifications fail, clergy and laity alike resort to quoting a litany of verses, each one of which can be summarily dismissed. For example, John 10:38 reads, "The Father is in me and I in the Father." John 14:11 reads much the same. But what does this mean? If we propose these verses support co-sharing of divinity, we have to factor John 14:20 into the equation, which reads, "At that day you (i.e., the disciples) will know that I am in my Father, and you in me, and I in you." Bearing in mind that Aramaic and Hebrew possess far greater capacity for metaphor than English, the only logical conclusion is that the language is figurative. Hence none of the above quotes can be used to defend Trinitarian doctrine. The only other option would be blasphemous—that the council of Nicaea failed to recognize a dozen disciples as partners with both Jesus and God. Infinitely more reasonable is to admit that two thousand-year-old colloquialisms are just that—flowery phrases which, if taken literally, distort reality. The Old English of seven centuries ago is incomprehensible to all but scholars. What, then, do we know of 1,600-year-old Greek translations of ancient Hebrew and Aramaic, much less their colloquialisms?

Let's look at another alleged piece of evidence.

John 14:9 relates Jesus as having said, "He who has seen me has seen the Father." Assuming the language to be literal, which is a bold assumption, we still have to rectify John 14:9 with John 5:37, which reads, "You have neither heard His voice at any time, nor seen His form." John 1:18 is even more emphatic, stating, "No one has seen God at any time." Disregarding our "no end of life" friend, Melchizedek, in Hebrews 7:3, Paul apparently agreed; "[God] alone has immortality, dwelling in unapproachable light, whom no man has seen or can see . . ." (1 Timothy 6:16). The "unapproachable" and "no man has seen or can see" descriptions certainly do not conform to the approachable and visible person of Jesus. The argument of John 14:9, when played out, reveals itself to be invalid. The one scriptural step forward slips three steps back when one learns that Jesus stood bodily in front of the eyes of his disciples and informed them, "You have neither heard His voice at any time, nor seen His form."

When all else fails, John 10:30 relates Jesus as having said, "I and the Father are one." Short, succinct, to the point, and terribly flawed. In this verse, the manuscript Greek for the English "one" is *heis*.[164] This word also occurs in John 17:11 and 17:21–23. John 17:11 reads, "Holy Father, keep through Your name those whom You have given me, that *they may be one* as we are" (italics mine). Literal or metaphorical? John 17:21 reinforces the metaphor with the words, "That they [i.e., all believers] *all may be one*, as You, Father, are in me, and I in You, that they [i.e., all believers] also *may be one in us*, that the world may believe that You sent me" (italics mine). If a person is faithful to the equation, the sum total adds up to a whole lot more than three-in-one; a person either has to think bigger and more blasphemous, or rewrite the rules of mathematics, if the Trinity is to be preserved.

John 10:30, being a widely misapplied verse, nonetheless

deserves a closer examination. Trinitarian Christianity argues that Jesus declared, "I and the Father are one," whereupon the Jews prepared to stone him for blasphemy according to their accusation that, "You, being a Man, make yourself God" (John 10:33). The argument is that the Jews recognized Jesus' claim to being God, so all should understand John 10:30 similarly. This might seem a reasonable argument at first glance, but only if the passage is taken out of context.

  To analyze the passage appropriately, we might begin with the preceding verse, John 10:29, which emphasizes the separate and distinct natures of God and Jesus—One the giver, the other the receiver. Many who subsequently read John 10:30 come away with the understanding that this verse relates Jesus and God to be in agreement, one in understanding, or one in purpose. And let us note Jesus' response to the Jews' accusation of claiming divinity. Did he stand up with divine confidence and insist, "You heard me right, I said it once, and I'll say it again!"? Just the opposite; he said that they had misunderstood, and quoted Psalm 82:6 to remind the Jews that the phrases "son of God" and "you are gods" are metaphors. In the words of the Bible,

> Jesus answered them, "Is it not written in your law, '*I (God) said, "You are gods"*'? [Psalm 82:6] If He called them gods, to whom the word of God came (and the Scripture cannot be broken), do you say of him whom the Father sanctified and sent into the world, "You are blaspheming," because I said, "I am the son of God"? (John 10:34–36).

135

Jesus included himself with those "to whom the word of God [i.e., revelation] came," who were identified in the referenced Psalm 82:6 as "gods" with a small G or "children of God." Psalm 82:1 makes a bold metaphor by identifying judges as "gods"—not as righteous men, not as prophets, not as sons of god, but as *gods*. Furthermore, Psalm 82:6–7 leaves no doubt that "sons of god" refers to mortal human beings: "I [God] said, 'You are gods, and all of you are children of the Most High. But you shall die like men, and fall like one of the princes.'" And lastly, let us not forget that the Greek *huios*, translated as "son" in the above quote, was "used very widely of immediate, remote or figurative kinship."[165]

So in reading John 10:30 in context, we find that Jesus identified himself with other righteous mortals, emphasized the figurative meaning of "son of God," denied divinity, and behaved as would be expected of a flesh-and-blood prophet. After all, if Jesus were a partner in Godhead, wouldn't he have defended his rank with the confidence of divine omnipotence?

Similarly, for every verse held as evidence of the Trinity, there is one or more that discredits or disqualifies. Much to the frustration of the Christian world, biblical confirmation of Jesus teaching the Trinity is not just scarce, it is absent. If anything, the opposite is the case. Three times Jesus is recorded as having emphasized the first commandment, saying, "The Lord our God, the Lord is one" (Mark 12:29; Matthew 22:37; and Luke 10:27). In none of these three instances did he even hint at the Trinity. And who has more biblical authority than Jesus?

Vain analogies similarly fall apart.

The Trinitarian argument that, "God is one, but One in a triune being, like an egg is one, but one in three separate and

136

distinct layers" is catchy, but unsatisfying.[166(EN)] Once upon a time the world was flat, and at the center of the universe. Base metals could be transmuted into gold, and a fountain of youth promised immortality to those who could find it. Or so people believed. But good explanations do not a reality make. The question is not whether a valid analogy to the concept of the Trinity exists, but rather whether the doctrine is correct in the first place. And did Jesus teach it? The answers, according to the information cited above, are No and No.

Consequently, proponents of Trinitarian doctrine have run out of arguments. Lacking biblical evidence, some have gone so far as to suggest Jesus taught the Trinity in secret. Even this claim has an answer, for the Bible reports Jesus having said, "I spoke openly to the world. I always taught in synagogues and in the temple, where the Jews always meet, and *in secret* I have said *nothing"* (John 18:20—italics mine).

So we have Moses teaching the oneness of God, Jesus teaching the oneness of God, but church authorities teaching us to believe what they tell us, and not what we read in the Bible with our own eyes. Who should we believe, Jesus or the Pauline theologians? And what should we trust, scripture or doctrine? And a doctrine based on non-biblical sources at that?

It is worth noting that the Holy Qur'an not only confirms the oneness of God (Allah) but refutes the Trinity, thereby establishing a common monotheistic thread between the teachings of Moses, Jesus and the Holy Qur'an:
1. "Do not say Trinity: desist . . ." (TMQ 4:171)
2. "They do blaspheme who say: God is one of three in a Trinity: for there is no god except one God (Allah)" (TMQ 5:73)
3. "Your God (Allah) is One God (Allah): whoever expects

to meet his Lord, let him work righteousness, and, in the worship of his Lord, admit no one as partner" (TMQ 18:110)[167(EN)]

Now, these are teachings from the Holy Qur'an, but it tickles the imagination to consider what Jesus Christ might say differently, were he to join us for a chat at a local café (our treat, of course). We can well imagine him sitting hunched over a decaf latté as he morosely stirs in a third packet of turbino sugar (he takes his coffee sweet, I have no doubt), slowly swaying his bowed head as he mutters, "I *told* them there's only one God. I said it once, twice, three times. What did they need me to do—carve it in stone? That didn't work for Moses, why would it have worked any better for me?"

It's far easier to imagine Jesus saying, "Do not say Trinity: desist . . ." or "They do blaspheme who say: God is one of three in a Trinity: for there is no god except one God" than to imagine him saying, "Well, sure, I said there was only one God, but what I really meant was . . ."

Understandably, some view the clarity of Islamic monotheism, once juxtaposed to the tangled and indefensible web of Trinitarian ideology, and wonder, "Well, what's wrong with Islam then?" Others continue to object, "But Jesus is God!"

Upon the foundation of such opposing viewpoints are the lines of religious differences drawn, wars waged, lives and, even more importantly, souls lost.

9 — Divinity of Jesus? An Inquiry

Man is made to adore and to obey: but if you will not command him, if you give him nothing to worship, he will fashion his own divinities, and find a chieftain in his own passions.

—Benjamin Disraeli, *Coningsby*

The critical difference between Jesus' teachings and the Trinitarian formula lies in elevating Jesus to divine status—a status Jesus denies in the gospels:

> "Why do you call me good: No one is good but One, that is, God." (Matthew 19:17, Mark 10:18, and Luke 18:19)

> "My Father is greater than I." (John 14:28)

> "I do nothing of myself, but as the Father taught me, I speak these things." (John 8:28)

> "Most assuredly, I say to you, the son can do nothing of himself. . . ." (John 5:19)

> "But I know Him, for I am from Him, and He sent me." (John 7:29)

139

"He who rejects me rejects Him who sent me." (Luke 10:16)

"But now I go away to Him who sent me. . . ." (John 16:5)

"Jesus answered them and said, 'My doctrine is not mine, but His who sent me.'" (John 7:16)

"For I have not spoken on my own authority; but the Father who sent me gave me a command, what I should say and what I should speak." (John 12:49)[168(EN)]

What does Pauline theology say? That Jesus is a partner in divinity, God incarnate. So whom should a person believe? If Jesus, then let's hear what else he might have to say:

"The first of all the commandments is: 'Hear O Israel, The Lord *our* God, the Lord is one." (Mark 12:29)

"But of that day and hour no one knows, neither the angels in heaven, *nor the Son*, but *only* the Father." (Mark 13:32)

"'You shall worship the Lord your God, and Him *only* you shall serve.'" (Luke 4:8)

"My food is to do the will of Him who sent me . . ." (John 4:34)

140

> "I can *of myself* do nothing . . . I do not
> seek my own will but the will of the
> Father who sent me." (John 5:30)

> "For I have come down from heaven, not
> to do my own will, but the will of Him
> who sent me." (John 6:38)

> "My doctrine is *not mine*, but His who
> sent me." (John 7:16)

> "I am ascending to *my* Father and your
> Father, and to *my* God and your God."
> (John 20:17)

My italics in the above verses do not imply that Jesus
spoke with that emphasis, although nobody can claim with
certainty that he didn't. Rather, the italics stress the fact that
Jesus not only never claimed divinity, but would be the first to
deny it. In the words of Joel Carmichael, "The idea of this new
religion, with himself as its deity, was something he [Jesus
Christ] could never have had the slightest inkling of. As Charles
Guignebert put it, 'It never even crossed his mind.'"[169]

So if Jesus never claimed divinity, then what was he
exactly? He answered that question himself:

> "A *prophet* is not without honor except in
> his own country, among his own relatives,
> and in his own house." (Mark 6:4)

> "But Jesus said to them, 'A *prophet* is not
> without honor except in his own country
> and in his own house.'" (Matthew 13:57)

"It cannot be that a *prophet* should perish outside of Jerusalem." (Luke 13:33)

Those who knew him acknowledged, "This is Jesus, the prophet from Nazareth of Galilee" (Matthew 21:11), and "A great prophet has risen up among us . . ." (Luke 7:16). The disciples recognized Jesus as "a prophet mighty in deed . . ." (Luke 24:19. Also see Matthew 14:5, 21:46, and John 6:14). If these statements were inaccurate, why didn't Jesus correct them? Why didn't he define his divinity if, that is, he truly was divine? When the woman at the well stated, "'Sir, I perceive that you are a prophet'" (John 4:19), why didn't he thank her for her lowly impression, but explain there was more to his essence than prophethood?

Or was there?

Jesus Christ, a mere man? Could it be? A good part of the religiously introspective world wonders, "Why not?" Acts 2:22 records Jesus as "Jesus of Nazareth, a man attested by God to you by miracles, wonders, and signs which God did through him in your midst, as you yourselves also know." Jesus himself is recorded as having said, "But now you seek to kill me, a man who has told you the truth which I heard from God . . ." (John 8:40). Strikingly, a similar quote is found in the Holy Qur'an: "He [Jesus] said: 'I am indeed a servant of Allah: He has given me Revelation and made me a prophet'" (TMQ 19:30).

So was Jesus a "servant of Allah (i.e., servant of God)?" According to the Bible, yes. Or, at least, that is what we understand from Matthew 12:18: "Behold! My servant whom I have chosen . . ." Furthermore, Acts of the Apostles traces the growth of the early church for the first thirty years following Jesus' ministry, but nowhere in Acts did Jesus' disciples ever call Jesus "God." Rather, they referred to Jesus as a man and God's servant.[170]

In fact, the *only* New Testament verse that supports the doctrine of the Incarnation is 1 Timothy 3:16.[171(EN)] However, with regard to this verse (which states that "God was manifest in the flesh"), Gibbon notes, "This strong expression might be justified by the language of St. Paul (I Tim. iii. 16), but we are deceived by our modern bibles. The word(*which*) was altered to(*God*) at Constantinople in the beginning of the sixth century: the true reading, which is visible in the Latin and Syriac versions, still exists in the reasoning of the Greek, as well as of the Latin fathers; and this fraud, with that of the *three witnesses of St. John*, is admirably detected by Sir Isaac Newton."[172]

Fraud? Now there's a strong word. But if we look to more modern scholarship, it's a word well applied, for "some passages of the New Testament were modified to stress more precisely that Jesus was himself divine."[173]

The Bible was *modified?* For doctrinal reasons? Hard to find a more appropriate word than "fraud," given the circumstances.

In a chapter entitled "Theologically Motivated Alterations of the Text" in his book, *Misquoting Jesus,* Professor Ehrman elaborates on the corruption of 1 Timothy 3:16, which was detected not only by Sir Isaac Newton, but also by the eighteenth-century scholar, Johann J. Wettstein. In Ehrman's words, "A later scribe had altered the original reading, so that it no longer read 'who' but 'God' (made manifest in the flesh). In other words, this later corrector changed the text in such a way as to stress Christ's divinity. . . . Our earliest and best manuscripts, however, speak of Christ 'who' was made manifest in the flesh, without calling Jesus, explicitly, God."[174]

Ehrman stresses that this corruption is evident in five early Greek manuscripts. All the same it was the corrupted, and not the "earliest and best," biblical manuscripts that came to dominate both the medieval manuscripts and the early English translations.[175] Consequently, from medieval times on, the tenets of Christian faith have suffered the corrupting influence of a church devoted more to theology than to reality.[176]

Ehrman adds: "As Wettstein continued his investigations, he found other passages typically used to affirm the doctrine of the divinity of Christ that in fact represented textual problems; when these problems are resolved on text-critical grounds, in most instances references to Jesus' divinity are taken away."[177]

Given the above, there should be little surprise that twentieth-century Christianity has expanded to include those who deny the alleged divinity of Jesus. A significant sign of this realization is the following report of the London*Daily News*: "More than half of England's Anglican bishops say Christians are not obliged to believe that Jesus Christ was God, according to a survey published today."[178] It is worth noting that it was not mere clergy that were polled but *bishops,* no doubt leaving many parishioners scratching their heads and wondering who to believe, if not their bishops!

Regardless of any devotee's romantic view of religious origins, the harsh reality isthat all prophets but Adam were born in the bath of amniotic fluid that flushes each and every child from the womb—Jesus Christ included. No doubt, the mother of Jesus suckled him at her breast in the natural act of nurturing a human child, but in what would be an oddly incongruous act for God, as the relationship would imply God's dependence upon His very own creation. One would suspect that Jesus crawled on a dirt floor and grew up in a human fashion complete with worldly eating and worldly drinking (most certainly followed by the occasional trip to a worldly bathroom). His human hunger, thirst, anger, pain, fatigue, sorrow, anxiety, and frustration are all well described in the Bible.

God is all-knowing, but in Mark 5:30, Jesus did not even know who had touched his clothes. God is all-powerful, but Mark 6:5 tells us Jesus could not perform any miracles (or, as per some translations, "no mighty work") in his own country. Furthermore, in Mark 8:22–25 Jesus failed to heal a blind man in his first attempt. God never weakens and yet, when Jesus needed strengthening, the angels ministered to him (Mark 1:13, Luke 22:43).

Jesus slept, but God never sleeps (Psalm 121:4). Jesus was tempted by Satan (Luke 4:1–13), and yet James 1:13 tells humankind, "God cannot be tempted with evil . . ." Jesus prayed and gave thanks (to whom?), fasted (why?), carried the teachings of God, and in the end helplessly suffered humiliation and torture at the hands of misguided tyrants. A man oppressed by tyrant rulers or a god oppressed by the very creation He will Himself condemn on the Day of Judgment? Many (and not just Muslims) argue that the Islamic view is more complimentary and noble of God as a supreme and transcendent being, and more realistic of Jesus as a prophet and a man.

The question begs an answer, "Why *must* Jesus be God? Why can't he just be human?"

Most Christians assert that humankind needed a sacrifice to redeem their sins, but an ordinary human sacrifice wouldn't do; only a divine sacrifice would suffice. Strict monotheists—be they Orthodox Jew, Unitarian Christian, or Muslim—may object, as in this typical exchange:

*Monotheist:*Oh. So you believe God died?

Trinitarian: No, no, perish the thought. Only the man died.

Monotheist: In that case, the sacrifice didn't need to be divine, if only the man-part died.

Trinitarian: No, no, no. The man-part died, but Jesus/God had to suffer on the cross to atone for our sins.

Monotheist: What do you mean "had to"? God doesn't "have to" anything.

Trinitarian: God needed a sacrifice and a human wouldn't do. God needed a sacrifice big enough to atone for the sins of humankind, so He sent His only begotten son.

Monotheist: Then we have a different concept of God. The God I believe in doesn't have needs. My God never wants to do something but can't because He needs something to make it possible. My God never says, "Gee, I want to do this, but I can't. First I need this certain something. Let's see, where can I find it?" In that scenario God would be dependent upon whatever entity could satisfy His needs. In other words, God would have to have a higher god. For a strict monotheist that's just not possible, for God is One, supreme, self-sufficient, the source of all creation. Humankind has needs, God doesn't. We need His guidance, mercy and forgiveness, but He doesn't *need* anything in exchange. He may desire servitude and worship, but he doesn't *need* it.

Trinitarian: But that's the point; God tells us to worship Him, and we do that through prayer. But God is pure and holy, and humankind are sinners. We can't approach God directly because of the impurity of our sins. Hence, we need an intercessor to pray through.

Monotheist: Question—did Jesus sin?

Trinitarian: Nope, he was sinless.

Monotheist: How pure was he?

Trinitarian: Jesus? 100% pure. He was God/Son of God, so he was 100% holy.

Monotheist: But then we can't approach Jesus any more than we can God, by your criterion. Your premise is that humankind can't pray directly to God because of the incompatibility of sinful man and the purity of anything 100% holy. If Jesus was 100% holy, then he's no more approachable than God. On the other hand, if Jesus *wasn't* 100% holy, then he

was himself tainted and couldn't approach
God directly, much less be God, the Son
of God, or partner with God.

A fair analogy might be that of going to meet a
supremely righteous man—the holiest person alive, holiness
radiating from his being, oozing from his pores. So we go to see
him, but are told the "saint" won't agree to the meeting. In fact,
he can't stand to be in the same room with a sin-tainted mortal.
We can talk with his receptionist, but the saint himself? Fat
chance! He's much too holy to sit with us lesser beings. So what
do we think now? Does he sound holy, or crazy?

Common sense tells us holy people are approachable—
the holier, the more approachable. So why should we need an
intermediary between us and God?

Frustration approaches critical mass for anyone who
attempts to argue such issues, for rational discussion gives way
to emotionally charged justifications. For example, when
scriptural evidence fails, those who argue based on non-biblical
doctrine are forced to close the book from which they claim to
take guidance (i.e., the Bible) and switch gears to the mystical.
Who can argue with such condescending questions as, "Haven't
you ever felt the power of Jesus in your life?"

Whether a person (including the one asking) understands
the question is a separate issue. Strict monotheists can be quick
to answer in the affirmative, but with the amendment that the
truth Jesus taught is more powerful than the blasphemies that
subsequently grew to dominate Christianity. The strict
monotheist, whether Orthodox Jew, Unitarian Christian or
Muslim, might also question what the power of Satan's
deception might feel like. Pretty slick and persuasive, we would

148

think, for how many souls could Satan win over if he didn't appear in a cloak of righteousness?

So how can we tell the difference between God's truth and Satan's deception? If we choose religion based on emotion and not rational thought, how can we be sure we're on the right path? The God-given faculty of judgment is based upon cognitive reason; to think otherwise is to assume that a rational creation was given an irrational law. God directs humankind in Isaiah 1:18, "Come now, and let us reason together . . ." Nowhere does God teach, "Feel your way along." Satan's doorway—the stress-cracks of human weakness through which he gains a handhold—consists of the base emotions, the lower desires. Nobody ever sits down over a hot cup of tea in the fading twilight of a pastel-colored sunset and tabulates the pros and cons of adultery, theft, or avarice. Nobody ever arrives at sin through deductive reasoning—it just doesn't happen. Humankind arrives at sin through following base desires to the compromise of better—that is, rational—judgment. Sins of the flesh are dangerous enough, from both worldly and after-worldly perspectives. How much more dangerous are errors of religion based upon the emotional appeal of proposals of spiritual exclusivity?

In the past, such claims of spiritual exclusivity were largely limited to the domain of the Gnostics, who were burned at the stake as heretics right up until the time (or so it would seem) that Trinitarian doctrine found itself naked and defenseless in the woods of theological debate. Dependence upon the "holy spirit" and "guiding light" mystical religious defenses, though previously considered a Gnostic heresy, became the trademark of Christian orthodoxy. And it has served them well. The claim that a person lacks the "holy spirit" if they do not accept a given ideology serves as the ultimate storm-wall of religious discussion, diverting the thrust of rational argument away from those who would prefer the evidence to go away than be confronted by its inconvenience. The claim that a person will understand Jesus if they only accept the "Holy Spirit" into their lives meets resistance from those who seek to avoid such Gnostic ideology—ideology which implies an arbitrary nature to God, Who grants mystical understanding to some while withholding it from others.

Strict monotheists may try to redirect discussion back to the main point. For example, many religious groups (Muslims included) accept Jesus, but as a prophet of God. They believe what he taught, including his oft-repeated declaration of himself as nothing more than a prophet and a man. In contrast, many *don't* believe what Pauline theologians taught, preferring to rely upon the clear truth of the prophets in preference to the turbulent contradictions of those who followed in their wake. No matter how sincere Paul may appear to have been, he wasn't a disciple, never met Jesus, and in fact persecuted, imprisoned, and killed his followers (Acts 22:19 and 26:9–11), consented to the stoning of Stephen (Acts 7:58–60 and 22:20), and made havoc of the church (Acts 8:3).

Many admit Paul may have had a mind-warping vision or dream, but that the engineer behind the curtain-of-illusion on *that* yellow brick road to Damascus couldn't be divine if the alleged inspiration contradicted revelation. In the creed of Unitarian Christians and Muslims, God is neither fickle nor inconsistent. Furthermore, we must remember that Jesus cautioned his disciples, "Take heed that no one deceives you. For many will come in my name, saying, 'I am the Christ,' and will deceive many." (Matthew 24:4-5. See also Luke 21:8).

Despite this caution, Paul based his inspiration upon an ethereal voice that told him, "I am Jesus." (Acts 9:5, 22:8, 26:15).

The "in a nutshell" view is that Jesus cautioned his disciples not to be deceived by those who claimed to be him, but that Paul took his inspiration from a voice that claimed . . . stay with me here . . . to be Jesus. Hm.

Those who deny Paul's claim to divine inspiration speculate that, following his alleged vision, he continued to make havoc of the church, but this time from within. Some would call it subterfuge. Others, apparently, consider his actions sufficient for sainthood. And not just any ordinary, run of the mill sainthood, but sainthood of the first rank.

Any such exchange of ideas usually ends abruptly, because disagreement between fiery emotionalism and calm rationality is doomed to frustrate both parties. One side speculates on an imagined "WWJD"—"What Would Jesus Do?" The other focuses on the documented "WDJD"—"What *Did* Jesus Do?" The vast majority of Christians claim to follow Jesus, when in actuality they follow not what he taught, but what others taught about him. Unitarian Christians and Muslims claim to follow Jesus, and then actually do so. Christians who claim to take their teachings from Jesus should feel humbled when they find his teachings better exemplified in the manners of the Islamic community than in those of the Christians themselves.[179(EN)] Practical examples include the following:

Appearance

1. It is commonly acknowledged that Jesus was bearded. Do we find this practice better maintained among Muslims or Christians?

2. Jesus is known to have dressed modestly. Nobody imagines Jesus Christ in shorts and a T-shirt. If we close our eyes and form a mental picture, we see flowing robes, from wrists to ankles. When Jesus delivered his Sermon of the Mount, did he have a paunch? We like to think not, but in fact nobody knows, and his loose clothes may be the reason. So, how many *practicing* Muslims does a person find dressed with Christ-like modesty? The traditional Arabian *thobes* and the Indio-Pakistani *shalwarkameez*are perhaps the best examples, whereas the revealing or seductive clothing so ubiquitous in Western cultures is perhaps the worst.

3. Jesus' mother wore a headscarf, and the Christian women of the Holy Land maintained this practice up to the middle of the twentieth century. Any photograph of an Orthodox Jewish or Palestinian Christian parade or congregation prior to 1950 shows a field of headscarves. But which women of piety cover now—practicing Christians or practicing Muslims?

Manners

1. Jesus placed emphasis on the next world, and was a man preoccupied with striving for salvation. How many "righteous" Christians fit this "It's not just on Sundays" profile? Now, how many "five prayers a day, every day of the year" Muslims?

2. Jesus spoke with humility and kindness. He didn't "showboat." When we think of his speeches, we don't imagine theatrics. He was a simple man known for quality and truth. How many preachers and how many

evangelists follow this example?

3. Jesus taught his disciples to offer the greeting of "Peace" (Luke 10:5). He then set the example by offering the greeting, "Peace be with you" (Luke 24:36, John 20:19, John 20:21, John 20:26). Who continues this practice to this day, Christians or Muslims? "Peace be with you" is the meaning of the Muslim greeting, *"Assalamalaikum."* Interestingly enough, we find this greeting in Judaism as well (Genesis 43:23, Numbers 6:26, Judges 6:23, 1 Samuel 1:17 and 1 Samuel 25:6).

Religious Practices

1. Jesus was circumcised (Luke 2:21). Paul taught it wasn't necessary (Rom 4:11 and Gal 5:2). Muslims believe it is. Which religious group follows Jesus and which follows Paul?

2. Jesus didn't eat pork, in keeping with Old Testament Law (Leviticus 11:7 and Deuteronomy 14:8). Muslims also believe pork is forbidden. Christians . . . well, you get the idea.

3. Jesus didn't give or take usury, in compliance with the Old Testament prohibition (Exodus 22:25). Usury is forbidden in the Old Testament and the Qur'an, as it was forbidden in the religion of Jesus. The economies of most Christian countries, however, are structured upon usury.

4. Jesus didn't fornicate, and abstained from extramarital contact with women. How many Christians adhere to this example? Note: the issue surpasses fornication, and extends to the least physical contact with the opposite

sex. With the exception of performing religious rituals and helping those in need, there is no record of Jesus ever having *touched* a woman other than his mother. Strictly practicing Orthodox Jews maintain this practice to this day in observance of Old Testament Law. Likewise, *practicing* Muslims don't even shake hands between the sexes. Can Christian "hug your neighbor" and "kiss the bride" congregations make the same claim?

Practices of Worship

1. Jesus purified himself with washing prior to prayer, as was the practice of the pious prophets who preceded him (see Exodus 40:31–32 in reference to Moses and Aaron), and as is the practice of Muslims.
2. Jesus prayed in prostration (Matthew 26:39), like the other prophets (see Nehemiah 8:6 with regard to Ezra and the people, Joshua 5:14 for Joshua, Genesis 17:3 and 24:52 for Abraham, Exodus 34:8 and Numbers 20:6 for Moses and Aaron). Who prays like that, Christians or Muslims?
3. Jesus fasted for more than a month at a time (Matthew 4:2 and Luke 4:2), as did the pious before him (Exodus 34:28, 1 Kings 19:8). So who follows the example of Jesus, if not those who annually fast the month of Ramadan?
4. Jesus made pilgrimage for the purpose of worship, as all Orthodox Jews aspire to do. In his day, pilgrimage was to Jerusalem (Acts 8:26–28). Muslims, if able, make pilgrimage to Makkah(more familiar to many by its alternate spelling, *Mecca)* as directed by Allah in the

Holy Qur'an. Should Christians have difficulty accepting the change of pilgrimage sites, Muslims cite Matthew 21:42–43. In Matthew 21:42 Jesus reminded his followers of Psalm 118:22–23 as follows: "The stone which the builders rejected has become the chief cornerstone. This is the Lord's doing, and it is marvelous in our eyes."

Matthew 21:43 then records Jesus as having predicted, "Therefore I say to you, the kingdom of God will be taken from you and given to a nation bearing the fruits of it."

The first quote references "the rejected," who for two thousand years have been understood by Jews and Christians alike to be the Ishmaelites—the bloodline of Muhammad and the majority of the Arab Muslims. Jesus foretells the kingdom of God being taken from the Jews and given to a more deserving nation. Muslims assert that no people could be more deserving than those who embrace the teachings and follow the example of all the prophets, Jesus and Muhammad included.

Furthermore, Muslims point out that Makkah is not without mention in the Bible. Makkah is pronounced "Bakka" in one of the Arabic dialects. Thus, the Holy Qur'an mentions "Makkah" by name in one passage (48:24) and as "Bakka" in another verse, which reads, "The first house (of worship) appointed for men was that at Bakka; full of blessing and of guidance for all kinds of beings" (TMQ 3:96). Psalm 84:5–6 provides the remarkable link between Old Testament and Qur'an: "Blessed *is* the man whose strength *is* in You, whose heart *is* set on *pilgrimage. As they* pass through the

Valley of Baca, they make it a spring . . ." The sacred "spring" of the well of Zamzam in Bakka/Makkah is well known. Additionally, as noted in the form of an editor's comment in Edward Gibbon's work, "Mecca cannot be the Macoraba of Ptolemy; the situations do not agree, and till the time of Mahomet, it bore the name of Becca, or the House, from its celebrated temple. It is so called even in some parts of the Koran."[180]

Matters of Creed

1. Jesus taught the oneness of God (Mark 12:29–30, Matthew 22:37 and Luke 10:27), as conveyed in the first commandment (Exodus 20:3).
2. Jesus declared himself a man and a prophet of God (see above), and nowhere claimed divinity or divine sonship. Which creed is the above two points more consistent with—the Trinitarian formula or the absolute monotheism of Islam?

Practical considerations arise. Questions like, "What was Jesus' religion?" and "If Jesus lived, preached, and completed his ministry faithful to the religious laws of his time, why are those who claim to follow in his name not living by his example?" After all, the Acts of the Apostles documents how strict the practices were among the early followers of Christ. Peter's avoidance of unclean animals is documented in Acts 10:14, the emphasis upon circumcision is found in Acts 11:2–3, 15:1 and 15:5, the conversion of priests and Pharisees into the faith is discussed in 6:7 and 15:5, and 21:20 emphasizes the zeal of the thousands of believers "for the Law." In this regard,

Carmichael notes, "The above passages are astonishing; they indicate that for a whole generation after Jesus' death his followers were pious Jews and proud of it, had attracted into their fold members of the *professional* religious classes, and did not deviate *even* from the burdensome ceremonial laws."[181]

So that was the first generation of followers. Yet despite the scriptural evidence, many Christians prefer the teachings of Paul, the pope, or select clergy over the recorded teachings of Jesus. As a result, common ground for discussion between the true followers of Jesus and the followers of what-somebody-else-says-about-Jesus is frequently lacking. And although some think this to be a fairly recent disagreement, it is in fact an old division, which Paul noted within his lifetime: "Now I say this, that each of you says, 'I am of Paul,' or 'I am of Apollos,' or 'I am of Cephas,' or 'I am of Christ'" (1 Corinthians 1:12).

So Paul, Apollos (an Alexandrian Jew), Cephas (Peter), and Jesus Christ all had their own separate and distinct group of followers, each according to his teachings and example. History weeded out the two groups in the middle, leaving a clean separation between those who live "of Paul" and those who are "of Christ." Whereas Jesus Christ proclaimed the Kingdom of God, Paul proclaimed the mysteries that became the foundation of the church and modern Christology.

Since Paul had such formative influence upon Trinitarian doctrine, one wonders what brought him to the mysteries of his belief. Reportedly a light from the heavens, a voice, a convincing message (Acts 9:3–9). But in 2 Corinthians 11:14–15, even Paul admits that "Satan himself transforms himself into an angel of light. Therefore it is no great thing if his ministers also transform themselves into ministers of righteousness . . ." So to whom was Paul speaking? An angel of light, a minister of righteousness, or Satan?

He didn't seem to question his vision, despite the sage advice, "Beloved, do not believe every spirit, but test the spirits, whether they are of God; because many false prophets have gone out into the world" (First Epistle of John 4:1). Regardless of who was behind Paul's vision, he was a changed man. And although many souls have reformed through religious observance, this isn't what happened with Paul, for one simple reason: Paul didn't *observe* the religion, he *transformed* it. James, the younger brother of Jesus and head of the new church, admonished Paul for his blasphemous teachings: "But they have been informed about you that you teach all the Jews who are among the Gentiles to forsake Moses, saying that they ought not to circumcise their children nor to walk according to the customs" (Acts 21:21). He then warned Paul of the assembly meeting to decide his punishment: "What then? The assembly must certainly meet, for they will hear that you have come" (Acts 21:22). Therefore, he directed him to repent, purify himself of sacrilege, and thereafter "walk orderly and keep the law" (Acts 21:23–24).

Unfortunately, Paul didn't hold to repentance, and returned to his sacrilegious ways.

A person wonders, W*WJD*—What *Would* Jesus Do? No doubt he wouldn't concede his revelation to the contrary opinions of Pauline theology. That being the case, why do some people continue to consider Jesus divine?

A brief summary, then, of these key points:

1. Jesus differentiated between himself and God. On one hand he exalted God, but on the other hand he humbled himself before his Creator in worship. To his followers, Jesus defined himself as nothing more than a man and a

prophet.

2. The disciples agreed, and acknowledged Jesus Christ as a man and a prophet.
3. The only New Testament verse (1 Timothy 3:16) held to support the doctrine of Incarnation is corrupt—even more, if it can be imagined, than the widely discredited John 1:14 and Colossians 2:9.
4. The Bible describes the life and history of Jesus in terms that can only be associated with humanity.
5. Rational arguments for the humanity of Jesus overwhelm the emotional defenses of those who seek to support the Incarnation.
6. The example of Jesus, in appearance, manners, religious practices, and creed, is better exemplified in the lives of practicing Muslims than in the lives of practicing Christians.
7. Pauline theology and that of Jesus Christ are separate and divergent, having resulted in different schools of thought—so much so that, from the time of Paul, a person had to choose between being a person "of Paul" or "of Christ."

Lacking an explicit Bible verse to support the doctrine of the Incarnation, the Christian world is forced to justify the theology on the basis of what they consider to be suggestive evidence. What follows, then, is a list of this evidence, followed by rebuttal.

10 – Divinity of Jesus? The "Evidence"

The truth that makes men free is for the most part the truth which men prefer not to hear.

—Herbert Agar

Exhibit #1 — Miracles

Some associate Jesus with divinity because he performed miracles. Many Unitarian Christians and all Muslims point out that Jesus did indeed perform miracles, but by the will of God and not through any divine powers of his own. To repeat the quote of Acts 2:22, "Jesus of Nazareth, a *man* attested by God to you by miracles, wonders, and signs which *God did* through him in your midst, as you yourselves also know" (italics mine). In conformity with both the Bible and Holy Qur'an, Muslims contend that the miracles of Jesus were performed by the power of God. As the Holy Qur'an states,

> Then will Allah say: "O Jesus the son of Mary! Recount My favor to you and to your mother. Behold! I strengthened you with the holy spirit, so that you spoke to the people in childhood and in maturity. Behold! I taught you the Book and Wisdom, the Law and the Gospel. And

160

> behold! You made out of clay, as it were,
> the figure of a bird, by My leave, and you
> breathed into it, and it became a bird by
> My leave, and you healed those born
> blind, and the lepers, by My leave. And
> behold! You brought forth the dead by
> My leave. (TMQ 5:110)

The Islamic perspective is that miracles can be God-given signs of prophethood, but don't imply divinity. *Hadith* (Islamic traditions relating the words, deeds, appearance, and approvals of Muhammad) relate numerous miracles of Muhammad with greater historical authenticity than found in biblical manuscripts. While the science of *hadith* authentication is regarded as a wonder of historical recordkeeping, the Bible doesn't satisfy many of the most basic standards of historical accuracy.[182(EN)] For example, the authors of most of the books of the Bible (gospels included) are unknown, the time period in which they were written is ill-defined, and the source of much of the information is ambiguous. These issues will be discussed later at greater length, but as a small teaser, let's examine the story of Judas' betrayal of Jesus to the chief priests. Who was the author, and why should we believe him? Was he present at the betrayal? If so, then what was he doing there, and why didn't he alert Jesus? And if not, then where did he get his information, and why should we trust it?

There are other private scenes recorded in the gospel narratives. But if these scenes were private, how did the gospel authors know the details? Who witnessed Jesus' temptation in the desert? Who stood by and recorded his prayers in the garden of Gethsemane?

Given all these unanswered questions, why should humankind trust its salvation to the gospels, considering that they are of unknown origin and authorship?

The Jesus Seminar is perhaps one of the most objective and sincere attempts of an ecumenical council of Christian scholars to determine the authenticity of the recorded acts and sayings of Jesus. Yet their methodology involves casting votes! Two thousand years after the ministry of Jesus, nearly two hundred scholars are formulating a collective Christian opinion regarding the reliability of the quotes and historical reports of Jesus by casting colored beads. For example, as regards the reported words of Jesus, the definitions of the bead colors are as follows:

> Red—Jesus said it or something very close to it. Pink—Jesus probably said something like it, although his words have suffered in transmission. Gray—these are not his words, but the ideas are close to his own. Black—Jesus did not say it; the words represent the Christian community or a later point of view.[183]

Other Christian committees have attempted to authenticate Bible texts by similar methodologies. The editors of the United Bible Societies' *The Greek New Testament: Second Edition* are alphabetically minded:

> By means of the letters A, B, C, and D, enclosed within "braces" {} at the beginning of each set of textual variants

> the Committee has sought to indicate the
> relative degree of certainty, arrived at the
> basis of internal considerations as well as
> of external evidence, for the reading
> adopted as the text. The letter A signifies
> that the text is virtually certain, while B
> indicates that there is some degree of
> doubt. The letter C means that there is a
> considerable degree of doubt whether the
> text of the apparatus contains the superior
> reading, while D shows that there is a
> very high degree of doubt concerning the
> reading selected for the text.[184]

Bruce M. Metzger describes using similar methodology in his *A Textual Commentary on the Greek New Testament*. "In fact," he writes, "among the {D} decisions sometimes none of the variant readings commended itself as original, and therefore the only recourse was to print the least unsatisfactory reading."[185]

Now doesn't *that* give us a warm, secure feeling in trusting the Bible with the salvation of humankind?

But I digress. The point is that these ranking systems are probably about the best possible, given the limitations of the biblical record, but what a sad comment that is! Compared to the exquisitely refined system of *hadith* authentication, these colored-bead and A-B-C-D classification systems are a bit wanting, to say the least.

The historical recordkeeping is relevant, for when a person hears a story—even a believable story at that—the first question is usually, "Where did you hear that?" Any reasonable set of historical standards includes the identification and verification of sources. The Holy Qur'an and many *hadith* traditions satisfy the highest degrees of authentication. The majority of Bible verses don't.[186(EN)]

How does this relate to the issue at hand? Simple. The miracles that occurred through Muhammad are no less numerous or impressive than those of Jesus, and are witnessed by an unimpeachable historical record that puts all others of similar time period to shame. So just as the miracles of Moses, Elisha, and Muhammad don't imply divinity, neither do those of Jesus.

Let's look at a few examples:

> **Jesus fed thousands with a few fish and loaves of bread.**But Elisha fed a hundred people with twenty barley loaves and a few ears of corn (2 Kings 4:44); granted a widow such an abundant flow of oil from a jar that she was able to pay off her debts, save her sons from slavery, and live on the profits (2 Kings 4:1–7); and gave increase to a handful of flour and spot of oil such that he, a widow and her son had enough to eat for many days, after which "The bin of flour was not used up, nor did the jar of oil run dry . . ." (1 Kings 17:10–16). So what does that make Elisha? The historical record of Muhammad feeding the masses with a handful of dates on one occasion, a pot of milk on another, and enough meat for a

164

small party on still another are equally miraculous. Likewise are the stories of his watering the masses (1,500 people on one occasion) from a single bowl of water. Yet no Muslim claims divinity for Muhammad.

Jesus healed the lepers. Likewise, Elisha healed Naaman (2 Kings 5:7–14). For that matter, the disciples were bidden to such service in Matthew 10:8. What does that make them?

Jesus cured a blind man. Elisha not only struck his enemies blind, but restored vision to the blind through prayer (2 Kings 6:17–20). Muhammad reportedly cured blindness through prayer as well.

Jesus raised the dead. Once again, Elisha beat him to it, having raised two children from the dead (1 Kings 17:22 and 2 Kings 4:34). Furthermore, the disciples were bidden to raise the dead (Matthew 10:8). So once again, what does that make them?

Jesus walked on water. Had he been around in the time of Moses, he wouldn't have had to.

Jesus cast out devils. So did his disciples (Matthew 10:8). So did the sons

of the Pharisees (Matthew 12:27 and
Luke 11:19). So, for that matter, do the
wayward followers whom Jesus will
reportedly disown (see Matthew 7:22)—a
disconcerting thought considering how
many priests and ministers perform such
theatrics, even if real.

So if we seek evidence of Jesus being divine, we are
forced to look beyond miracles.

Exhibit #2 — Scriptural Predictions
The Old Testament predicted the coming of Jesus. It also
predicted the coming of John the Baptist in the book of Malachi.
More importantly, many Old and New Testament references to a
final prophet do not match the profile of either John the Baptist
or Jesus (see "Messengers" in the sequel to this book, *God'ed*).

Exhibit #3 — Savior
The Bible describes God as "Savior" and Jesus as
"savior." Conclusion? God is "Savior," Jesus is "savior,"
therefore Jesus is God? The problem with this proposal is that
we have to invite Othniel, Ehud, Shamgar, Gideon, and other
anonymous "saviors" to the party. Why? The Hebrew word by
which the Old Testament identifies God as savior is *yasha*.
Yasha appears 207 times in the Old Testament Hebrew,
including references to Othniel (Judges 3:9), Ehud (Judges
3:15), Shamgar (Judges 3:31), Gideon (Judges 8:22), and
anonymous individuals (2 Kings 13:5, Neh 9:27, Oba 1:21).
Why is *yasha* translated differently for these individuals than for
Jesus and for God? Only the translators know for sure, but the

166

motivations appear less than honorable, for selective mistranslation conceals the fact that Jesus and God are far from having exclusive rights to the term.

Exhibit #4 — "I Am"

John 8:58 reports Jesus as having said, "Before Abraham was, I Am," and Exodus 3:14 records God as having informed Moses, "I am who I am." First of all, according to the words of Jesus, is a person to conclude that Jesus had a pre-human existence? According to Jeremiah 1:5, so did Jeremiah. According to the Islamic religion, so did all of us. Next, is a person to draw a parallel between the "I Am" attributed to Jesus and that attributed to God? Once again, the foundational text pokes fun at the translation. Jesus is *not* recorded to have said "I Am" in capital "makes me look like God" letters. Jesus is *translated* as having said "I Am" in a "looks like God's words in Exodus, think they'll buy it?" effort at textual synchronization. What Jesus *is* recorded to have said is *eimi*, anuncapitalized, humble, unprepossessing and nonexclusive (152 times in the New Testament) Greek word that doesn't justify capitals *or* comparison with the supposed words of God in Exodus (which are not capitalized, either in the Hebrew *hayah* or the Greek Septuagint *ho ohn*. For that matter, neither the Ancient Hebrew nor Greek even *have* capital letters). By no means can the New Testament Greek *eimi* attributed to Jesus be compared with the Old Testament Greek *ho ohn* attributed to God in the Septuagint. By no means of honesty or accuracy, that is. Likewise, neither of these phrases can honestly be capitalized "I Am," for the 151 other instances of *eimi* are translated to the uncapitalized, "I am." Why is *eimi* capitalized once and not capitalized 151 times, if not due to doctrinal prejudice? To their own credit, most

167

reputable bibles avoid this textual game-playing. The New International Version, the Revised Standard Version, the New Revised Standard Version, the American Standard Version, and many others do not capitalize the *eimi* of Jesus to "I AM."

Exhibit #5 — The Right Hand Man

Mark 16:19 and Luke 22:69 report that Jesus was received into heaven, where he sat at the right hand of God. Let's begin by pointing out that Mark 16:9–20 has been rejected from many bibles for being of doubtful scriptural authority.[187] Bart Ehrman puts it more simply, stating, "But there's one problem. Once again, this passage was not originally in the Gospel of Mark. It was added by a later scribe."[188]

Barring the consideration that the entire passage might be illegitimate to begin with, the argument that closeness to God makes one equal to, partners with, or part of God breaches clear from the waters of reason. The Bible says Jesus sat with God, which, if Jesus *were* God, could only mean that God sat beside Himself, on his own right side. In conflict with this bizarre thought is Isaiah 44:6, which reads with blinding clarity, "Thus says the Lord . . . 'I am the First and I am the Last; besides Me there is no God.'" Isaiah 43:11 records, "I, even I, am the Lord, and besides Me there is no savior." So what's the argument again? That Jesus sat beside Himself, Theirselves, Godselves, whatever—but he sat beside God *without* sitting beside God because, "Besides Me there is no God," and "besides me there is no savior"? A true dilemma arises—either Jesus sat beside God and therefore is neither God *nor* savior, or he didn't sit beside God and the Bible is unreliable. In the first case the theology fails, in the second case the Bible fails, and either way we're left confused, whereas the purpose of revelation is to clarify. In addition, the Bible says, "And Enoch *walked* with God . . ." (Genesis 5:24). So what does that make him?

Exhibit#6 — Forgiving Sins

Some attribute divinity to Jesus because they believe he forgave sins. Luke 5:20 reads, "So when he saw their faith, he said to him, 'Man, your sins are forgiven you.'" Luke 7:47–48 states, "Therefore I say to you, her sins, which are many, are forgiven. . . . And he said to her, 'Your sins are forgiven.'" The claim is that, by these words, Jesus forgave sins. Others suggest he informed the individuals concerned that their sins were forgiven, but by whom, he didn't say. Significantly, Jesus didn't say, "I forgive your sins." Were we to assume Jesus conveyed the forgiveness of the Creator, of which he was informed through revelation, we fall into agreement with Jesus in John 12:49—"For I have not spoken on my own authority, but the Father who sent me gave me a command, what I should say and what I should speak." On the other hand, were we to assume Jesus forgave sins on his own initiative, we contradict his statement, "I can of myself do nothing . . ." (John 5:30).

A deeper question is not whether Jesus had the power to forgive sins, but whether that would make him equal to God. The Pharisees allegedly thought so, but Jesus corrected them, as Luke 5:21 records: "And the scribes and the Pharisees began to reason, saying, 'Who is this who speaks blasphemies? Who can forgive sins but God alone?'" Again, the argument is that the Pharisees believed Jesus claimed to be God, so we should believe as they did. However, it's a peculiar argument. The Pharisees hated Jesus, defied him and obstructed his mission, lied against him at his trial and plotted his capture, humiliation, beating and murder. And yet, we're supposed to trust their opinion? Let's remember, it's the defiant Pharisees who teach, to this day, that Jesus Christ was a bastard child and his mother was either a fornicator or a prostitute. And yet the Christian is supposed to accept their opinion? Jesus didn't. In the very next verse, Luke 5:22, he rebuked the Pharisees with the words, "Why are you reasoning in your hearts?"—the rough scriptural equivalent of calling them blithering idiots, for they allowed their emotions to override rational judgment.

And again, what better place for Jesus to have asserted his divinity if, that is, he were in fact divine? What better place for him to have stood tall with the confidence of divine omnipotence and said, "That's right, who *can* forgive sins but God alone? *Finally*, you've figured it out. Now, let me explain. . . ."

But he didn't, and we have to assume he had good reason not to, for in fact he stated the exact opposite.

Exhibit #7 — "Lord"

In the Bible, God was called "Lord" (Greek *kurios*) and Jesus was also called "lord." Is this evidence for divinity of Jesus? Apparently not, for a lot of other people were also called "lord" in the Bible. However, once again, selective capitalization where it suited the doctrinal purpose of the translators distorts the reality. "Lord" is a biblical title of respect, as evidenced by numerous stories throughout the Bible (ex. Matthew 18:23–34 and Luke 19:11–21). The title "Lord" does not in itself imply divinity, and we see this when Sarah called Abraham "Lord" (1 Peter 3:6). Nonetheless, Christians present John 20:28 as evidence, in which Thomas is quoted as having identified Jesus as "My Lord and my God!" One problem. 1 Corinthians 8:6 reads, "Yet for us there is only one

God, the Father . . . and one Lord Jesus Christ. . . ." "Lord" and "God" are separate and distinct in one verse, but one and the same in the other. Exodus 4:16 compounds this confusion, for the Greek literally translates to Moses being *Elohim* (God) to Aaron. Substitution of the word "as" to distort the translation to "as God" has no manuscript authority, but does serve to throw readers off the unmistakable scent of an overripe theology gone bad. In a book where pagan gods (e.g., Ex. 12:12; 18:11; 20:3), judges (Psalms 82:1 and 6), angels (Psalm 8:5), and prophets (Exodus 4:16) are identified with the same *Elohim* as The One True God, who can trust a doctrine based on human interpretations of ancient colloquialisms?

Exhibit #8 — Worship

People "worshipped" Jesus, and he didn't object. Well, that's not quite true, is it? What the biblical manuscripts record is that people *proskuneo*'ed Jesus, and he didn't object. *Proskuneo* is selectively translated in some bibles as "worship" or "worshipped," but that doesn't hint at the full range of meanings:

> *proskuneo, pros-koo-neh'-o*; from G4314 and a prob. der. of G2965 (mean. to kiss, like a dog licking his master's hand); to fawn or crouch to, i.e. (lit. or fig.) prostrate oneself in homage (do reverence to, adore):—worship.[189]

It's a fair assumption that few conceive the faithful to have kissed, much less licked Jesus' hand. So assuming that some of the faithful crouched or prostrated themselves to Jesus,

we have to wonder what such a gesture would have signified.
Matthew 18:26 records the story of a slave who
proskuneo'ed his master, begging for forgiveness of his debts.
Mark 15:16–20 records the humiliation of Jesus prior to the
alleged crucifixion as follows:

> Then the soldiers led him away into the
> hall called Praetorium, and they called
> together the whole garrison. And they
> clothed him with purple; and they twisted
> a crown of thorns, put it on his head, and
> began to salute him, "Hail, King of the
> Jews!" Then they struck him on the head
> with a reed and spat on him; and bowing
> the knee, they worshiped [*proskuneo*'ed]
> him. And when they had mocked him,
> they took the purple off him, put his own
> clothes on him, and led him out to crucify
> him.

Acts 10:25 records this: "As Peter was coming in,
Cornelius met him and fell down at his feet and worshiped
[*proskuneo*'ed] him." Old Testament references include
1 Samuel 25:23, in which Abigail "fell on her face before David,
and bowed down to the ground." 2 Kings 4:37 speaks of a
Shunammite woman who, after God revived her child through
Elisha's prayer, "fell at his [Elisha's] feet, and bowed to the
ground . . ." Genesis 50:18 and 2 Samuel 19:18 weigh into the
equation as well.

Taken in total, *proskuneo* can only imply divinity if
Peter, David, and Elisha, among others, are included. Otherwise,

selective translation must be assumed, for when the Roman soldiers *proskuneo*'ed to Jesus, they didn't worship him, as the Bible translates. Rather, they mocked him with the salute offered to the kings and leaders of their time. Likewise, when others *proskuneo*'ed to Peter, David, Elisha, the slave-master, *et al.* they showed their respect according to custom. So, too, with Jesus.

This subject can be summed up with the question, "When people *proskuneo*'ed to Jesus, did they revere him as God?" If so, why didn't they pray to him? It is worth noting that the Bible never records anyone having prayed to Jesus, and the rights due to God were directed to Him alone. By both Jesus and his followers. Luke 4:8 records Jesus saying, "You shall worship the Lord your God, and Him only you shall serve."

What jumps out at us from this verse is not only that Jesus directed worship to God, but service—or in Greek, *latreuo*, which is defined, "to minister (to God), i.e., render religious homage:—serve, do the service, worship (-per)."[190] Unlike the aforementioned *proskuneo*, *latreuo* means to render *religious* homage. And significantly, out of twenty-two uses in the New Testament, nowhere is *latreuo* applied to Jesus. So while some people may have crouched or prostrated to Jesus in accordance with the custom of their day, they didn't *latreuo*, or render religious homage, to him. They reserved that honor for God alone. And for that matter, so did Jesus himself.

Exhibit #9 — The Resurrection

Some attribute divinity to Jesus based upon his alleged resurrection. This subject is critical, for the keystone of orthodox Christianity is the belief that Jesus died for the sins of humankind. The concepts of the crucifixion, resurrection, and

173

atonement are discussed later in depth. For now, the important point is that many early Christians doubted the crucifixion, for none of the gospels is an eyewitness account. In the words of Joel Carmichael, author of *The Death of Jesus,* "Who could the witnesses have been? . . . .. Not only do [the disciples] 'all forsake' Jesus and flee; they do not—even more surprisingly—reappear during Jesus' trial nor are they present at his execution, nor are they the ones who bury him."[191] Nor, for that matter, are they the authors of the gospels in the first place, but we'll come to that point later.

Most scholars agree that the gospel writers worked off nothing but hearsay in recording the alleged crucifixion. Even the *New Catholic Encyclopedia* admits, "The four Evangelists differ slightly in the wording of the inscription (on top of the cross), which shows that they were citing from memory and hearsay evidence."[192]

This fact has been well recognized since the time of Jesus, but thoroughly covered up by those who would have humankind believe the authors of the gospels had front-row seats and photographic memories. In reality, all of the disciples deserted Jesus at the garden of Gethsemane, as recorded in Mark 14:50: "Then they all forsook him and fled." Peter may have followed Jesus at a distance, but only as far as the courtyard of the high priest Caiaphas. Here the "Rock" (on which Jesus promised to build his church—Matthew 16:18–19) thrice denied having known Jesus. (Did Jesus say "rock"? Perhaps what he really meant to say was "Satan" and "an offense," as he declared a scant five verses later.) Anyway, Peter wasn't one of the gospel authors. So where were *they*? Matthew 27:55 and Luke 23:49 tell us the "observers" were not present at the crucifixion, so we can only guess.

174

Regarding the alleged resurrection, the four gospels (Matthew 28, Mark 16, Luke 24, and John 20) don't agree on what happened following the crucifixion. For example:

Who went to the tomb?
Matthew: "Mary Magdalene and the other Mary"
Mark: "Mary Magdalene, Mary the mother of James, and Salome"
Luke: "The women who had come with him from Galilee" and "certain other women"
John: "Mary Magdalene"

Why did they go to the tomb?
Matthew: "To see the tomb"
Mark: They "brought spices, that they might come and anoint him"
Luke: They "brought spices"
John: no reason given

Was there an earthquake (something that would not easily go unnoticed)?
Matthew: Yes
Mark: no mention
Luke: no mention
John: no mention

Did an angel descend (again, would any self-respecting gospel author have failed to mention this)?
Matthew: Yes
Mark: no mention
Luke: no mention

175

John: no mention

Who rolled back the stone?
>*Matthew:* The angel
>*Mark:* unknown
>*Luke:* unknown
>*John*: unknown

Who was at the tomb?
>*Matthew:* "an angel"
>*Mark:* "a young man"
>*Luke:* "two men"
>*John:* "two angels"

Where were they?
>*Matthew:* The angel was sitting on the stone, outside the tomb.
>*Mark:* The young man was in the tomb, "sitting on the right side."
>*Luke:* The two men were inside the tomb, standing beside them.
>*John:* The two angels were "sitting, one at the head and the other at the feet, where the body of Jesus had lain."

By whom and where was Jesus first seen?
>*Matthew:* Mary Magdalene and the "other Mary," on the road to tell the disciples.
>*Mark:* Mary Magdalene only, no mention where.
>*Luke:* Two of the disciples, en route to "a village called Emmaus, which was about seven miles from Jerusalem."
>*John:* Mary Magdalene, outside the tomb.

There is depressingly little or no consistency to the stories, which leads one to ask whether the Bible is a book of viewpoints or a book of God. Ehrman concludes the Bible is a very human book, riddled with errors, of which the most egregious are scriptural additions and deletions (both intentional and not).[193] Heinz Zahrnt agrees as follows:

> The days of the unhistorical doctrine of
> verbal inspiration as held by Old
> Protestant theology are over. From now
> onwards the Bible is understood as an
> historical book, written and transmitted
> by men and therefore subject to the same
> laws of tradition, the same errors,
> omissions and alterations as any other
> historical source. The men who produced
> it were no automata, instruments of God,
> but individual writers, men of flesh and
> blood who had their own decided aims
> and tendencies in writing, who lived
> within the limited horizons of their time
> and were moulded by the ideas of their
> environment.[194]

Many who examine the evidence with an open mind agree. After all, would God have inspired inconsistencies such as those listed above? But if the Bible is a book of human viewpoints, then who can fault people for any opinion they construct from the framework of contradictory teachings found therein?

177

One can assert that despite the differences, all four gospels teach the crucifixion, and this is true. Many satisfy their beliefs with such thoughts. Others wonder what alternative viewpoints were burned to ashes in the destruction of an estimated 250 to 2,000 acts, epistles, and gospels the council of Nicaea excluded from canonization, and why the alleged crucifixion was debated among early first-century Christians. In other words, what did they know that we don't?

With regard to the alleged divinity of Jesus, none of these points matter. Even if the crucifixion were true, Jesus being raised from the dead would not imply divinity any more than it would for the children raised through the prayers of Elisha, the dead man revived through contact with Elisha's bones, or Lazarus resurrected at the hands of Jesus. For that matter, God promises to raise all humankind come the Day of Judgment—what will that make us?

Exhibit#10 — Foreknowledge

Some attribute divinity to Jesus because he had foreknowledge of certain events. However, isn't that what prophets do—prophesy? And isn't this the example of previous prophets, even though none of them were divine? Significantly, prophets only have foreknowledge of that which is revealed to them, whereas God's knowledge is absolute. Were Jesus divine, we would expect his knowledge to have been comprehensive. Yet we encounter teachings that cancel this expectation, as follows:

> Particularly difficult to explain would be
> the logion [one of Jesus' sayings] of Mk
> 13:31 concerning the Last Day: "But of

that day or hour no one knows, neither the
angels in heaven, nor the Son, but the
Father only." The authenticity of this
passage can hardly be questioned, for a
community bent on exalting its Lord
would scarcely have constructed a saying
in which He confesses ignorance.[195]

Summary of Evidence

Some suggest that, despite the objections, the sheer
amount of "evidence" suggests that Jesus was divine. This might
be a fair argument, if each piece of evidence contributed
something to support the conclusion. It wouldn't have to be a
lot, but there has to be some buoyancy to float the argument.
Either a couple of big logs or a million twigs bundled together
will bear a man down a river. An ounce of gold can be had from
one huge nugget, or from smelting a ton of crude ore. A court
case can be concluded with one perfect photo or a hundred
suggestive testimonies. But a million worthless testimonies
won't support a verdict, and basing a doctrine on ten, or a
hundred, or even a thousand pieces of "evidence," each one of
which brings nothing to support the conclusion, is as futile as
trying to float a raft of rocks, or smelt salt for gold. Add more
rocks, smelt more salt, and the desired result will remain elusive,
just as a conclusion evades a million "evidences" if each one
lacks the slightest validity.

Do any other "proofs" for the presumed divinity of Jesus
remain? When all else fails, some clergy claim that Jesus was
filled with the Holy Spirit, and therefore must be divine. But
was Jesus filled with the Holy Spirit differently from Peter (Acts

4:8), Stephen (Acts 6:5 and 7:55), Barnabas (Acts 11:24), Elizabeth (Luke 1:41), and Zacharias (Luke 1:67)?

Some distinguish Jesus from the above individuals by claiming he was filled with the Holy Spirit before his birth. Others point out that John the Baptist was not associated with divinity, though Luke 1:15 records, "He [John the Baptist] will also be filled with the holy spirit, even from his mother's womb."

Some regard the Holy Spirit as integral with God. Others struggle to grasp the concept, certain only that whatever the Holy Spirit is, it is sent to all of the righteous, as is written, "And we are His witnesses to these things, and so also is the holy spirit whom God has given to those who obey Him." (Acts 5:32). The conclusion that the Holy Spirit is given to all who obey God has the clear ring of reason, and at least this concept stands up to scripture. The question then arises, "What *is* this 'holy spirit'?"

11 – Holy Spirit

Free from desire, you realize the mystery.

Caught in desire, you see only the manifestations.

—Lao-Tzu, *Tao TeChing*

Everyone knows the term "Holy Spirit," but few attempt to define it. Those who do usually produce a mix of personal opinion and ambiguous, though doctrinally sanctioned, apologetics. In the minds of most, this "oil and water" theology fails to gel into a homogeneous reality. The Islamic understanding, on the other hand, is remarkably concrete, teaching that the "Holy Spirit" is Gabriel, the angel of revelation. When we come to *Rûh-ul-Qudus* in the Holy Qur'an (see ayah 2:87), some (like Yusuf Ali) translate "holy spirit," others (like Muhammad Al-Hilali and Muhammad Khan) translate "Gabriel" and still others (like Saheeh International) offer both "holy spirit" and "Gabriel"—reflecting that, in the creed of the Muslim, the two terms are synonymous.

While Islam teaches that the Bible is to one degree or another corrupted, many Muslims contend that the truth of Islam can nonetheless be found *in the Bible*. And since Muslims frequently argue Islamic ideology on the basis of biblical teachings, we might ask, "How does Islam explain the use of 'Holy Spirit' in the Bible?" For "Angel Gabriel" cannot be substituted for "Holy Spirit" without rendering many Bible passages implausible or nonsensical.

The challenge, then, is for Muslims to either make sense of this discrepancy, *from a biblical perspective*, or to stop arguing Islam on the basis of the Bible. This would seem an ultimately fair challenge, for otherwise Muslims can be accused of the same disingenuousness with which they charge Christians—namely, picking and choosing only those Bible verses that suit their purpose, while dismissing without legitimately discrediting verses that prove ideologically uncomfortable. However, at least two points need to be considered in order to understand the Islamic perspective. The first concerns the questionable reliability of the Bible, which will be addressed in later chapters devoted to that subject. The second point, which dovetails with the first, is that Muslims do not claim the Bible to be unadulterated revelation from God pointing the way to the Holy Qur'an and Islam. Rather, Muslims believe the Bible contains both divine truths and human corruptions. Indeed, biblical corruptions run the gamut from copying errors to doctrinally motivated additions, deletions, tailored translation and, in some cases, even forgery.[196]

The thrust of Unitarian Christian and Muslim argument, then, focuses not only upon faithful adherence to revealed truth, but also upon recognition and disavowal of scriptural corruptions.

Take, for example, the Greek word *pneúma*. In the Bible, *pneúma* is translated "spirit." However, Kittel and Friedrich's *Theological Dictionary of the New Testament* informs us *pneúma* can mean a great deal more (as well as a great deal *less*): wind, breath, life, soul, transferred (in a metaphorical sense) sense of spirit, mantic*pneúma* (the spirit that stirs and inspires—"mantic" pertaining to prophecy), divine*pneúma*(about which the authors comment, "But there is in Greek no sense of a personal holy spirit"), the *pneúma* of Stoicism (an ancient Greek philosophy to which few today subscribe), and non-Greek development of meaning (which is to say, unauthentic, for even Greek wasn't the language of Jesus).[197]

In reading the above, we find Bible translators assumed considerable literary license, for the correct translation of *pneúma* is nowhere "holy spirit." According to the above text (which is widely considered one of the most scholarly references on this subject worldwide), the word *pneúma* bears diverse possibilities in translation. Of course, "holy wind" or "holy breath" don't support Trinitarian doctrine as does "holy spirit," but what's a translator to do? Seek the truth of God's revelation or manipulate translation to support institutional decree?

Let's let Jason BeDuhn answer that question. In his landmark work, *Truth in Translation*, he wrote:

> In our survey of the use of "spirit" in the New Testament, we have found no translation that heeds grammar, syntax, literary context, and cultural environment with complete consistency. The translators of all of the versions we are comparing allowed theological bias to interfere with their accuracy. At one point or another, they all imported the "Holy Spirit" into passages where "spirit" is being used in a different sense. . . . no translation emerged with a perfectly consistent and accurate handling of the

many uses and nuances of "spirit" and
"holy spirit."[198]

Then, there's the startling "coincidence" between the
book of "John" being dramatically more poetic than any of the
other gospels and "John's" unique utilization of the mantic
pneúma, as described above. So great is the disparity that expert
theologians admit surprise at the infrequent mention of the Spirit
in "Mark" and "Matthew" compared to "John."[199] Couple this
with the fact that the doctrines of the Trinity and the Incarnation
stem primarily from strained interpretations of the poeticisms of
"John" with little, if any, scriptural support from the other
gospels, and the weight of these doctrines overstresses their
shoddy foundation.

Undeniably, there is ample room for interpretation of
scripture. There are those who read the Bible and understand
"Holy Spirit" to be a somewhat indefinable third element of
divinity, akin to the *pneúma* of Stoicism or the unauthentic
meaning developed following the period of revelation. Others
understand God to be One, without partner or subdivision, and
search for what is rational and justified according to logic. For
this latter group, "Holy Spirit" cannot be understood except in
reference to a tangible entity separate and distinct from God.

An example of how the Bible suffers in translation, and
why conclusions vary as consequence, is the fact that *paraclete*
(from the Greek *parakletos*) can mean "helper, defender,
mediator, consoler."[200] Elsewhere it is translated "advocate,
helper."[201] Harper's concurs with "advocate."[202] Why is this
important? Because "the word Paraclete occurs only five times
in the Bible, and all five occurrences are in the purported
writings of St. John: 1st Epistle of John 2:1; and the Gospel

according to John 14:16, 14:26, 15:26, 16:7."[203]

Should we assume this word slipped the minds of the other gospel authors? If so, we would suspect it must not have been very important. On the contrary, these five passages are *critical*. In fact, Trinitarian emphasis on the need to accept the Holy Spirit hinges on these few quotes. A person can appreciate the peculiarity of this incongruity, for if the concept of the Paraclete is so crucial to the creed that God wants man to gain from revelation, we have to wonder why it didn't make enough of an impression on the other three gospel authors to be worthy of mention. Even once.

Whatever the reasons, *paraclete* is one more word frequently mistranslated "Holy Spirit" or "Holy Ghost." Even as modern translation of the Bible tends toward greater academic integrity, *paraclete* is still often mistranslated "counselor" or "comforter". The correct translation as "helper," "defender," "mediator," "consoler" or "advocate" would imply an actual physical entity, which would be consistent with the fact that "some trace the origin of the use of *parakletos* in the Johannine works back to the concept of heavenly helpers."[204] And who could be a greater "heavenly helper" than Gabriel, the angel of revelation himself?

Similarly, in its first-century Greek usage, "*Parakletos* was a legal term used mainly of advocate, defender, or intercessor. True to its basic meaning one 'called out to stand beside, defend, advise or intercede,' it was used of legal counsel and witnesses alike."[205]

These quotes help us to understand what *paraclete* meant in the period of revelation. But somewhere in the passage of time, select theologians claimed to know better, and developed a radically different understanding of the word. Association of *parakletos* with a physical entity proved inconvenient to those who sought to bolster the Trinitarian argument, and appears to have been avoided at all costs.

And so, to review:

1. The definition of "holy spirit" is elusive in Christianity, but concrete in Islam, being synonymous with Gabriel, the angel of revelation.
2. There are many definitions of *pneúma*, but nowhere is it "holy spirit" in its original Greek meaning.
3. Only according to the derived and unauthentic, "non-Greek development of meaning" is *pneúma* translated to "holy spirit."
4. Christian theology regarding the Holy Spirit depends almost exclusively on the Gospel and First Epistle of "John."
5. The Paraclete is not mentioned in any of the other books of the New Testament.
6. Correct translation of *paraclete* appears to imply a material entity, which could be human or angelic.

With these points firmly in mind, what remains is to trace the meaning of *Paraclete* in the five NT verses in which it appears. Taken in order:

1. The First Epistle of John, 2:1 (I Jn 2:1) identifies Jesus Christ as a "paraclete" (herein translated "advocate"): "And if anyone sins, we have an advocate [i.e., paraclete] with the Father, Jesus Christ the righteous." So whatever a "paraclete" is—advocate, helper, comforter, *whatever*—Jesus was one, according to this verse.

2. John 14:16–17 reads, "And I will pray the Father, and He will give you another helper [i.e., paraclete], that he may abide with you forever, even the Spirit of truth, whom the world cannot receive, because it neither sees him nor knows him; but you know him, for he dwells with you and will be in you."

Note the qualifying adjective "another" in the phrase "another helper." The Greek word used in this verse is *allos*, the meaning of which is "'the other,' strictly where there are many, as distinct from *heteros*, where there are only two . . ."[206] The wording is specific and leaves no room for interpretation. In this verse, Jesus advised his disciples—and, by extension, all humankind—to anticipate another paraclete (i.e., helper) following his ministry. Not just another helper, but one characterized by honesty (i.e., "the spirit of truth") and bearing an eternal (i.e., that he may abide with you forever) message.

Can we conclude that this "other" (i.e., "'the other,' strictly where there are many") is the final prophet in the long line of prophets, bearing a final revelation? Is this not a more comfortable conclusion than the strained claim that Jesus describes some mystical "holy spirit," as derived from an unauthentic, "non-Greek development of meaning?" On the other hand, the conclusion that Jesus is unique in a "begotten, not made, son of God" sense if there is another, "strictly where there are many . . .," all of whom bear the exact same description as Jesus (i.e., the description of "paraclete") is not just unfounded, it is contrary to scripture.

Lest there be any confusion over this point, the New Testament confirms that the Greek *pneúma* (translated below as "spirit") is not restricted to mystical beings but can refer to flesh and blood humans, both good and bad. For example, the First Epistle of John 4:1–3 states:

> Beloved, do not believe every spirit, but

187

> test the spirits, whether they are of God;
> because many false prophets have gone
> out into the world. By this you know the
> Spirit of God: every spirit that confesses
> that Jesus Christ has come in the flesh is
> of God, and every spirit that does not
> confess that Jesus Christ has come in the
> flesh is not of God. And this is the spirit
> of the Antichrist, which you have heard
> was coming, and is now already in the
> world.

This verse not only clarifies the human nature of some "spirits" (i.e., *pneúma*), but Muslims claim that this verse admits Muhammad into the company of those who are "of God," for *every* spirit that "confesses that Jesus Christ has come in the flesh is of God." Muhammad said it, all Muslims affirm it, the Holy Qur'an documents it, and in the minds of a billion Muslims, that settles it.

3.& 4. The third reference to "paraclete" is in John 14:26, which reads, "But the helper [i.e., Paraclete], the holy spirit, whom the Father will send in my name, he will teach you all things, and bring to your remembrance all things that I said to you."

The fourth reference, John 15:26, reads much the same. Once again, Trinitarians may justify their mysticisms with this verse. Others perceive reference to a prophet who will remind the world of Jesus' true message, as opposed to the misdirection which developed in the beliefs and doctrines of later generations. Once again, Muslims suggest Christians should consider Muhammad and the Holy Qur'an. The union of the comments, "He will bear witness to the truth of what Jesus did and said and was,"[207] and "even though this divine Advocate is the very 'Spirit of truth' (John 14:16; 15:26; 16:13), the world will not listen to him (14:17)"[208] would make perfect sense if the prophethood of Muhammad were assumed to be true. As discussed above, both Muhammad and the Holy Qur'an witnessed "to the truth of what Jesus did and said and was." Furthermore, Muhammad bore the reputation of honesty (i.e., the "spirit of truth")—throughout his life he was known, even among his enemies, as *As-Saadiq Al-Ameen*, which means "the truthful; the trustworthy." And yet, the majority of humankind will neither "listen to him" nor entertain his message.

5. The final mention of *paraclete* is in John 16:7: "Nevertheless I tell you the truth. It is to your advantage that I go away; for if I do not go away, the helper will not come to you; but if I depart, I will send him to you."

This last reference to the Paraclete, like a small but high-velocity projectile, lays waste to surrounding doctrines far in excess of the innocent entrance wound. Trinitarians may continue to assert that *paraclete* refers to the mystical Holy Spirit, but John 16:7 negates that possibility. How? Jesus reportedly stated that unless he goes away the "Paraclete" will not come; even though multiple, *multiple* Bible passages speak of the presence of the "holy spirit" in or before Jesus' time.[209] Both cannot be true, and the most logical conclusion, if the Bible is to be trusted, is that "holy spirit" and "paraclete" are anything but synonymous.

To compound the confusion, Jesus seems to have contradicted himself. In John 14:17, the Paraclete is preexistent: "but you know him [i.e., the Paraclete], for he dwells with you and will be in you," and this makes sense considering that Jesus is himself identified as Paraclete in 1 John 2:1. However, in John 16:7 the Paraclete is foretold: "If I do not go away, the helper [i.e., the Paraclete] will not come to you; but if I depart, I will send him to you." The church's conclusion? "The Paraclete is another Paraclete in whom Jesus comes but who is not Jesus (14:18, 16:7)."[210] Some accept that explanation. Others believe Jesus spoke of himself in one case and of a prophet to follow in the other. Billions of Muslims have voted Muhammad as the fulfillment of this prophecy, just as a few million Mormons vote for John Smith, a smattering of Ahmadi'ites for MirzaGhulam Ahmad, the Baha'i for Mirza Ali Muhammad and Mirza Husain Ali, and small handfuls for David Koresh, Jim Jones, Luc Jouret, Marshall Applewhite and similar cultists (and look at what happened to them). The critical issue, then, may not be whether Jesus predicted a prophet to follow, but over which of the many claimants to the title fulfilled the prophecy.

12 – Crucifixion

The report of my death was an exaggeration.

—Mark Twain, letter to the *New York Journal,* in
response to rumors of his death while in Europe

If there is a keystone to orthodox Christianity, it is the
doctrine of the crucifixion. However, if Christians expect others
to adopt their belief, they have to satisfy the demand for
supporting evidence. Everyone knows the story. Everyone
knows the biblical record. But everyone also knows that other
myths have been propagated over longer periods of religious
history, and the duration and popularity of a deception in no way
validates it. So while many accept the crucifixion
unquestioningly, many others are not satisfied. Such individuals
read, "that Christ died for our sins according to the Scriptures"
(1 Corinthians 15:3), and ask, "Umm, according to exactly
which scriptures?" In Carmichael's words, "For that matter the
whole insistence, in the Gospels as well as in Paul's Epistles,
that everything had been accomplished in fulfillment of the
Scriptures seems puzzling. No such belief—in the death and
resurrection of the Messiah—is recorded among the Jews at all,
and certainly not in the Hebrew Scriptures."[211]

Paul himself invited criticism of the concept of the
crucifixion and its related mysteries when he wrote, "For Jews
request a sign, and Greeks seek after wisdom; but we preach

Christ crucified, to the Jews a stumbling block and to the Gentiles (Greeks) foolishness" (1 Corinthians 1:22–23).

In other words, "We preach something without signs and without wisdom—who's with us?"

No surprise, then, that so many consider the crucifixion incompatible with God's mercy. Muslims, for example, believe Jesus was saved from crucifixion, in accordance with the following: "But they did not kill him [Jesus], nor crucified him, but so it was made to appear to them, and those who differ therein are full of doubts, with no (certain) knowledge, but only conjecture to follow, for of a surety they did not kill him:Nay, Allah raised him up unto Himself; and Allah is Exalted in Power, Wise . . . " (TMQ 4:157–158)

Should a person believe Jesus to have been God, one wonders why God would have allowed His own death when He had the power to save Himself. Should a person believe Jesus to have been the "Son of God," why would God not answer the prayer of His son, when Jesus is quoted as saying, "Ask, and it will be given to you; seek, and you will find; knock, and it will be opened to you. For everyone who asks receives, and he who seeks finds, and to him who knocks it will be opened" (Matthew 7:7–8). Jesus reportedly *did* ask—to the point of sweating "like great drops of blood" in prayer (Luke 22:44)—and he clearly sought to be saved. But nowhere is Jesus quoted as saying, "Everyone who asks receives, except for me." Matthew 7:9 reads, "Or what man is there among you who, if his son asks for bread, will give him a stone?" Put another way, who imagines that God would answer a prophet's plea for rescue with a short weekend on a cross instead? Plenty of sunshine and all the vinegar a person can sip from a sponge? There's an incompatibility issue here; if people believe God, or the son of

God, was born in a bath of his own urine (which is what amniotic fluid consists of), then they will have no problem believing God committed suicide (and what else would the act of allowing Oneself to die be called when, being omnipotent, able to save Oneself?). Similarly, such people will have no difficulty believing that God turned His back on His Son in the time of greatest need. The rest of the world wonders: "Whose concept of God is this compatible with, anyway?"

Well, Tertullian, the aforementioned originator of the Trinitarian formula, for one. The comment has been offered that, "Tertullian enjoyed paradox. To him the divine character of Christianity was vindicated not by its reasonableness but by the very fact that it was the kind of thing no ordinary mind could have invented. The crucifying of the Son of God sounds ridiculous and scandalous: 'I believe because it is outrageous.'"[212]

I believe because it is outrageous. If such is the methodology of God, are we not justified in believing each and every outrageous theory of divinity—the more "ridiculous and scandalous" the better?

Somewhere, someone is bound to say, "But Jesus had to die for our sins!" One wonders, "Why? Because God can't forgive us otherwise? Because God *needs* a sacrifice?" This isn't what the Bible teaches. Jesus reportedly taught the message of Hosea 6:6, "I desire mercy, and not sacrifice." And not just once—the lesson was worthy of two mentions, the first in Matthew 9:13, the second in Matthew 12:7. Why, then, are clergy teaching that Jesus had to be sacrificed? And if he was sent for this purpose, why did he pray to be saved?

Furthermore, why do we have to believe to be saved? On one hand, original sin is held to be binding, whether we believe in it or not. On the other hand, salvation is held to be conditional upon acceptance (i.e., belief) of the crucifixion and atonement of Jesus. In the first case, belief is held to be irrelevant; in the second, it's required. The question arises, "Did Jesus pay the price or not?" If he paid the price, then our sins are forgiven, whether we believe or not. If he didn't pay the price, it doesn't matter either way. Lastly, forgiveness doesn't *have* a price. A person can't forgive another's debt and still demand repayment. The argument that God forgives, but only if given a sacrifice He says He doesn't want in the first place (see Hosea 6:6, Matthew 9:13 and 12:7) drags a wing and cartwheels down the runway of rational analysis. From where, then, does the formula come? According to scripture, it's not from Jesus. So do people believe teachings *about* the prophet in preference to those *of* the prophet? The Bible condemns such inverted priorities, for Matthew 10:24 records Jesus having declared, "A disciple is not above his teacher, nor a servant above his master."

What, then, should we understand from the verse, "Then he said to them, 'Thus it is written, and thus it was necessary for the Christ to suffer and to rise from the dead the third day" (Luke 24:46)? Given a choice between literal or figurative interpretation, only the metaphor makes sense if we are to reconcile God not desiring sacrifice with Jesus having to "die" for the sins of humankind. Furthermore, biblical reference to death is frequently metaphorical, as in Paul's statement of his suffering as, "I die daily" (1 Corinthians 15:31).

So perhaps "rising from the dead" doesn't mean literally rising from the state of actual death, but from a metaphorical death, such as:

1. Having been unconscious or sleeping (as in "He slept like a dead man").

2. Having been suffering (as in the many biblical analogies between suffering and death).
3. Having been incapable (as in "I couldn't do a thing last night, I was just dead").
4. Or having been in the tomb, left for dead, but in fact alive (as in "He recovered miraculously—he came back from the dead").

In any case, Matthew 12:40 reports Jesus having taught, "For as Jonah was three days and three nights in the belly of the great fish, so will the Son of Man be three days and three nights in the heart of the earth." This simple verse opens the gates to a relatively uncharted territory of thought. "Three days and three nights" must be assumed to mean exactly what it says, for otherwise it wouldn't have been stated with such clarity. However, if we believe the Bible, Jesus spent only one day and two nights—Friday night, Saturday day and Saturday night—in the sepulcher following the alleged crucifixion. Does this pose a difficulty? We should think so, because the above quote is Jesus' response to the request for a sign, to which he reportedly answered, "An evil and adulterous generation seeks after a sign, and no sign will be given to it except the sign of the prophet Jonah. For as Jonah was three days and three nights in the belly of the great fish, so will the Son of Man be three days and three nights in the heart of the earth" (Matthew 12:38–40). The above, "No sign will be given to it except . . ." declares, in no uncertain terms, that this is the *only* sign Jesus offers. Not the healing of the lepers, not the curing of the blind, not the raising of the dead. Not the feeding of the masses, not the walking on water, not the calming of the storm. No . . . *no* sign would be given but the sign of Jonah.

Many Christians base faith on something they perceive to be a miracle, whether written in the Bible, attributed to saints, or borne of personal experience. And yet, Jesus strikingly isolates the sign of Jonah as the only sign to be given. Not the weeping statues, not the visions of Mary, not the faith healing. Not the speaking in tongues, not the exorcising of spirits, not the receiving of the Holy Ghost. Just the sign of Jonah. That's all. Those who adopt different signs must realize that, according to the Bible, they do so against the teaching of Jesus. And considering the emphasis he placed on the sign of Jonah, we should examine it.

The Bible tells us that Jesus was crucified on a Friday, which explains why the Jews were under pressure to expedite his death, along with that of the two criminals crucified with him. Friday sunset ushers in the Jewish Sabbath, for the Hebraic calendar is lunar, which means their days end at sunset. Hence, Friday sunset heralds the beginning of Saturday, the Jewish Sabbath. The problem facing the Jews was that Jewish law forbade leaving dead bodies hanging overnight (either on a cross or on gallows—Deuteronomy 21:22–23), but also forbade taking the bodies down and burying them on the Sabbath. It was an Old Testament Catch-22. Had any of the crucified died on the Sabbath, the Jews could neither leave the corpse nor bury it. The only practical solution was to speed the death of the condemned, and this is why the Roman soldiers were sent to break their legs.

The rapidity by which crucifixion kills depends not only upon the individual's fortitude, which is unpredictable, but also upon his physical strength. Most crosses were constructed with a small seat or a wood block for the feet, to partially bear the victim's weight in order to prolong the torture. In Jesus' case, Christian tradition has it that his feet were nailed to the cross.

The reason for this brutality is that the condemned would be forced to support his weight on impaled feet, greatly compounding the agony. However, the Romans would often expedite death by breaking the victims' legs. With no means of supporting his body, the crucified would hang with his body weight suspended on outstretched arms, which fatigues the respiratory muscles. Eventually, the victim would no longer be able to draw his breath. The mechanism of death, therefore, is slow asphyxiation—slower still in individuals with greater endurance and the will to live.

The Bible records that the Roman soldiers were sent to break the legs of the condemned, but upon their arrival, they found Jesus already dead. Subsequently, he was removed from the cross and placed in the sepulcher. When? Late Friday afternoon, prior to sunset.

Sunday morning, *before sunrise*, Mary Magdalene returned to the tomb, having rested on the Sabbath in accordance with the law (Luke 23:56 and John 20:1), and found the tomb empty. She is told that Christ is risen (Matthew 28:6, Mark 16:6, Luke 24:6). The arithmetic works out to one night (Friday sunset to Saturday sunrise), plus one day (Saturday sunrise to sunset), plus one night (Saturday sunset to slightly before Sunday sunrise). Grand total? Two nights and one day—a far cry from the "three days and three nights" referenced in Jesus' "sign of Jonah." Once again, a person either has to admit that the evidence doesn't add up, or rewrite the rules of mathematics.

One more piece of this scriptural puzzle deserves consideration. The quote, "For as Jonah . . ." (or, as per the New Revised Standard Version, "For just as Jonah . . .") compares the state of Jesus with that of Jonah. Even schoolchildren know that Jonah was alive from the time his comrades reduced the ship's

197

ballast by the measure of his weight, to the somewhat rough moment of regurgitation onto the sandy shore. Since Jonah was alive throughout the entire ordeal, a person could speculate that Jesus, "just as Jonah . . ." was alive throughout as well. It is worth noting that when the tomb was visited on Sunday morning, each of the gospels describes Jesus as "risen," which is hardly surprising given the fact that cold rock slabs, unlike warm, wave-suppressed waterbeds, don't exactly invite a person to punch the snooze button and sleep in. What is missing from the Bible, however, is the statement that Jesus was resurrected. Jesus reportedly said, "I came forth from the Father and have come into the world. Again, I leave the world and go to the Father" (John 16:28). But how is that different from any of us? And where does Jesus say he would die and be resurrected in the process? The word "resurrected" is nowhere to be found. "Risen from the dead" is mentioned a handful of times, but never by Jesus himself. And notably, many second and third-century Christians believed Jesus didn't die.[213]

This may not change anyone's way of thinking, but it should at least illustrate the reasonable viewpoints that result from assigning priority to the recorded words of Jesus over those of others. The Islamic understanding is one such viewpoint—one which affirms the prophethood of Jesus while pointing out that his scriptural teachings not only discredit many elements of established "Christian" doctrine, but reinforce Islamic ideology as well.

In recent years, many have found their doubts strengthened by a trail of engaging theories in books of critical Christian challenge. One such work, *The Jesus Conspiracy* by HolgerKersten and Elmar R. Gruber, is of particular interest with regard to the subject of this chapter, for the authors present powerful evidence that whoever was wrapped in the Shroud of Turin did not die. Kersten and Gruber proposed that the Catholic Church realized the devastating impact this theory, if true, could have. After all, if the evidence suggested that Jesus had been wrapped in the shroud but did not die, the church would be left without a death, without an atoning sacrifice, without a resurrection and, in short, the church would be left without a church. In the words of First Corinthians 15:14, "And if Christ is not risen, then our preaching *is* empty and your faith *is* also empty. Yes, and we are found false witnesses of God. . . ."

The authors claim the church responded by deliberately discrediting the shroud, even to the extent of falsifying carbon dating tests.

Well . . . maybe. The authors' evidence is substantial, and . . . their logic is compelling, and . . . they may be wrong. Then again, they may be right. Chances are, we'll never know. About the only thing we *do* know about the shroud is that the Catholic church has not taken a position on the authenticity of the shroud, and we have to wonder why it objects to more independent testing. If unauthentic, the shroud is little more than an oddity, so why not trim some insignificant snippets off the edges and pass them around? But no, the custodians keep the shroud under lock and key, and we have to wonder why, if not because they fear the results.

In any case, Muslims believe that Jesus was never crucified in the first place, "but so it was made to appear . . ." (TMQ 4:157). If the proposal sounds outlandish to those who have been raised to think the opposite, the doctrine of the crucifixion sounds stranger still when placed beside Deuteronomy 21:23, which states, "He who is hanged [i.e., either on a gallows or crucified] is accursed of God."

Simultaneous claims to biblical inerrancy and to the divine sonship of the crucified Jesus cast a truly peculiar light on anyone who supports such beliefs, for the contradiction is obvious. Either Jesus was not crucified, the Bible is in error, or, according to the scripture, Jesus was accursed of God. To hold that God's prophet, son, or partner (however a person regards Jesus) is also accursed of God can only achieve acceptance among those with synaptic sterility. The above pieces simply do not fit the package. Something has to give—one or more of the non-conforming elements need to be recognized for what it is— a sham—and cast out. Otherwise, the package as a whole bears the impossible qualities of make-believe, or perhaps we should say, "make-belief."

Similarly confounding is Hebrews 5:7, which states that because Jesus was a righteous man, God answered his prayer to be saved from death: "In the days of his flesh, Jesus offered up prayers and supplications, with loud cries and tears, to the one who was able to save him from death, and he was heard because of his reverent submission" (Hebrews 5:7, NRSV). Now, what does "God heard his prayer" mean—that God heard it loud and clear and ignored it? No, it means God answered his prayer. It certainly can't mean that God heard and refused the prayer, for then the phrase "because of his reverent submission" would be nonsensical, along the lines of, "God heard his prayer and refused it because he was a righteous man."

Now, while Muslims deny the crucifixion of Jesus, they don't deny that *someone* was crucified. So who do Muslims think was crucified in his place? It's a moot point, and not terribly important. Some suggest that Allah raised Jesus up and altered Judas' features to resemble those of Jesus, with the end result that Judas was crucified in his place, to the deception of the audience. Well, maybe. But then again, maybe not. There's no compelling evidence to support this opinion, even though it does conform to the biblical and Qur'anic principles of people reaping what they sow.

Notably, there are those who object to the suggestion of Judas being crucified on the basis that, as per Matthew 27:5, Judas threw his ill-gotten silver back at the priests and "went and hanged himself." So he wasn't around to be crucified. On the other hand, Acts records that Judas "purchased a field with the wages of iniquity; and falling headlong, he burst open in the middle and all his entrails gushed out" (Acts 1:18). So if the authors of Acts and Matthew don't agree on the matter, what really happened is anybody's guess.

Perhaps we can look at this issue from a different angle. If the idea of Judas being crucified in Jesus' place sounds technically strained, maybe it shouldn't; God is described as having restrained the eyes of two disciples (i.e., intimate companions who should have readily recognized their teacher) when they met the allegedly "risen" Jesus on the road to Emmaus, "so that they did not know him" (Luke 24:16). Another biblical example would be that Mary Magdalene reportedly failed to recognize Jesus outside of the tomb, "supposing him to be the gardener . . ." (John 20:15). Mary Magdalene? Shouldn't *she* have been able to identify him, even in the early morning light?

Interestingly enough, this concept of a crucifixion switch isn't entirely foreign to Christianity. Among early Christians, the Corinthians, the Basilidians, the Paulicians, the Cathari and the Carpocratians all believed Jesus Christ's life was spared. The Basilidians believed that Simon of Cyrene was crucified in his place, which may not be an unreasonable suggestion, considering that Simon carried Jesus' cross (see Matthew 27:32, Mark 15:21 and Luke 23:26). Typically, all of the dissenting sects mentioned above were judged to have been Gnostics and/or heretics by the church, and were violently suppressed by a Trinitarian majority that systematically burned dissenters into oblivion for the first fifteen centuries of Catholic rule (the most recent roasting having taken place in Mexico in 1850 CE).

To be fair, Gnostic ideology did have a place in many, if not most, or even all groups regarded as dissenters from orthodoxy. But then again, Gnosticism has a place in orthodoxy as well, for what is *gnosis* if not the belief that its initiates possess some esoteric but essential knowledge necessary for salvation, which can neither be explained nor justified? And what has this discussion thus far exposed, if not the lack of scriptural foundation for the canon of Trinitarian orthodoxy?

Of the above groups, the Paulicians (whose name possibly derived from their devotion to Paul of Samosata) hold special interest. Paul of Samosata reportedly took his teaching from Diodorus, head of the Nazarene Church in Antioch. His teachings in turn branched off the trunk of apostolic ideology through individuals such as Lucian (who in turn taught Arius), Eusebius of Nicomedia, and even Nestorius (whose influence expanded from Eastern Europe as far east as China and as far south as Abyssinia). The Paulician influence eventually spread to occupy most, if not all, of Europe and North Africa. Yet so complete was their annihilation by the Roman Catholic Church during the period of persecution, both they and their books were virtually completely destroyed. Only in the mid-nineteenth century was one of their sacred books, *The Key of Truth*, discovered in Armenia and translated. From this document, a view of their beliefs and practices can be appreciated.

The Paulicians may invite condemnation for their
dualistic ideology, acceptance of suicide and excess of
asceticism. Notable is the peculiar Paulician concept of Jesus
Christ having been a phantasm, and not a man. On the other
hand, the Paulicians adhered to belief in divine unity, the virgin
birth, baptism, and other creeds and practices that date from the
apostolic age. Included in the list of their particulars is the
apparent lack of an organized priesthood or hierarchy of clergy.
The leaders married and had families. Their services were
characterized by simplicity of worship and lack of sacraments:
they didn't even use holy water. The Paulicians refused to adopt
any visible object of worship—no relics, no images, not even
the cross. They considered the use of images, whether two or
three dimensional, to be idolatrous, foreign to the teachings of
Jesus, and in violation of the second commandment. The
doctrine of Incarnation appears to have been denied, as were the
doctrines of original sin and the Trinity—all rejected on the
basis of lacking scriptural foundation. The Paulicians denied the
alleged crucifixion of Jesus, and consequently rejected the
doctrines of the resurrection, atonement, and redemption of
sins.They also shunned infant baptism as an innovation foreign
to the teachings and practice of Jesus, and claimed it was
worthless since children lack the capacity for mature faith and
repentance. They boycotted Christmas on the grounds that it was
an illegitimate holiday constructed as a concession to the
pagans, who worshipped the rebirth of their Sun-god three days
following the winter solstice, on December 25, at the annual
festival of *Sol Invictus* (The Invincible Sun). They neither
solicited nor accepted tithes, maintained a strict diet, stressed
devotion to worship in all aspects of life and aspired to
cleanliness of temper, thoughts, words, and work.

A better model of the carpenter-King would be difficult to find, but for their creed, they were killed. Over a period of centuries the Paulicians were hounded wherever they were found. The Byzantine Empress Theodora reestablished image worship in Constantinople during the ninth century and, as Gibbon notes, "Her inquisitors explored the cities and mountains of the Lesser Asia, and the flatterers of the empress have affirmed that, in a short reign, one hundred thousand Paulicians were extirpated by the sword, the gibbet, or the flames."[214]

The Paulicians eventually were driven from Armenia to Thrace, and on to Bulgaria. From there they spread to Serbia, Bosnia and Herzegovinia, then north to Germany, west to France and south into Italy. By sea they found routes to Venice, Sicily and Southern France. The rapid expansion of Paulician theology, which seems to have been revived in the Cathari (meaning "the Pure") in or around the eleventh century, became a serious threat to the Catholic Church, and was condemned at the Councils of Orleans in 1022, of Lombard in 1165, and of Verona in 1184. St. Bernard of Clairvaux described the Cathari thusly: "If you interrogate them, nothing can be more Christian; as to their conversation, nothing can be less reprehensible, and what they speak they prove by deeds. As for the morals of the heretic, he cheats no one, he oppresses no one, he strikes no one; his cheeks are pale with fasting, he eats not the bread of idleness, his hands labour for his livelihood."[215]

Nonetheless, the church condemned the Cathari, not for their ethics and sincerity, but for their theology. Not until the Medieval Inquisition of the thirteenth century was the church able to act upon their condemnation, but then, opening floodgates on the hostility of several centuries, they applied the full force of their hatred with a vengeance sufficient to establish their authority and destroy their enemies. The loss of the Paulicians, Cathari, and the various other "heretic" Christian sects testifies to the terrible efficacy of the religious cleansing of the Medieval Inquisition and subsequent periods of persecution. F. C. Conybeare comments,

> It was no empty vow of their elect ones, "to be baptized with the baptism of Christ, to take on themselves scourgings, imprisonments, tortures, reproaches, crosses, blows, tribulation, and all temptations of the world." Theirs the tears, theirs the blood shed during more than ten centuries of fierce persecution in the East; and if we reckon of their number, as well we may, the early puritans of Europe, then the tale of wicked deeds wrought by the persecuting churches reaches dimensions which appall the mind. And as it was all done, nominally out of reverence for, but really in mockery of, the Prince of Peace, it is hard to say of the Inquisitors that they knew not what they did.[216]

That the Catholic Church was so effective in eliminating their opposition is of no surprise to those who study their methodology. Their degree of savagery did not even spare their own people, at times sacrificing members of the orthodoxy to insure complete elimination of the Unitarians. For example, the mixed population of Catholics and Unitarians of the people of

Beziers, in the South of France, were attacked mercilessly. In his *History of the Inquisition of the Middle Ages,* Henry Charles Lea brings the full horror of the invaders' overzealousness into sharp focus:

> From infancy in arms to tottering age, not one was spared—seven thousand, it is said, were slaughtered in the Church of Mary Magdalen to which they had fled for asylum—and the total number of slain is set down by the legates at nearly twenty thousand. . . .
>
> A fervent Cistercian contemporary informs us that when Arnaud was asked whether the Catholics should be spared, he feared the heretics would escape by feigning orthodoxy, and fiercely replied, "Kill them all, for God knows his own!" In the mad carnage and pillage the town was set on fire, and the sun of that awful July day closed on a mass of smouldering ruins and blackened corpses—a holocaust to a deity of mercy and love whom the Cathari might well be pardoned for regarding as the Principle of Evil.[217]

The inquisitors' use of torture was equally horrific, for it did not end at confession. Once they procured a confession, they began torture anew, to extract names of associates until the last drop of information was squeezed from the mangled husk of what had once been a human being.

Once accused, the pitiful defendant was guaranteed to suffer. Torture yielded the required confession—if not out of truth, then out of the victim's desperation to bring an end to the pain. Horrifically, protestations of innocence and even the oath of orthodoxy did not bring relief, for suspects professing orthodox belief were committed to a test of faith, and here the church demonstrated the full measure of its creativity. Trials by water and fire were popularized and sanctioned by the Catholic Church for the testing of faith by way of *Judicium Dei*—Judgment of God, a concept based upon superstition. It was believed that the purity of water would not accept a guilty body into its midst, and so floaters were judged guilty and executed, sinkers were considered innocent, and if rescued before drowning, spared. It was believed that earthly fire, like the flames of Hell, would not harm those who were (in their view) the faithful Christians bearing the promise of paradise. The "hot iron test" was the most commonly employed, as it was simple and readily available. In this test, the accused was required to carry a red-hot piece of iron for a certain number of steps, usually nine. Judgment was offered either at the time of the test (those burned were judged guilty) or several days later (those whose wounds were healing were declared innocent, whereas those whose wounds became infected were deemed guilty). Other variations existed, such as determining whether a person suffered a burn when an arm was immersed up to the elbow in boiling water or boiling oil.

Lest a person presume such insane methods were rarely employed, the Council of Rheims in 1157 ordered "trials by ordeal" to satisfy all cases of suspected heresy.[218]

Now, why all this discussion about what are now littleknown and dead sects? Well, the intent is neither to glorify them beyond the merits of their ideology, nor to evoke sympathy for their cause, but rather to draw attention to the alternate Christian ideologies that have become obscure in the shadow of prevailing Trinitarianism. The Corinthians, the Basilidians, the Paulicians, the Cathari, and the Carpocratians may be littleknown today, but they were dynamic Christian ideologies that shared a significant place in history. But history, as the saying goes, is written by the victors. "Moreover," writes Ehrman, "the victors in the struggles to establish Christian orthodoxy not only won their theological battles, they also rewrote the history of the conflict . . ."[219] The Catholic Church attempted to systematically erase the memory of all other sects and scriptures contrary to their own, and at this, they were largely successful. Given their vicious methodology, we should not be surprised.

Additionally, historical attempts to vilify all other religions or Christian sects prejudiced the minds of the populace. So successful were these efforts that the records and holy books of those who appear to have been closest to the teachings of the apostolic fathers have been largely lost. Similarly, those closest to embodying the practices and creed of the prophet Jesus have come to be regarded as heretics, simply because they did not embrace the "evolved" doctrines of the Trinitarian victors. In other words, they were condemned for nonconformity with views which, though lacking scriptural authority, were selected by men of position and propagated for reasons of political expediency.

One of the curious elements of Trinitarian history lies in the fact that in all its travels throughout the Christian world, it had to be forced upon a previously Unitarian people. The Visigoths, Ostrogoths and Vandals, the Arians, Donatists, and

Paulicians—all had to be muscled aside prior to the imposition of Trinitarian rule. Even in England and Ireland there is suspicion that, contrary to official historical accounts, a good percentage of the population were staunch Unitarian Christian prior to receiving Trinitarian "encouragement." Whereas Unitarians attempted to spread faith through example and invitation, the Catholic Church spread Trinitarian faith by shearing the populace with the sharp blades of compulsion and elimination.

Reviewing unprejudiced historical accounts, a large population of the religious throughout the known world voiced their opposition to Trinitarian Christianity, and those who denied Jesus Christ's crucifixion and death were not necessarily a minority. Many would argue that from a gut level it makes more sense for God to have punished Judas for his treachery than to have tortured Jesus for his innocence. The argument would be more convincing if the doctrines of atonement and original sin could be shown to be invalid, for these two doctrines hinge off the doorframe of the alleged death of Jesus. The first hurdle for many people in considering such revolutionary notions is the age-old assertion that Jesus Christ was the "Lamb of God who takes away the sins of the world" (John 1:29), for in the mind of the Trinitarian, this verse can have no relevance other than to that of the doctrine of atonement. Unitarians, however, conceive Jesus to have lived a life of sacrifice in order to bear a purifying teaching which, if adopted, would put humankind on the path of God's design.

13 – Lamb of God

There is nothing worse than a sharp image of a fuzzy concept.

—Ansel Adams

Many Christians claim to find proof of the crucifixion and atonement in John 1:29, which calls Jesus Christ the "Lamb of God who takes away the sins of the world." Others are more speculative, and for good reason.

To begin with, Christians disagree on the meaning and significance of this concept of "lambness." Some question the Bible translation while still others fail to link Old and New Testament "Lamb of God" references into a reasonable chain of logic. Even John the Baptist, whom this verse quotes, seemed to have trouble with the term. The Christian claim is that John the Baptist knew who Jesus was, and identified him as the "Lamb of God" in John 1:29. But if he knew Jesus so well as to identify him with certainty in one verse, why did he question Jesus years later: "Are You the Coming One, or do we look for another?" (Matthew 11:3)

Among those who have difficulty rectifying Old and New Testament inconsistencies are Catholic clergy themselves. The *New Catholic Encyclopedia* admits inability to determine the origin of the title "Lamb of God," for although attempts are made to trace the term through Isaiah (Chapter 53) by way of

Acts 8:32, "this text is incapable of explaining the expression. . ."[220]

The *Theological Dictionary of the New Testament* has this to say: "The Aramaic might also offer a basis with its use of the same word for both 'lamb' and 'boy or servant.' Thus the Baptist in Jn. 1:29, 36 might have been describing Jesus as the servant of God who takes away the sin of the world in vicarious self-offering (Is. 53)."[221] Excuse me, but was that *servant* of God? Hm . . . lamb/servant; animal/human . . . Perhaps we should be content that the translators confined their differences within the same animal kingdom, but all the same . . .

So could John the Baptist's native Aramaic have been corrupted in translation to the New Testament Greek *amnos*? Could the correct translation be "boy" or "servant" rather than "lamb?" If so, any link between Old and New Testament references to "Lamb of God" would shred faster than ticker tape in a turboprop. Hence, it is with great interest that we encounter the *New Catholic Encyclopedia* agreeing that the Aramaic word *talya'* can be translated to "boy" or "servant," as well as "lamb."[222] Furthermore, the proposal that the phrase uttered by the Baptist was "Behold the Servant of God," and not "Behold the Lamb of God" is, in their words, "very plausible" and "much easier to explain."[223]

As with *paistheou*, the first translation of which is "servant of God" rather than "Son of God," could this be yet one more instance of theologically prejudiced mistranslation? Quite possibly.

Finally, there is the now-familiar pattern of Jesus being labeled "Lamb of God" in the Gospel of John but in none of the other gospels, which implies a minority opinion or, at the very least, lack of substantiation. Once again, the vote is three gospel

211

authors to one that the phrase was never spoken in the first place, or not stated with the meaning into which it has been translated. Had the original meaning been "servant of God," (assuming the phrase was uttered in the first place) the other three gospel authors are to be applauded for refusing to corrupt the message into an abstract recipe of "lambness." On the other hand, if we are to trust the Bible as the word of God, we have to wonder why God didn't inspire this knowledge to the other three gospel authors. Assuming God's objective to be that of spreading His truth as widely and precisely as possible, we have to ask which is more likely:

1. Our infallible God failed to propagate His truth three times (uh—no).
2. The author of the book of John, verses 1:29 & 1:36, espoused a false doctrine twice. (Possible, but let's assume not, for if this were the case it becomes difficult to trust any part of the Bible.)
3. The true meaning is "servant of God," but doctrinal prejudice resulted in the translation "lamb of God."

Perhaps we should consider this issue in the context of Christian creed as a whole, for the doctrine of Jesus being the "Lamb of God who takes away the sins of the world" bleeds into those of original sin and atonement. After all, what's the need for a sacrificial lamb, if not to atone for the (original) sin of the world?

14 – Original Sin

He that falls into sin is a man; that grieves at it, is a
saint; that boasteth of it, is a devil.

—Thomas Fuller, *The Holy State and the*
Profane State

The concept of original sin is completely foreign to
Judaism and Eastern Christianity, having achieved acceptance in
only the WesternChurch. Furthermore, Christian and Islamic
concepts of sin are virtual opposites with respect to certain
nuances. For example, there is no concept of "sinning in the
mind" in Islam; to a Muslim, an evil thought becomes a *good*
deed when a person refuses to act upon it. Overcoming and
dismissing the evil thoughts which forever assail our minds is
considered deserving of reward rather than punishment.
Islamically speaking, an evil thought only becomes sinful when
fulfilled.

Conceiving good deeds is more contrary to the base
nature of man. Since our creation, if not bound by societal or
religious restrictions, humankind has historically dined on the
banquet of life with lust and abandon. The orgies of self-
indulgence that have carpeted the corridors of history envelop
not only individuals and small communities, but even major
world powers which ate their fill of deviancy to the point of self-
destruction. Sodom and Gomorrah may top most lists, but the

greatest powers of the ancient world—to include the Greek, Roman and Persian empires, as well as those of Genghis Khan and Alexander the Great—certainly bear dishonorable mention. But while examples of communal decadence are innumerable, cases of individual corruption are exponentially more common.

So, good thoughts are not always the first instinct of humankind. As such, the Islamic understanding is that the very conception of good deeds is worthy of reward, even if not acted upon. When a person actually commits a good deed, Allah multiplies the reward even further.

The concept of original sin simply does not exist in Islam, and never has. For the Christian readers, the question is not whether the concept of original sin exists in present day, but whether it existed during the period of Christian origins. Specifically, did Jesus teach it?

Apparently not. Whoever dreamt up the concept, it certainly wasn't Jesus, for he reportedly taught, "Let the little children come to me, and do not forbid them, for of such is the kingdom of heaven" (Matthew 19:14). We may well wonder how "for of such" could be "the kingdom of heaven" if the unbaptized are hell-bound. Children are either born with original sin or are bound for the kingdom of heaven. The church can't have it both ways. Ezekiel 18:20 records, "The son shall not bear the guilt of the father, nor the father bear the guilt of the son. The righteousness of the righteous shall be upon himself, and the wickedness of the wicked shall be upon himself."

Deuteronomy 24:16 repeats the point. The objection may be raised that this is Old Testament, but it's not older than Adam! If original sin dated from Adam and Eve, one wouldn't find it disavowed in *any* scripture of *any* age!

Islam teaches that each person is born in a state of

spiritual purity, but upbringing and the allure of worldly pleasures may corrupt us. Nonetheless, sins are not inherited and, for that matter, not even Adam and Eve will be punished for their sins, for God has forgiven them. And how can humankind inherit something that no longer exists? No, Islamically speaking, all of us will be judged according to our deeds, for "man can have nothing but what he strives for" (TMQ 53:38–39), and "Who receives guidance, receives it for his own benefit: who goes astray does so to his own loss: no bearer of burdens can bear the burden of another . . ." (TMQ 17:15). Each person will bear responsibility for his or her actions, but no infant goes to hell for being unbaptized and burdened with sin as a birthright—or should we say a birthwrong?

15 – Atonement

*Must then a Christ perish in torment in every age to
save those that have no imagination?*

—George Bernard Shaw, *Saint Joan, Epilogue*

The atonement—what a concept. Who wouldn't like
someone else to pick up the tab for their every indulgence and
transgression? However, no matter how good the atonement
sounds, no matter how much people want it to be true, the
critical question is whether it has a basis in revealed truth. Will
the atonement be there on the Day of Judgment for those who
rely upon it for their salvation? Or will the untold billions of
anxious human souls be struck with downcast faces when God
announces He never promised any such thing?

Some believe that, should the atonement not be there for
them on the Day of Judgment, God will accept their apology.
Others understand life to be a proving ground for the hereafter,
and that our books of deeds close when we die. After all, if an
apology on the Day of Judgment will suffice for salvation, what
need for hell? For what sinner won't offer sincere repentance
when faced with the reality of God's punishment? But what
weight will such an apology have, really? A righteous life
demands denial of sinful pleasures and sacrifice of time, effort,
and worldly priorities. Forgoing hedonistic delights for the sake
of honoring God testifies to a person's faith. That testimony will

have weight. But what weight will a person's repentance have on the Day of Judgment, when the game is over, leaving no sins to be avoided, no worldly effort or compromise to be made, no righteous life to be lived and, in short, no deeds to be performed that might testify to a person's faith?

So authenticating the atonement is of critical importance. If valid, it's God's greatest blessing to humankind. But if false, the atonement has no more value than a forged check—it might convey a sense of security and satisfaction as long as we carry it around in our pocket, but the moment we try to cash it, it will prove worthless.

Who, then, authored the atonement? If God, we would be foolish not to endorse it. But if authored by man, we would have to question the authority of those who claim to speak for God, if not the prophets.

As discussed in the previous chapter, the chain of responsibility is clear in this life. Both the Old and New Testaments, as well as the Holy Qur'an, stress individual responsibility and teach that nobody bears the burden of another's iniquities. But where does *Jesus* say his case is different? And if he was never crucified in the first place (as discussed in previous chapters), the doctrine of atonement crumbles from the foundation.

Those who find satisfaction in the loose interpretation of the alleged words of the disciples, Paul, and other para-prophet personages may not research their individual codes of religion any further. Those who find firmer footing on the teachings of the prophets perceive that God promises nothing of good in the hereafter to those who duck accountability to Him in this life. Jesus reportedly stated that belief, in and of itself, is *not* sufficient for salvation: "Not everyone who says to me, 'Lord,

Lord,' shall enter the kingdom of heaven, but he who does the will of my Father in heaven" (Matthew 7:21). When asked how to achieve salvation, he reportedly taught, "But if you want to enter into life [eternal life, that is—i.e., salvation] keep the commandments" (Matthew 19:17).

But where in the New Testament did Jesus counsel his followers that they could relax, for in a few days he would pay the price and they could all go to heaven on nothing more than belief? Nowhere. For that matter, when Jesus was allegedly resurrected after his alleged crucifixion and returned to his disciples, why didn't he announce the atonement? Why didn't he declare that he had paid for the sins of the world, past, present and future, so now it's time to party atonement-style? But he didn't, and we should wonder why. Could it be the atonement isn't true? Could it be that someone scribbled wishful thoughts into the margins of scripture?

It wouldn't be the first time.

So where did the atonement come from in the first place? And would anyone be surprised to hear the name, "Paul"? Another questionable doctrine coming from the same questionable source? So it would seem. Acts 17:18 reads, "Then certain Epicurean and Stoic philosophers encountered him [Paul]. And some said, 'What does this babbler want to say?' Others said, 'He seems to be a proclaimer of foreign gods,' because he preached to them Jesus and the resurrection.'"

Paul directly claims to have conceived the doctrine of resurrection as follows: "Remember that Jesus Christ, of the seed of David, was raised from the dead according to my gospel" (2 Timothy 2:8). Sure enough, the concept of Jesus Christ dying for the sins of humankind is found in the epistles of Paul (e.g., Romans 5:8–11 and 6:8–9), and nowhere else.

Nowhere else? Not from Jesus? Not from the disciples? Is it possible they neglected the critical details upon which Christian faith rests? Curiouser and curiouser!—as Alice would say.

At this point, discussion should properly return to the law, for nobody can be faulted for suspecting that someone played fast and loose with the design of Christian thought. Jesus, being a Jew, lived by Old Testament (Mosaic) Law. Among his recorded teachings are, "But if you want to enter into life, keep the commandments" (Matthew 19:17), and, "Do not think that I came to destroy the Law or the Prophets. I did not come to destroy but to fulfill. For assuredly, I say to you, till heaven and earth pass away, one jot [Greek *Iota*—the ninth letter of the Greek alphabet] or one tittle [a stroke or dot] will by no means pass from the law till all is fulfilled" (Matthew 5:17–18). Some apologists assert that all was "fulfilled" upon the alleged death or resurrection of Jesus, allowing the laws to be restructured subsequently. But that reasoning doesn't work, for every Christian believes Jesus will return to vanquish the Antichrist close to the Day of Judgment. So if Jesus' mission upon planet Earth is the endpoint, all has not yet been fulfilled. More likely, "all being fulfilled" is exactly what any sensible person would assume it to mean: the conclusion of worldly existence at the Day of Judgment. And referencing the above quote, heaven and earth have not yet passed away. Furthermore, there's no sign of a returned Jesus on the horizon. Yet two thousand years ago, Paul said that not just a jot or a tittle, but the entire law has changed.

Paul's amendment to the teaching of Moses *and* Jesus reads, "And by him [Jesus Christ] everyone who believes is justified from all things from which you could not be justified by the law of Moses" (Acts 13:39). A more permissive blanket

statement would be hard to conceive. We can easily imagine the
voice of the collective public screaming, "Please, let's have
more of that!" And here it is: "But now we have been delivered
from the law, having died [i.e., suffered] to what we were held
by, so that we should serve in the newness of the Spirit and not
in the oldness of the letter" (Romans 7:6). Or, if I may freely
paraphrase: "But now I tell you to forget this old law, the
inconveniences of which we have lived with for too long, and
live by the religion of our desires, rather than by the old,
uncomfortable mandates of revelation." According to Paul,
God's law was apparently good enough for Moses and Jesus, but
not for the rest of humankind.

There should be little wonder that a person who
considered himself qualified to negate the law of the prophets
also considered himself to be all things to all people, as he so
clearly stated:

> For though I am free with respect to all, I
> have made myself a slave to all, so that I
> might win more of them;
>
> To the Jews I became as a Jew, in
> order to win Jews.
>
> To those under the law I became as
> one under the law (though I myself am
> not under the law) so that I might win
> those under the law.
>
> To those outside the law I became as
> one outside the law (though I am not free
> from God's law but am under Christ's
> law) so that I might win those outside the

law.

>To the weak I became weak, so that I
>might win the weak.

>I have become all things to all people,
>that I might by all means save some
>(NRSV; 1 Corinthians 9:19–23).

And what's wrong with trying to be all things to all people? What's wrong is that those who try to be all things to all people fail to be the most important thing to the most important person—they fail to be true to themselves. This scenario is a surefire gambit in politics, where the most successful politicians are the ones who sell themselves to the largest number of interest groups, some of them conflicting. The problem is that politicians typically sell not only the truth, but their souls in the process.

So in one corner we have the true prophets, Jesus Christ included, teaching salvation through adhering to God's laws as conveyed through revelation—that is, salvation through faith and works. In the other corner we have the challenger, Paul, promising an effortless salvation following a life unrestricted by commandments—in other words, salvation through faith alone. No wonder Paul gained a following!

James taught that faith alone was *not* sufficient for salvation. In the passage sometimes titled "Faith Without Works is Dead" (James 2:20), the author sarcastically condemns those who rely solely upon faith for salvation: "You believe that there is one God. You do well. Even the demons believe—and tremble!" (James 2:19). A modern paraphrase might read more like, "You believe in God? So what? So does Satan. How are

221

you different from him?" James clarifies that "a man is justified by works, and not by faith only" (James 2:24). Why? Because, "For as the body without the spirit is dead, so faith without works is dead also" (James 2:26).

Jesus Christ didn't compromise *his* values to appeal to the masses. He taught simplicity and good sense, such as, "As the Father gave me commandment, so I do . . ." (John 14:31) and, "If you keep my commandments, you will abide in my love, just as I have kept my Father's commandments and abide in His love" (John 15:10). To repeat: "If you keep *my* commandments . . ." (italics mine). Yet, nowhere did Jesus command belief in divine sonship, the Trinity, the crucifixion, resurrection, atonement, and other tenets of Trinitarian dogma. If anything, in fact, he taught the exact opposite.

Furthermore, in stark contrast to Paul, Jesus didn't try to be all things to all people. He appears to have been *one* thing to all people—a prophet bearing the truth of God. He wasn't afraid to voice the harsh truth, to speak his mind, or to convey revelation without putting a more appealing spin on it. In the short passage of Matthew 23:13–33, Jesus labeled the Pharisees "hypocrites" no less than eight times, "blind" five times, "fools" twice, topped off with "serpents" and "brood of vipers." Strong words? Maybe not in Western nations, but try those insults in the Palestine that was Jesus' homeland and see what happens, even in the present day.

Now *that* is the forthright example of a true prophet. And yet, there are those who view Paul as the main voice of revelation, despite the clear warning, "A disciple is not above his teacher, nor a servant above his master" (Matthew 10:24).

So why does Trinitarian Christianity assign priority to the teachings of Paul, who wasn't a disciple or a servant, and for that matter never even *met* Jesus—over those of "the teacher," despite the Bible warning us against such inverted priorities? And what does Paul propose with regard to the doctrine of atonement? Not just an amendment to Jesus' teachings. No, it's a whole new religion, and a whole new law—or lack thereof! It's so easy and alluring, a person *wants* to believe it. And given the bloody history of Roman Catholic intolerance, for fifteen hundred years a person *had* to believe it, *or else*! Consequently, the church appears to have succeeded in mixing a seemingly innocent hardener of satisfying falsehoods into the resinous minds of the receptive masses, cementing convictions upon an unsupported creed—a creed far from Jesus' teaching: "Most assuredly, I say to you, he who believes in me, the works that I do he will do also . . ." (John 14:12). One wonders, did Jesus really mean things like living according to revealed law, keeping the commandments, praying *directly* to God—things like that?

What can we imagine Jesus will say, upon his return, when he finds a group of his "followers" preferring Pauline theology to his own? Perhaps he will quote Jeremiah 23:32— "'Behold, I am against those who prophesy false dreams,' says the Lord, 'and tell them, and cause My people to err by their lies and by their recklessness. Yet I did not send them or command them; therefore they shall not profit this people at all,' says the Lord."

Whenever Jesus does return, we can safely assume that whatever else he says will catch a lot of people by surprise.

16 – Return of Jesus

If Jesus Christ were to come today, people would not
even crucify him. They would ask him to dinner, and
hear what he had to say, and make fun of it.

—D.A. Wilson, *Carlyle at his Zenith*

There is one thing upon which Christians and Muslims
agree, and that is the return of Jesus Christ. Interestingly
enough, both religions expect Jesus to return in a victory of faith
to defeat the Antichrist, correct the deviancies in religion, and
establish the truth of God throughout the world. Christians
expect this truth to echo their evolved doctrines, whereas
Muslims expect Jesus to remain consistent with his earlier
teachings and refute the false doctrines derived by those who
claimed to speak in his name. To this end, Muslims expect Jesus
will validate Muhammad as the final messenger Jesus predicted
in the New Testament, and endorse submission to God (i.e.,
Islam) as the religion for all humankind.

In the mind of the Muslim, Jesus' return will go hard on
those who embrace the doctrines of men in preference to the
teachings of the prophets. In particular, those who blaspheme
through associating a son and partner with God, despite Jesus'
teachings to the contrary, will deserve punishment.

The Holy Qur'an records that Allah will question Jesus
in this regard, as follows:

> And behold! Allah will say: "O Jesus the
> son of Mary! Did you say to men,
> 'Worship me and my mother as gods in
> derogation of Allah'?"
>
> He will say: "Glory to You! Never
> could I say what I had no right (to say).
> Had I said such a thing, You would
> indeed have known it. You know what is
> in my heart, though I do not know what is
> in Yours. For You know in full all that is
> hidden. Never said I to them anything
> except what You commanded me to say,
> to wit, 'Worship Allah, my Lord and your
> Lord'" (TMQ 5:116–117).

Until Jesus returns with *prima facie* evidence—namely,
his irrefutable human reality—one question assaults the
doctrinal defense system. It's the same question, perhaps, that
Jesus will ask of those who claim to have followed in his name:
Where in the Bible did Jesus say, in *clear* and *unambiguous*
terms, "I am God, worship me?" Nowhere. So why is he
considered divine? Would he have forgotten to pass on such an
essential teaching, if it were true? Unlikely. If Jesus never
claimed to be God and the doctrine of his divinity was contrived
by men, then we can expect God to object. Perhaps He would
repeat Isaiah 29:13 (as Jesus did in Matthew 15:8–9 and Mark
7:6–7)—"These people draw near to Me with their mouth, and
honor Me with their lips, but their heart is far from Me. And in
vain they worship Me, teaching as doctrines the commandments

of men." One wonders what doctrines are more the "commandments of men" than the Trinity, divine sonship, divinity of Jesus, original sin, resurrection and atonement. And what does God say of those who adopt such doctrines? "In vain they worship Me."

In Luke 6:46, Jesus posed a question that similarly challenges his "followers": "But why do you call me 'Lord, Lord,' and not do the things which I say?" In subsequent verses, Jesus describes the security of those who follow his teachings and the ruin of those who "heard and did nothing." And truly, should we be surprised? Let us recall Matthew 7:21–23, in which Jesus promised to disown his heretical followers in the hereafter:

> Not everyone who says to me, "Lord,
> Lord," shall enter the kingdom of heaven,
> but he who does the will of my Father in
> heaven. Many will say to me in that day,
> "Lord, Lord, have we not prophesied in
> your name, cast out demons in your name,
> and done many wonders in your name?"
> And then I will declare to them, "I never
> knew you; depart from me, you who
> practice lawlessness!"

Of course, there are those who assert that faith is faith; it's not to be pushed, manipulated, or reasoned with. Mark Twain addressed such attitudes with the words, "It was the schoolboy who said, 'Faith is believing what you know ain't so.'"[224] The point is that there is a huge difference between believing *in* God without proof, and believing doctrines *about*

226

God which are not only lacking proof, but for which there is evidence to the contrary in the teachings of the prophets. Perhaps it is the latter group referred to in Matthew 13:13: "Seeing they do not see, and hearing they do not hear, nor do they understand." Yet they remain sure in their belief, smugly hibernating until the season of reckoning.

Remember that scripture directs our faith through logic rather than emotion. The Bible says, "Test [some versions say "prove"] all things; hold fast what is good" (1 Thessalonians 5:21). Isaiah 1:18 tells us, "'Come now, and let us reason together,' says the Lord." So belief in God may be based upon faith, but after that, truth should be sought in the teachings of His prophets. Accept and follow those teachings, and a person will be ranked among the righteous. Submit to alternate teachings, and a person forfeits salvation, for the Bible cautions, "'If you are willing and obedient, you shall eat the good of the land; but if you refuse and rebel, you shall be devoured by the sword;' for the mouth of the Lord has spoken" (Isaiah 1:19–20).

The sincere seeker, then, will climb the staircase of stacked evidences, holding firmly to the handrail of reason. Recognizing that although, in the words of Shakespeare, "The devil can cite Scripture for his purpose,"[225] truth becomes evident through examination of the complete scripture. The conclusion as to which devils have been citing precisely which scriptures, and for what purpose, will vary from one individual to another. Thousands of years of theological disagreement will never be resolved to the satisfaction of all people, no matter how comprehensive the analysis. Trinitarians and Unitarians will continue to vie for recognition as representing the one "true" Christianity, and Muslims will continue to assert that both versions are corrupted by non-biblical doctrines. Meanwhile, the Jews remain content with their conviction of being "the chosen people."

If this analysis has shown nothing else, it has exposed the fact that both Moses and Jesus taught pure monotheism and predicted a final prophet. Could this final prophet be Muhammad, and the final revelation the Holy Qur'an? To even approach an answer to this question, we must first evaluate the books of scripture, and move from there to an examination of the prophets themselves.

Part IV: BOOKS OF SCRIPTURE

There is only one religion, though there are a hundred versions of it.

—George Bernard Shaw, *Plays Pleasant and Unpleasant*, Vol. 2, Preface

The common theme that runs through all religions is that if we believe in God and submit to His decree—obeying the commanded and avoiding the forbidden, and repenting our transgressions to Him—we will achieve salvation. The difference is in defining God's decree. Jews consider the Old Testament the endpoint of revelation at present, whereas Christians and Muslims alike contend that if the Jews followed their scripture, they would accept Jesus as a prophet and embrace his teachings.

Muslims carry the thought a step further by asserting that anybody (Jewish, Christian, or otherwise) who *does* embrace Jesus' teachings has to acknowledge that he taught strict monotheism, Old Testament Law, and the coming of the final prophet. But in fact, most who claim to follow Jesus don't follow what *Jesus* taught, but rather what others taught *about* Jesus. In this manner, Paul (and the Pauline theologians who followed in his wake) usurped Jesus in the derivation of Christian canon. And yet we find the Old Testament cautioning us:

> Whatever I command you, be careful to
> observe it; you shall not add to it nor take
> away from it. If there arises among you a
> prophet or a dreamer of dreams, and he
> gives you a sign or a wonder, and the sign
> or the wonder comes to pass, of which he
> spoke to you, saying, "Let us go after
> other gods"—which you have not
> known—"and let us serve them," you
> shall not listen to the words of that
> prophet or that dreamer of dreams, for the
> LORD your God is testing you to know
> whether you love the LORD your God
> with all your heart and with all your soul.
> You shall walk after the LORD your God
> and fear Him, and keep His
> commandments and obey His voice; you
> shall serve Him and hold fast to Him
> (Deut. 12:32–13:4).

Despite this warning, Paul proclaimed a construct of God that "you have not known." The theological morass derived from Paul's mysticisms is unavoidably thick and confusing. Many, if not most, worshippers are not aware of the questionable origins of their religion's doctrine, and simply trust a charismatic leader (pastor, priest, pope, etc.) and commit their path to his (or hers). Once that choice is made, the followers become confirmed believers in a religious construct of men, which, as we have seen, significantly conflicts with the teachings of Jesus himself. Monotheistic Christians, on the other hand, recognize that charismatic leaders, though convincing, are frequently astray, and struggle to adhere to scripture instead.

This isn't always easy, as anyone who attempts to distill God's teachings from the Old and New Testaments knows. The broad guidelines (to believe in God, His prophets and revelation) and laws (e.g., the Ten Commandments) are clear. The finer points are not, and to this the tremendous variety of Jewish and Christian sects and churches, and the depth and breadth of their differences, testifies.

Where, then, does this leave the serious seeker? To give up on religion, as many have? Or to seek a final, clarifying book of revelation, as conveyed by the final prophet predicted by both Old and New Testaments?

What follows is an analysis of the Old and New Testaments, not to validate them as scripture, but rather to expose the many errors and inconsistencies that betray their corruption. The purpose of this book is not to shake the faith of those who revere these texts as scripture, but to redirect that faith where these texts direct it themselves. In the face of modern textual criticism, we deceive ourselves (as well as invite ridicule and condemnation) if we believe the Old or New Testaments to be the unadulterated Word of God. However, if we recognize the errors of the Jewish and Christian bibles and understand the significance of these errors, this understanding might direct our search for guidance.

After reading the following chapters, those wishing to continue that search may do so inthe sequel to this book, which extends the analysis first to the Holy Qur'an, and then to the prophets. In the same manner that the scriptures demand analysis, so too must we validate the prophets if we are to trust the revelation they claimed to have transmitted.

1 — The Old Testament

*[The Bible] has noble poetry in it; and some clever
fables; and some blood-drenched history; and a wealth
of obscenity; and upwards of a thousand lies.*

—Mark Twain, *Letters from the Earth*, Vol. II

Let's begin by putting "two of every sort (of animal) into
the ark," and then . . . Oh, wait. Was that "*two* of *every* sort," as
per Genesis 6:19, or seven of clean and two of unclean animals,
as per Genesis 7:2–3?

Hmm. Well, we've got up to 120 years to think about it,
because that's the limit of the human lifespan, as per God's
promise in Genesis 6:3. So, just like Shem . . .

Oops. Bad example. Genesis 11:11 states, "Shem lived
five hundred years . . . ."

Oookay, forget Shem. So, just like Noah . . . Double
Oops. Genesis 9:29 teaches, "So all the days of Noah were nine
hundred and fifty years; and he died." So let's see, Genesis 6:3
promised a lifespan limited to 120 years, but a few verses later
both Shem and Noah broke the rule?

Whoa, time out.

Let's look at Old Testament dates from a different angle.
Here's Genesis 16:16: "Abraham was eighty-six years old when
Hagar bore Ishmael to Abraham." Genesis 21:5 tells us, "Now
Abraham was one hundred years old when his son Isaac was

born to him." So let's see, one hundred minus eighty-six, subtract the six from the first ten, nine minus eight . . . I get fourteen. So Ishmael was fourteen when Isaac was born.

A bit later, in Genesis 21:8, we read, "So the child (Isaac) grew and was weaned." Now, weaning in the Middle East takes two years, according to ethnic custom. So tack two onto fourteen, and Ishmael was sixteen before Sarah ordered Abraham to cast him out (Genesis 21:10).

Fine.

So far.

A couple more verses, and Genesis 21:14–19 portrays the outcast Ishmael as a helpless infant rather than an able-bodied sixteen-year-old youth, as follows:

> So Abraham rose early in the morning,
> and took bread and a skin of water; and
> putting it on her shoulder, he gave it and
> *the boy* to Hagar, and sent her away. Then
> she departed and wandered in the
> Wilderness of Beersheba. And the water
> in the skin was used up, and she *placed
> the boy under one of the shrubs*. Then she
> went and *sat down across from him* at a
> distance of about a bowshot; for she said
> to herself, "Let me not see the *death of
> the boy*." So she sat opposite him, and
> lifted her voice and wept.
>
> And God heard the voice of *the lad*.
> Then the angel of God called to Hagar out
> of heaven, and said to her, "What ails
> you, Hagar? Fear not, for God has heard

> *the voice of the lad* where he is. Arise, *lift up the lad* and *hold him with your hand,* for I will make him a great nation."
>
> Then God opened her eyes, and she saw a well of water. And she went and filled the skin with water, and *gave the lad a drink.*

A sixteen-year-old youth described as a "boy" or a "lad"? In a time and place when sixteen-year-olds were commonly married and awaiting their second or third child while supporting a growing family? In addition to being hunters, soldiers and, albeit rarely, even kings on occasion? Sixteen years equated to manhood in Ishmael's day. So how exactly did his father give the sixteen-year-old "boy," Ishmael, to Hagar? And how did she leave him crying (i.e., "the voice of the lad") like a helpless baby under a shrub? And how, precisely, did his mother lift him up and hold him with her hand? Lastly, are we truly expected to believe that Ishmael was so frail, his mother had to give him a drink because he was unable to get it himself?

Uh, yes, that's the gist of it. That's what we're supposed to believe.

But wait, there's more.

2 Chronicles 22:2 teaches that "Ahaziah was forty-two years old when he became king. . . ." Hunh. Forty-two years old. Hardly seems worthy of mention. Unless, that is, we note that 2 Kings 8:26 records, "Ahaziah was *twenty-two years old* when he became king . . ." So which was it? Forty-two or twenty-two?

Let's take a hint from the Bible. 2 Chronicles 21:20 teaches that Ahaziah's father, King Jehoram, died at the age of

234

forty.

Ahem.

King Jehoram died at the age of forty and was succeeded by his son, who was forty-two? In other words, King Jehoram fathered a child two years older than himself? Arithmetic, according to Mickey Mouse, is "Being able to count up to twenty without taking off your shoes." But between the reader's toes and all appendages of the family cat, there's no way to make sense of these figures. And while the logical conclusion approaches ramming speed, 2 Chronicles 22:1 points out that Ahaziah was King Jehoram's *youngest* son, for raiders had killed all Jehoram's older sons.

So if Ahaziah was two years older than dear departed Dad, how many years did his older brothers have on their father?

Obviously, 2 Chronicles 22:2 can't be trusted and 2 Kings 8:26, which teaches that Ahaziah was twenty-two when he became king, must be the correct version.

So King Jehoram died at forty (2 Chronicles 21:20) and was succeeded by Ahaziah, who was twenty-two (2 Kings 8:26). Which means King Jehoram was eighteen when Ahaziah was born, and roughly seventeen when he was conceived. Not only that, but Jehoram had older sons (2 Chronicles 22:1), so he must have started his family at the age of fifteen or less. So much for Ishmael having been a helpless lad at the age of sixteen. It was a time when teenagers were men.

But what about 2 Chronicles 22:2, which states that Ahaziah was forty-two when he assumed the throne?

A copying error, no doubt.

But that's not the point.

Isaiah 40:8 claims that "the word of our God stands

forever." This assertion doesn't excuse copying errors, or any other error, regardless how slight. In fact, according to Isaiah 40:8, any "word" which has not "stood forever" is disqualified as having been from God.

Which should make us question the authorship.

If "the word of our God stands forever," and the "word" of Ahaziah's age doesn't stand the test of time, whose word is it? God's or Satan's?

Don't look now, but even the Old Testament seems uncertain on this point.

2 Samuel 24:1 reads, "Again the anger of the *LORD* was aroused against Israel, and He moved David against them to say, 'Go, number Israel and Judah.'" However, 1 Chronicles 21:1 states, "Now *Satan* stood up against Israel, and moved David to number Israel."

Uhhh, which was it? The Lord, or Satan? There's a slight (like, total) difference.

Talk about identity theft.

But seriously, the mistake is understandable. After all, it's pretty hard to know who you're talking to when you can't put a face to revelation. And, as God said in Exodus 33:20, "You cannot see My face; for no man shall see Me, and live."

So there we have it.

No man can see God's face, and live.

Well, except for Jacob, of course. As Genesis 32:30 states, "So Jacob called the name of the place Peniel: 'For I have seen God face to face, and my life is preserved.'"

And we mustn't forget Moses, as per Exodus 33:11: "So the LORD spoke to Moses face to face, as a man speaks to his friend."

So no man can see God's face, and live.

Brown / MisGod'ed

Except for Jacob and Moses.
But God didn't mention that exception, did He?
So maybe He changed His mind.
And then again, maybe not.
On one hand, Genesis 6:6–7 suggests that God makes mistakes for which He repents, as follows: "And the LORD *was sorry* that He had made man on the earth, and He was grieved in His heart. So the LORD said, 'I will destroy man whom I have created from the face of the earth, both man and beast, creeping thing and birds of the air, *for I am sorry* that I have made them'" (italics mine).
On the other hand, Numbers 23:19 records, "God *is* not a man, that He should lie, nor a son of man, that He should repent."
The point, if not already obvious, is that the Old Testament is fraught with errors. Perhaps the simplest errors are numerical, and these are plentiful. For example, 2 Samuel 8:4 speaks of David taking seven hundred horsemen and 1 Chronicles 18:4, describing the exact same event, makes it seven thousand.
Big deal.
Seven *hundred* in one verse, seven *thousand* in another—obviously some scribe flubbed a zero.
Wrong.
The Old Testament doesn't have zeros. Nor, for that matter, does it have numerals. In the time of the Old and New Testaments, the Arabic numerals we are all familiar with weren't in common use. The clumsy Roman numerals were the language of mathematics, and the earliest evidence of the zero dates from 933 CE.
In ancient Hebrew, numbers were written *longhand*.

Seven hundred was *sheba' me'ah* and seven thousand was *sheba' eleph*. So this scriptural difference may indeed represent a scribal error, but it's not a simple error of a zero. Rather, it's the difference between *me'ah* and *eleph*.

Similarly, 2 Samuel 10:18 speaks of seven *hundred* charioteers and forty thousand *horsemen,* and 1 Chronicles 19:18 speaks of seven *thousand* charioteers and forty thousand *foot soldiers.* 2 Samuel 23:8 records *eight* hundred men, 1 Chronicles 11:11 numbers them at *three* hundred. And in case the reader suspects they are speaking about different events, Josheb-Basshebeth and Jashobeam are cross-referenced, clarifying that both passages describe the same person. 2 Samuel 24:9 describes *eight hundred thousand* men "who drew the sword" in Israel and *five hundred thousand* in Judah; 1 Chronicles 21:5 puts the numbers at *one million one hundred thousand* in Israel and *four hundred and seventy thousand* in Judah. 2 Samuel 24:13 describes *seven* years of famine, 1 Chronicles 21:11–12 states it was *three.* 1 Kings 4:26 numbers Solomon's horse stalls at *forty* thousand, 2 Chronicles 9:25 numbers them at *four*thousand. 1 Kings 15:33 teaches that Baasha reigned as king of Israel until the *twenty-seventh*year of Asa, king of Judah; 2 Chronicles 16:1 states Baasha was still king of Israel in the *thirty-sixth* year of Asa's reign. 1 Kings 5:15–16 speaks of 3,300 deputies to Solomon, 2 Chronicles 2:2 records 3,600. In 1 Kings 7:26 we read of *two* thousand baths, but in 2 Chronicles 4:5 the number is *three* thousand. 2 Kings 24:8 states "Jehoiachin was *eighteen* years old when he became king, and he reigned in Jerusalem*three months.*" 2 Chronicles 36:9 records, "Jehoiachin was *eight* years old when he became king, and he reigned in Jerusalem*three months and ten days.*" Ezra 2:65 writes of *two hundred* men and women singers,

Nehemiah 7:67 states they were *two hundred and forty-five*.

Now, are these differences important?

Answer: Yes, and no. For the most part, we could care less how many baths, singers, and foot soldiers there were, or whether one scribe made a slip of the stylus while another rounded numbers off to the nearest hundred. From the point of conveying useful information, these discrepancies are insignificant. However, from the point of validating the Old Testament as the inerrant word of God, these discrepancies are highly significant.

Furthermore, there are numerous discrepancies which are not numerical in nature.

For example, Genesis 26:34 tells us Esau's wives were *Judith* and *Basemath;* Genesis 36:2–3 records his wives as A*dah, Aholibamah* and *Basemath*. 2 Samuel 6:23 states that Michal was childless until the day she died; 2 Samuel 21:8 attributes five sons to Michal. 2 Samuel 8:9–10 speaks of Toi as king of Hamath, and *Joram* as an emissary of King David; 1 Chronicles 18:9–10 records the king's name as *Tou*, and that of the emissary as *Hadoram*.

Again, not a big deal.

But here's something that is:

2 Samuel 17:25 tells us Jithra (a.k.a. Jether; both names are cross-referenced, so we know these two passages speak of the same individual) was an *Israelite*, whereas 1 Chronicles 2:17 identifies him as an *Ishmaelite*. Now, if Old Testament authors couldn't get *this* straight, we might wonder how much more inclined they might have been, being Jewish, to calculated lineage-switching in the case of Abraham sacrificing his "only begotten son," Isaac. In the "Jesus Begotten?" chapter earlier in this book, I discussed the fact that at no time was Isaac

the only begotten son of Abraham. And we find here that Old Testament authors substituted "Israelite" with "Ishmaelite" when there was no obvious motivation. How much more likely would they have been to have switched lineages when their birthright and covenants with God were at stake?

Incidentally, once this contradiction became known, Bible translators tried to make it disappear. For example, the New Revised Standard Version translates the Hebrew *yisre'eliy* in 2 Samuel 17:25 to "Ishmaelite," and then acknowledges in a discreet footnote that the correct translation is "Israelite." *Yishma'e'li* is "Ishmaelite." The evidence against the translators' integrity is strengthened by the fact that practically any Bible published prior to the mid-twentieth century (including the American Standard Version of 1901, upon which the RSV and NRSV are based) translate *yisre'eliy* to "Israelite." Only after the scriptural inconsistency was identified was the translation corrupted to "Ishmaelite."

By this modern deception, the New Revised Standard Version avoids conflict in their translation, but not in the source documents. And we would do well to note this deceit, for will we truly be surprised if future Bible translations attempt to gloss over the other errors exposed in this present work?

Now, here's the point. 2 Kings 19 and Isaiah 37 contain a sequence of thirty-seven verses which correspond virtually to the letter. This correspondence is so exact that Bible critics have suggested that the authors plagiarized either from one another or from the same source document. And while plagiarism would explain the consistency, a more generous suggestion might be that these two chapters exemplify the exquisite accuracy we expect from a book of God. Whether a story is retold once, twice or a thousand times, as long as the origin of the tradition lies in revelation from the Almighty, it shouldn't change. Not in the smallest detail. The fact that stories *do* change, both in Old and New Testaments, threatens the claim to biblical inerrancy.

And then there are the simple questions. Questions like, "Does anybody really believe that Jacob wrestled with God, and Jacob prevailed (Genesis 32:24–30)?" The Creator of a universe 240,000,000,000,000,000,000,000,000 miles in diameter with all its intricacies, with the measly, middleweight planet Earth alone weighing in at 5,976,000,000,000,000,000,000,000,000 kg—and someone believes that a paltry blob of protoplasm not only wrestled with The One who created him, but *prevailed?*

Another simple question: Genesis 2:17 records God warning Adam, "but of the tree of the knowledge of good and evil you shall not eat, for in the day that you eat of it you shall surely die." Genesis 3:3 contributes, "but of the fruit of the tree which is in the midst of the garden, God has said, 'You shall not eat it, nor shall you touch it, lest you die.'" So which is it? Did Adam bite the apple or didn't he? The way the story is told, he bit the apple and lived. Yet God promised death the *very same day*. So did he bite it or not? If he did he should have died, and if he didn't, humankind should still be in paradise. Is the word "die" an error of translation, a metaphor or an inconsistency? If an error, then let the translators admit it. If a metaphor, then we can acknowledge the metaphorical nature of Hebrew idiom and suggest that Jesus, similarly, didn't "die" any more than Adam did. And if an inconsistency, well . . .

Next point—who wrote the Old Testament? Tradition relates that Moses wrote the Pentateuch (the first five books), but we can assume he encountered a slight technical difficulty (like the fact that he was *dead*) when it came to recording his own obituary in Deuteronomy 34:5–12. So who authored his death, burial, wake, and the aftermath? Is this author to be trusted, and what does this say about authorship of the Old Testament as a whole?

Then there are the tales of naked drunkenness, incest, and whoredom that no person of modesty could read to their mother, much less to their own children. And yet, a fifth of the world's population trusts a book which records that Noah "drank of the wine and was drunk, and became uncovered (naked) in his tent" (Genesis 9:22), and that Lot . . .

> . . . went up out of Zoar and dwelt in the mountains, and his two daughters were with him; for he was afraid to dwell in Zoar. And he and his two daughters dwelt in a cave. Now the firstborn said to the younger, "Our father is old, and there is no man on the earth to come in to us as is the custom of all the earth. Come, let us make our father drink wine, and we will lie with him, that we may preserve the lineage of our father." So they made their father drink wine that night. And the firstborn went in and lay with her father, and he did not know when she lay down or when she arose. It happened on the next day that the firstborn said to the younger, "Indeed I lay with my father last night; let us make him drink wine tonight also, and you go in and lie with him, that we may preserve the lineage of our father." Then they made their father drink

242

> wine that night also. And the younger
> arose and lay with him, and he did not
> know when she lay down or when she
> arose. Thus both the daughters of Lot
> were with child by their father (Genesis
> 19:30–36).

Tales of debauchery and deviancy include adultery and prostitution (Genesis 38:15–26), more prostitution (Judges 16:1), wholesale depravity (2 Samuel 16:20–23), whoredom (Ezekiel 16:20–34 and 23:1–21), and whoredom spiced with adultery (Proverbs 7:10–19). The incestuous rape of Tamar in 2 Samuel 13:7–14 bears a most interesting moral, for Tamar was counseled to "hold her peace," for "He [the rapist, Amnon] *is* your brother; (so) do not take this thing to heart" (2 Samuel 13:20). Oh, whew, the rapist was her brother—no problem, then . . . Say *WHAT?* Are we to believe that such "pearls of wisdom" are the fruits of revelation—or the stuff of deviant dreams?

And on the subject of dreaming, 2 Timothy 3:16 reads, "All scripture is given by inspiration of God, and is profitable for doctrine, for reproof, for correction, for instruction in righteousness." Now *that* makes sense. That's the way it should be. But can anyone conceive the "profit, reproof, correction, or instruction in righteousness" conveyed in the above passages? Those who think they can probably should be in jail.

Another curiosity—according to Genesis 38:15–30, Perez and Zerah were born to Tamar after incestuous fornication with her father-in-law, Judah. Passing over the fact that, according to Leviticus 20:12, both Judah and Tamar should have been executed (and prophets are not above the law), let's inspect the lineage of Perez and Zerah. After all, the alleged "word of

God" tells us, "One of illegitimate birth shall not enter the congregation of the Lord; even to the tenth generation none of his descendants shall enter the congregation of the Lord" (Deuteronomy 23:2).

So who was the tenth generation from Zerah?

No one important.

Well, then, who was the tenth generation from Perez?

Someone *very* important. Someone named Solomon. His father (the ninth generation) also has a familiar-sounding name: David.

If we trust Matthew 1:3–6, David was the ninth generation of a bastard, and as such, should by no way enter the "congregation of the Lord." The same goes for Solomon. And yet, both are held to have been patriarchs, if not prophets.

Hmm. An awkward understanding, at best.

Furthermore, if we are to believe the Old Testament, Solomon was not only the tenth generation of illegitimacy through Perez, but also the first generation of illegitimacy through his father, David's, adulterous union with Bathsheba, the wife of Uriah (2 Samuel 11:2–4). Once again, breezing past the unfulfilled death penalty (Leviticus 20:10), Solomon is portrayed as having a double-dose of illegitimacy.

Or does he?

Something doesn't sound right. Either David and Solomon were not prophets or the Old Testament is not to be trusted. The pieces of God-given revelation shouldn't require reshaping and force to fit together. They should snap together in congruence with the perfection of the One who created the heavens and earth in perfect harmony. That's the way it should be, and the average Christian suggests that such is precisely the case with the New Testament.

However, that assertion deserves inspection as well. Having examined the above, we can readily understand why the author of Jeremiah bewails, "How can you say, 'We are wise, and the law of the Lord is with us?' Look, the false pen of the scribe certainly works falsehood" (Jeremiah 8:8). The New Revised Standard Version, unlike the New King James Version, doesn't soften their words, and records this verse as, "How can you say, 'We are wise, and the law of the Lord is with us,' when in fact, the false pen of the scribes has made it into a lie?"

So that is the Old Testament—so full of errors that even one of the authors bemoans the scriptural corruption generated by the "false pens of the scribes."

Many claim that similar problems plague the New Testament—that weaknesses, inconsistencies, and contradictions upset the claim of divine inerrancy. If true, Christians face the challenge, "Are you a person of God, or of Christianity?"

This question demands testimony.

Followers of God will submit to the truth He conveyed, when made clear, while those who follow any man-made religion will defend their doctrine against reason and revelation. Discussion of the frail or nonexistent foundation of the most passionately defended Christian doctrines has already been offered. What remains to be examined is the authority, or lack thereof, of the New Testament.

2 — The New Testament

Both read the Bible day and night,

But thou read'st black where I read white.

—William Blake, *The Everlasting Gospel*

Of course, Blake's sentiment in the quote above is nothing new. The New Testament contains enough inconsistencies to have spawned a dizzying variety of interpretations, beliefs and religions, all allegedly Bible-based. And so, we find one author offering the amusing observation:

> You can and you can't,
>
> You shall and you shan't,
>
> You will and you won't,
>
> And you will be damned if you do,
>
> And you will be damned if you don't.[226]

Why such variance in viewpoints? To begin with, BeDuhn tells us, "I made it clear that every translation has been created by vested interests, and that none of the translations represent the ideal of a scholarly, neutral project."[227] More importantly, different theological camps disagree on which books should be included in the Bible. One camp's apocrypha is

246

another's scripture. Furthermore, even among those books that *have* been canonized, the many variant source texts lack uniformity. This lack of uniformity is so ubiquitous that *The Interpreter's Dictionary of the Bible* states, "It is safe to say that there is not one sentence in the NT in which the MS [manuscript] tradition is wholly uniform."[228]

Not one sentence? We can't trust a single *sentence* of the Bible? Hard to believe.

Maybe.

The fact is that there are over 5,700 Greek manuscripts of all or part of the New Testament.[229] Furthermore, "no two of these manuscripts are exactly alike in all their particulars. . . . And some of these differences are significant."[230] Factor in roughly ten thousand manuscripts of the Latin Vulgate, add the many other ancient variants (i.e., Syriac, Coptic, Armenian, Georgian, Ethiopic, Nubian, Gothic, Slavonic), and what do we have?

A lot of manuscripts.

A lot of manuscripts that fail to correspond in places and not infrequently contradict one another. Scholars estimate the number of manuscript variants in the hundreds of thousands, some estimating as high as 400,000.[231] In Bart D. Ehrman's now famous words, "Possibly it is easiest to put the matter in comparative terms: there are more differences in our manuscripts than there are words in the New Testament."[232]

How did this happen?

Poor recordkeeping. Dishonesty. Incompetence. Doctrinal prejudice. Take your pick.

None of the original manuscripts have survived from the early Christian period.[233],[234],[235]As a result, "we will never be able to claim certain knowledge of exactly what the original text of any biblical writing was.[236]

The most ancient complete manuscripts (Vatican MS. No. 1209 and the SinaiticSyriac Codex) date from the fourth century, three hundred years after Jesus' ministry. But the originals? Lost. And the copies of the originals? Also lost. Our most ancient manuscripts, in other words, are copies of the copies of the copies of nobody-knows-just-how-many copies of the originals.

No wonder they differ.

In the best of hands, copying errors would be no surprise. However, New Testament manuscripts were *not* in the best of hands. During the period of Christian origins, scribes were untrained, unreliable, incompetent, and in some cases illiterate.[237] Those who were visually impaired could have made errors with look-alike letters and words, while those who were hearing-impaired may have erred in recording scripture as it was read aloud. Frequently scribes were overworked, and hence inclined to the errors that accompany fatigue.

In the words of Metzger and Ehrman, "Since most, if not all, of them [the scribes] would have been amateurs in the art of copying, a relatively large number of mistakes no doubt crept into their texts as they reproduced them."[238] Worse yet, some scribes allowed doctrinal prejudice to influence their transmission of scripture.[239] As Ehrman states, "The scribes who copied the texts changed them."[240] More specifically, "The number of deliberate alterations made in the interest of doctrine is difficult to assess."[241] And even more specifically, "In the technical parlance of textual criticism—which I retain for its significant ironies—these scribes 'corrupted' their texts for theological reasons."[242]

Errors were introduced in the form of additions,

deletions, substitutions, and modifications, most commonly of words or lines, but occasionally of entire verses.[243],[244] In fact, "numerous changes and accretions came into the text,"[245] with the result that "all known witnesses of the New Testament are to a greater or lesser extent mixed texts, and even several of the earliest manuscripts are not free from egregious errors."[246] The scope of these errors is so vast that the two hundred Jesus Seminar scholars concluded that "Eighty-two percent of the words ascribed to Jesus in the gospels were not actually spoken by him."[247]

Let's look at some examples. According to biblical scholar J. Enoch Powell, regarding the book of Matthew,

> At the cost of sometimes severe
> disruption wherever they appear, passages
> about John the Baptist have been inserted.
> All have the function of displaying him as
> having recognized in Jesus the fulfillment
> of his own mission.[248]

Even worse, "It is in fact possible that *all* the long discourses put into the mouth of Jesus are artificially introduced."[249] This would, of course, include the 'great sermon,' the 'missionary charge,' and every parable the book of Matthew records Jesus having spoken.

In *Misquoting Jesus*, Ehrman presents persuasive evidence that the story of the woman taken in adultery (John 7:53–8:12) and the last twelve verses of Mark were not in the original gospels, but added by later scribes.[250] Furthermore, these examples "represent just two out of thousands of places in which the manuscripts of the New Testament came to be changed by scribes."[251]

In fact, entire books of the Bible were forged.[252] This doesn't mean their content is necessarily wrong, but it certainly doesn't mean it's right. So which books were forged? Ephesians, Colossians, 2 Thessalonians, 1 and 2 Timothy, Titus, 1 and 2 Peter, and Jude—a whopping nine of the twenty-seven New Testament books and epistles—are to one degree or another suspect.[253]

Forged books? In the Bible?

Why are we not surprised? After all, even the gospel authors are unknown. In fact, they're anonymous.[254]Biblical scholars rarely, if ever, ascribe gospel authorship to Matthew, Mark, Luke, or John. As Ehrman tells us, "Most scholars today have abandoned these identifications, and recognize that the books were written by otherwise unknown but relatively well-educated Greek-speaking (and writing) Christians during the second half of the first century."[255] Graham Stanton affirms, "The gospels, unlike most Graeco-Roman writings, are anonymous. The familiar headings which give the name of an author ('The Gospel according to . . .') were not part of the original manuscripts, for they were added only early in the second century."[256] Added by whom? "By unknown figures in the early church. In most cases, the names are guesses or perhaps the result of pious wishes."[257]

So what, if anything, did Jesus' disciples have to do with authoring the gospels? Little or nothing, so far as we know. According to Ehrman, "Moses did not write the Pentateuch (the first five books of the Old Testament) and Matthew, Mark, Luke, and John did not write the Gospels."[258]Furthermore, "Of the twenty-seven books of the New Testament, only eight almost certainly go back to the author whose name they bear:

the seven undisputed letters of Paul (Romans, 1 and 2 Corinthians, Galatians, Philippians, 1 Thessalonians, and Philemon) and the Revelation of John (although we aren't sure who this John was)."[259]

And why are we not sure who the John who authored the 'Gospel according to John' was? Let's come back to that in a moment. For now, it is enough to understand that we have no reason to believe the disciples authored any of the books of the Bible. To begin with, let us remember Mark was a secretary to Peter, and Luke a companion to Paul. The verses of Luke 6:14–16 and Matthew 10:2–4 catalogue the twelve disciples, and although these lists differ over two names, Mark and Luke don't make *either* list. So only Matthew and John were true disciples. But all the same, modern scholars pretty much disqualify them as authors anyway.

Why?

Good question. John being the more famous of the two, why should we disqualify him from having authored the Gospel of "John"?

Umm . . . because he was dead?

Multiple sources acknowledge there is no evidence, other than questionable testimonies of second-century authors, to suggest that the disciple John was the author of the Gospel of "John."[260],[261] Perhaps the most convincing refutation is that the disciple John is believed to have died in or around 98 CE,[262] whereas the Gospel of John was written twelve years later, circa 110 CE.[263] Another line of reasoning is that Acts 4:13 tells us that John and Peter were (and let's not play with the translation, here – read this one in the Greek) "unlettered." In other words, they were illiterate. So whoever Luke (Paul's companion), Mark (Peter's secretary), and John (the unknown,

251

but certainly not theilliterate, long-dead one) were, we have no reason to believe any of the gospels were authored by Jesus' disciples.

To this end, Stanton poses a compelling question: "Was the eventual decision to accept Matthew, Mark, Luke, and John correct? Today it is generally agreed that neither Matthew nor John was written by an apostle. And Mark and Luke may not have been associates of the apostles."[264]

Professor Ehrman is more direct in his assertion:

> Critical scholars are fairly unified today
> in thinking that Matthew did not write the
> First Gospel or John the Fourth, that Peter
> did not write 2 Peter and possibly not 1
> Peter. No other book of the New
> Testament claims to be written by one of
> Jesus' earthly disciples. There are books
> by the apostle of Paul, of course. Thirteen
> go by his name in the New Testament, at
> least seven of which are accepted by
> nearly all scholars as authentic.[265]

Why, then, do our bibles label the four gospels as Matthew, Mark, Luke, and John? Some scholars, Ehrman being just one, suggest something similar to branding—the modern advertising term for the commercial practice of soliciting celebrity endorsements to sell the product.[266] Second-century Christians who favored these four gospels had a choice—either acknowledge the gospels' anonymous authorship or fake it. The bluff proved irresistible, and they chose to assign the gospels to apostolic authorities, thereby illegitimately "branding" the gospels as authoritative.

So let's see—we have no evidence *any* book of the Bible, gospels included, were authored by Jesus' disciples. Furthermore, most scholars accept Paul's authorship in only half of the works attributed to him. Regardless of who authored what, corruptions and inconsistencies have resulted in more manuscript variants than words in the New Testament. Lastly, even scholars of textual criticism fail to agree.[267] Why? Because "considerations depend, it will be seen, upon probabilities, and sometimes the textual critic must weigh one set of probabilities against another."[268] Furthermore, with regard to the more complex textual problems, "the probabilities are much more evenly divided and the critic must sometimes be content with choosing the least unsatisfactory reading or even admitting that there is no clear basis for choice at all."[269]

Expanding on this thought, "Occasionally, none of the variant readings will commend itself as original, and one [i.e., a textual critic] will be compelled either to choose the reading that is judged to be the least unsatisfactory or to indulge in conjectural emendation."[270] Hmm. Conjectural emendation, conjectural emendation—isn't that scholar-talk for "educated guess"?

So perhaps we shouldn't be surprised that, just as Jeremiah bemoaned the "false pens" of the Old Testament scribes, the third-century church father, Origen, bemoaned the "false pens" of New Testament scribes:

> The differences among the manuscripts have become great, either through the negligence of some copyists or through the perverse audacity of others; they

either neglect to check over what they
have transcribed, or, in the process of
checking, they make additions or
deletions as they please.[271]

That was the voice of a third-century church father,
commenting on just the first couple hundred years. We have to
wonder what other corruptions occurred in the seventeen to
eighteen centuries that followed. But whatever happened in the
centuries that followed, by the third-century, scribes entrusted to
copy and preserve New Testament manuscripts modified them.
    Sure, many copying errors were unintentional and/or
inconsequential. But Ehrman tells us many others were not only
deliberate, and not only significant, but doctrinally motivated.[272]
And this is the scriptural vandalism we care about—the
additions, omissions and alterations, whether deliberate or not,
that changed the intended message of the New Testament
manuscripts.
    These changes had tremendous impact on the course of
Christianity. The insertion of the Johannine Comma (The First
Epistle of John, verses 5:7–8, as discussed in Chapter 8: Trinity)
lent false support to the doctrine of the Trinity. The addition of
the last twelve verses of Mark misguided some Appalachian
sects into snake-handling, and many evangelical denominations
into the unintelligible practice of "speaking in tongues." The
altered spin on Jesus' existence steered theology toward
deification of Jesus and the doctrine of atonement. In the
process, the scribes didn't transmit the message of Jesus, they
transformed it.
    One case in which a corruption has been identified and
corrected is Acts 8:37. This verse is not found in the most

ancient manuscripts, and appears to be an insertion by a later scribe. For this reason, it has been dropped from many modern translations, including the New International Version and the New Revised Standard Version. Should we look it up, we'll find the NIV and NRSV, as well as other respected translations, enumerate Acts 8:37, but leave it blank.

Take another example. Bruce M. Metzger tells us Acts 15:34 was unquestionably inserted by copyists.[273] He is not alone in this opinion. Again, both the New International Version and the New Revised Standard Version enumerate this verse, but leave it blank. The New King James, however, retains it, as do the Latin bibles.

In similar fashion, many other New Testament verses have been dropped from the most reputable bibles, such as the NIV and NRSV, but retained in the New King James version. The most notable omissions are: Matthew 17:21, 18:11; Mark 7:16, 9:44, 9:46, 11:26; part of Luke 9:56, 17:36, 23:17; John 5:4; Romans 16:24; part of 1 John 5:7.

Whereas illegitimate insertions are recognized and omitted by some bibles, others ignore them. In fact, they not only ignore the illegitimate insertions, but they sanction them.

Should we wish to document some of these errors, the logical place to start is with the most respected books of the New Testament, the gospels.

We have already disclosed the fact that Jesus' disciples did not appear to have authored the gospels. However, even if they *had* authored the gospels, Jesus did not seem to feel his disciples could handle everything he wanted to tell them (John 16:12—"I still have many things to say to you, but you cannot bear them now"). He considered them to be of little faith (Matthew 8:26, 14:31, 16:8, and Luke 8:25), lacking understanding (Matthew 15:16), and despaired over having to bear with that "faithless and perverse generation . . ." (Luke 9:41).

So perhaps we shouldn't be particularly disturbed to learn that the disciples did not author the gospels. Perhaps they weren't the best men for the job. After all, those who should have known Jesus best—his own relatives—thought him crazy (Mark 3:21 and John 8:48), and the very people to whom he was sent rejected him (John 1:11). So the issue of greatest concern shouldn't be who authored the gospels, but whether they are reliable. The answer, apparently, is "No." The Jesus Seminar analyzed the words attributed to Jesus in the Gospel of John, and "were unable to find a single saying they could with certainty trace back to the historical Jesus. . . . The words attributed to Jesus in the Fourth Gospel are the creation of the evangelist for the most part."[274] Now, why would he do such a thing? Because, "Jesus' followers were inclined to adopt and adapt his words to their own needs. This led them to invent narrative contexts based on their own experience, into which they imported Jesus as the authority figure."[275] The Jesus Seminar documents hundreds of examples in the gospels, including cases where "the followers of Jesus borrowed freely from common wisdom and coined their own sayings and parables, which they then attributed to Jesus."[276]

So much for "John." Now let's look at some specific difficulties, beginning with the book of Matthew. Matthew 2:15 asserts that Jesus was taken to Egypt "to fulfill what had been spoken by the Lord through the prophet, 'Out of Egypt I have called my son.'" Well, that's the proposal. However, exactly which scripture was Jesus' detainment in Egypt supposed to fulfill? Hosea 11:1. So what does Hosea 11:1 say, exactly?

"When Israel was a child, I loved him, and out of Egypt I called my son."

A scriptural match—no?

No.

The match only looks good if we stop reading. Should we continue to the next verse, the full passage reads, "When Israel was a child, I loved him, and out of Egypt I called my son.The more I called them, the more they went from me; they kept sacrificing to the Baals, and offering incense to idols" (Hosea 11:1–2, NRSV). Taken in context, we can only apply this passage to Jesus Christ if, at the same time, we assert that Jesus worshipped idols.

Similar errors abound. A short two verses later, Matthew 2:17 comments on Herod's genocide of the infants of Bethlehem with the words, "Then was fulfilled what had been spoken through the prophet Jeremiah: 'A voice was heard in Ramah, wailing and loud lamentation, Rachel weeping for her children; she refused to be consoled, because they are no more'" (Matthew 2:17, NRSV).

One minor problem.The referenced Old Testament passage, Jeremiah 31:15, refers to an actual event in history, namely the abduction of Rachel's children, along with those of the Israelite community, by Sargon, the king of Assyria. The scriptural parallel is not just strained and stressed, it is nonexistent. So too with Matthew 27:10, which references a quote in Jeremiah 32:6–9. In this case, the referenced quote simply isn't there. Furthermore, Matthew 27:10 speaks of a *potter's* field, priced at *thirty* pieces of silver. Jeremiah 32:6–9 speaks of *Hanamel's* field, priced at *seventeen* shekels of silver. Both were actual transactions separate in time and place. Any effort to claim "fulfillment" of previous scripture is capricious at best.

And the list goes on.

We can well understand why some New Testament authors may have sought validation through claiming fulfillment of Old Testament prophecies. However, this tactic backfires when referenced scripture turns out to be misremembered, misapplied or frankly nonexistent. Rather than conferring legitimacy, such errors render the document, as well as the author, sadly suspect.

Having touched on some of these errors, now let's look at a short (and by no means complete) list of transparent inconsistencies.

3—Inconsistencies Within the New Testament: Part 1

Even if it's grim, we'll bare it

—Advertisement for *The Times*,Leo Burnett
Advertising Agency[277]

The following list identifies some of the more glaring
New Testament conflicts. The purpose, as before, is not to
slander the Bible, but to expose it for what it is. Those who
consider the New Testament the inerrant word of God need to
consider this list in light of the fact that God doesn't err. Not
once.

That being the case, recognizing New Testament errors
should motivate the serious seeker to look a little further.

1. **Matthew 1:16 and Luke 3:23 – Who was Joseph's
    father?**
        Matthew 1:16: And *Jacob* begot Joseph the
    husband of Mary, of whom was born Jesus who is called
    Christ.
        Luke 3:23: Now Jesus himself began his ministry
    at about thirty years of age, being (as was supposed) the
    son of Joseph, the *son of Heli*. . .

2. **Matthew 2:14 and Luke 2:39 – To Egypt or
    Nazareth?**
        Matthew 2:14: When he arose, he took the young

259

child and his mother bynight and departed for *Egypt*, and was there until the death of Herod . . .

Luke 2:39: So when they had performed all things according to the law of the Lord, they returned to Galilee, to their own city, *Nazareth*.

3. **Matthew 4:3–9 and Luke 4:3–11 – Stones to bread, throw himself down, *then* worship Satan, or stones to bread, worship Satan, *then* throw himself down?**

   Matthew 4:3–9: Satan tells Jesus to "command that these stones become bread," then "throw yourself down," and lastly "fall down and worship me."

   Luke 4:3–11: Satan tells Jesus to "command this stone to become bread," then to "worship before me," and lastly to "throw [himself] down from here."

4. **Matthew 6:9–13 and Luke 11:2–4 – Which is the correct version of the "Lord's Prayer?"**

   Matthew 6:9–13: Our Father in heaven, Hallowed be Your name. Your kingdom come. Your will be done on earth as *it is* in heaven. Give us **this day** our daily bread. And forgive us our **debts, as we forgive our debtors.** And do not lead us into temptation, but deliver us from the evil one. **For Yours is the kingdom and the power and the glory forever. Amen.**

   Luke 11:2–5: Our Father in heaven, Hallowed be Your name. Your kingdom come. Your will be done on earth as *it is* in heaven. Give us **day by day** our daily bread. And forgive us our **sins, for we also forgive everyone who is indebted to us.** And do not lead us into temptation, but deliver us from the evil one.

260

5. **Matthew 7:7–8 and Luke 13:24 – All who seek will find, or not?**

Matthew 7:7–8: Ask, and it will be given to you; seek, and you will find; knock, and it will be opened to you. For *everyone who asks receives*, and he who seeks finds, and to him who knocks it will be opened.

Luke 13:24: Strive to enter through the narrow gate, for many, I say to you, *will seek* to enter *and will not be able*.

6. **Matthew 8:5 and Luke 7:3–7 – The centurion came himself, or sent messengers?**

Matthew 8:5: Now when Jesus had entered Capernaum, a centurion came to him, pleading with him . . .

Luke 7:3–7: So when he heard about Jesus, *he sent elders* of the Jews to him, pleading with him to come and heal his servant. And when they came to Jesus, they begged him earnestly, saying that the one for whom he should do this was deserving, "for he loves our nation, and has built us a synagogue." Then Jesus went with them. And when he was already not far from the house, *the centurion sent friends* to him, saying to him, "Lord, do not trouble yourself, for I am not worthy that you should enter under my roof. Therefore *I did not even think myself worthy to come to you*."

7. **Matthew 8:28 and Luke 8:27 – One or two men?**

Matthew 8:28: When he had come to the other side, to the country of the Gergesenes, there met him *two demon-possessed men*, coming out of the tombs, exceedingly fierce, so that no one could pass that way.

Luke 8:27: And when he stepped out on the land, there met him *a certain man* from the city who had demons for a long time. And he wore no clothes, nor did he live in a house but in the tombs.

8. **Matthew 9:18 and Mark 5:22–23 – Dead or not?**

Matthew 9:18: While he spoke these things to them, behold, a ruler came and worshiped him, saying, "My daughter *has just died*, but come and lay your hand on her and she will live."

Mark 5:22–23: And behold, one of the rulers of the synagogue came, Jairus by name. And when he saw him, he fell at his feet and begged him earnestly, saying, "My little daughter *lies at the point of death*. Come and lay your hands on her, that she may be healed, and she will live."

9. **Matthew 10:2–4 and Luke 6:13–16 – Who was a disciple, Lebbeus (whose surname was Thaddeus) or Judas, the son of James?**

Matthew 10:2–4: Now the names of the twelve apostles are these: first, Simon, who is called Peter, and Andrew his brother; James the son of Zebedee, and John his brother; Philip and Bartholomew; Thomas and Matthew the tax collector; James the son of Alphaeus, and *Lebbaeus, whose surname was Thaddaeus*; Simon the Cananite, and Judas Iscariot, who also betrayed him.

Luke 6:13–16: And when it was day, he called his disciples to himself; and from them he chose twelve whom he also named apostles: Simon, whom he also named Peter, and Andrew his brother; James and John; Philip and Bartholomew; Matthew and Thomas; James the son of Alphaeus, and Simon called the Zealot; *Judas the son of James*, and Judas Iscariot who also became a traitor.

10. Matthew 10:10 and Mark 6:8 – Bring a staff or not?

Matthew 10:10: . . . nor bag for your journey, nor two tunics, nor sandals, *nor staffs*; for a worker is worthy of his food.

Mark 6:8: He commanded them to take nothing for the journey *except a staff*—no bag, no bread, no copper in their money belts . . .

11. Matthew 11:13–14, 17:11–13 and John 1:21 – John the Baptist was Elijah or not?

Matthew 11:13–14: For all the prophets and the law prophesied *until John*. And if you are willing to receive it, *he is Elijah who is to come*.

Matthew 17:11–13: Jesus answered and said to them, "Indeed, Elijah is coming first and will restore all things. But I say to you that *Elijah has come already*, and they did not know him but did to him whatever they wished. Likewise the Son of Man is also about to suffer at their hands." Then the disciples understood that *he spoke to them of John the Baptist*.

John 1:21: And they asked him (i.e., John the Baptist), "What then? Are you Elijah?" He said, "*I am not*."

12. **Matthew 12:39 (the sign of Jonah being the *only* sign) vs. Mark 8:12 (no sign to be given) vs. Luke 7:22 and 11:20 (holding up miracles to be signs) – which is it?**

Matthew 12:39: But he answered and said to them, "An evil and adulterous generation seeks after a sign, and no sign will be given to it *except the sign of the prophet Jonah.*"

Mark 8:12: But he sighed deeply in his spirit, and said, "Why does this generation seek a sign? Assuredly, I say to you, *no sign* shall be given to this generation."

Luke 7:22: Jesus answered and said to them, "Go and tell John the things you have seen and heard: that the blind see, the lame walk, the lepers are cleansed, the deaf hear, the dead are raised, the poor have the gospel preached to them."

Luke 11:20: But if I cast out demons with the finger of God, surely the kingdom of God has come upon you.

13. **Matthew 15:22 and Mark 7:26 – The woman was from Canaan or Greece?**

Matthew 15:22: And behold, a woman *of Canaan* came from that region and cried out to him, saying, "Have mercy on me, O Lord, Son of David! My daughter is severely demon-possessed."

Mark 7:26: The woman was *a Greek*, a Syro-Phoenician by birth, and she kept asking him to cast the demon out of her daughter.

14. **Matthew 20:29–30 and Mark 10:46–47 – One or two beggars?**

Matthew 20:29–30: Now as they went out of Jericho, a great multitude followed him. And behold, *two blind men* sitting by the road, when they heard that Jesus was passing by, cried out, saying, "Have mercy on us, O Lord, Son of David!"

Mark 10:46–47: As he went out of Jericho with his disciples and a great multitude, *blind Bartimaeus*, the son of Timaeus, sat by the road begging. And when he heard that it was Jesus of Nazareth, he began to cry out and say, "Jesus, Son of David, have mercy on me!"

15. **Matthew 21:1–2 and Mark 11:1–2 – A donkey present or not? Bring "him" (i.e., the colt) or "them" (i.e., the colt and the donkey)?**

Matthew 21:1–2: Now when they drew near Jerusalem, and came to Bethphage, at the Mount of Olives, then Jesus sent two disciples, saying to them, "Go into the village opposite you, and immediately you will find a *donkey* tied, and *a colt with her*. Loose *them* and bring *them* to me."

Mark 11:1–2: Now when they drew near Jerusalem, to Bethphage and Bethany, at the Mount of Olives, he sent two of his disciples; and he said to them, "Go into the village opposite you; and as soon as you have entered it you will find *a colt* tied, on which no one has sat. Loose *it* and bring *it*."

16. **Matthew 26:74–75 and Mark 14:72 – Before the cock crows once or twice?**

Matthew 26:74–75: Then he began to curse and swear, saying, "I do not know the Man!" *Immediately a rooster crowed.* And Peter remembered the word of Jesus who had said to him, "*Before the rooster crows, you will deny me three times.*" So he went out and wept bitterly.

Mark 14:72: *A second time the rooster crowed.* Then Peter called to mind the word that Jesus had said to him, "*Before the rooster crows twice, you will deny me three times.*" And when he thought about it, he wept.

17. Matthew 27:5 and Acts 1:18 – How did Judas die?

Matthew 27:5: Then he threw down the pieces of silver in the temple and departed, and went and *hanged himself.*

Acts 1:18: Now this man purchased a field with the wages of iniquity; and *falling headlong*, he burst open in the middle and all his entrails gushed out.

18. Matthew 27:11–14 (Jesus answered Pilate "It is as you say," and *not one word more*), vs. John 18:33–37 (Jesus and Pilate held a conversation).

Matthew 27:11–14: Now Jesus stood before the governor. And the governor asked him, saying, "Are you the King of the Jews?" Jesus said to him, "It is as you say." And while he was being accused by the chief priests and elders, *he answered nothing*. Then Pilate said to him, "Do you not hear how many things they testify against you?" But he answered him *not one word*, so that the governor marveled greatly.

John 18:33–37: Then Pilate entered the Praetorium again, called Jesus, and said to him, "Are you the King of the Jews?" Jesus answered him, "Are you

266

speaking for yourself about this, or did others tell you this concerning me?" Pilate answered, "Am I a Jew? Your own nation and the chief priests have delivered you to me. What have you done?" Jesus answered, "My kingdom is not of this world. If my kingdom were of this world, my servants would fight, so that I should not be delivered to the Jews; but now my kingdom is not from here." Pilate therefore said to him, "Are you a king then?" Jesus answered, "You say rightly that I am a king. For this cause I was born, and for this cause I have come into the world, that I should bear witness to the truth. Everyone who is of the truth hears my voice."

19. Matthew 27:28 (scarlet robe) vs. John 19:2 (purple robe)

Matthew 27:28: And they stripped him and put a *scarlet robe* on him.

John 19:2: And the soldiers twisted a crown of thorns and put it on his head, and they put on him a *purple robe*.

20. Matthew 27:34 and Mark 15:23 – Gall or myrrh in the wine? Tasted it or not?

Matthew 27:34: They gave him sour wine *mingled with gall* to drink. But when he had *tasted it*, he would not drink.

Mark 15:23: Then they gave him wine *mingled with myrrh* to drink, but he *did not take it*.

21. Mark 15:25 and John 19:14–15 – Jesus crucified before the third hour or after the sixth hour?

Mark 15:25: Now it was the *third hour*, and they crucified him.

John 19:14–15: Now it was the Preparation Day of the Passover, and *about the sixth hour*. And he said to the Jews, "Behold your King!" But they cried out, "Away with him, away with him! Crucify him!"

22. Luke 1:15, 1:41, 1:67, 2:25 and John 7:39 – the "Holy Ghost/Spirit" given or not?

Luke 1:15: He (John the Baptist) will also be *filled with the Holy Spirit*, even from his mother's womb.

Luke 1:41: And it happened, when Elizabeth heard the greeting of Mary, that the babe leaped in her womb; and Elizabeth was *filled with the Holy Spirit*.

Luke 1:67: Now his father Zacharias was *filled with the Holy Spirit* . . .

Luke 2:25: And behold, there was a man in Jerusalem whose name was Simeon, and this man was just and devout, waiting for the Consolation of Israel, and the *Holy Spirit was upon him*.

John 7:39: But this he spoke concerning the Spirit, whom those believing in him would receive; for the Holy Spirit was *not yet given*, because Jesus was not yet glorified.

23. Luke 2:10–14 and Luke 12:49–53 – a prophet announced by angels as heralding peace on earth, good will to men, or one who brings fire and division?

Luke 2:10–14: Then the angel said to them, "Do not be afraid, for behold, I bring you good tidings of great joy which will be to all people. For there is born to you this day in the city of David a Savior, who is Christ the Lord. And this will be the sign to you: you will find a babe wrapped in swaddling cloths, lying in a manger." And suddenly there was with the angel a multitude of the heavenly host praising God and saying: "Glory to God in the highest, and *on earth peace, goodwill toward men*!"

Luke 12:49–53: I (Jesus Christ) *came to send fire on the earth*, and how I wish it were already kindled! But I have a baptism to be baptized with, and how distressed I am till it is accomplished! *Do you suppose that I came to give peace on earth?* I tell you, *not at all*, but rather division. For from now on five in one house will be divided: three against two, and two against three. Father will be divided against son and son against father, mother against daughter and daughter against mother, mother-in-law against her daughter-in-law and daughter-in-law against her mother-in-law.

24. Luke 23:39–40 and Mark 15:31–32 – One thief defended Jesus or not?

Luke 23:39–40: Then one of the criminals who were hanged *blasphemed him*, saying, "If you are the Christ, save yourself and us." *But the other, answering, rebuked him*, saying, "Do you not even fear God, seeing you are under the same condemnation?"

Mark 15:31–32: Likewise the chief priests also, mocking among themselves with the scribes, said, "He saved others; himself he cannot save. Let the Christ, the King of Israel, descend now from the cross, that we may see and believe." *Even those who were crucified with him reviled him*.

269

25. Luke 14:26 and 1 John 3:15 – To hate one's brother or not?

Luke 14:26: If anyone comes to me (Jesus Christ) and *does not hate his* father and mother, wife and children, *brothers* and sisters, yes, and his own life also, he cannot be my disciple.

1 John 3:15: *Whoever hates his brother* is a murderer, and you know that no murderer has eternal life abiding in him.

26. Luke 23:26, Matthew 27:32, Mark 15:21 vs. John 19:17 – Who carried the cross, Simon or Jesus?

Luke 23:26: Now as they led him away, they laid hold of a certain man, *Simon a Cyrenian*, who was coming from the country, and on him they laid the cross that he might bear it after Jesus.

Matthew 27:32: Now as they came out, they found a *man of Cyrene, Simon by name*. Him they compelled to bear his (Jesus Christ's) cross.

Mark 15:21: Then they compelled a certain man, *Simon a Cyrenian*, the father of Alexander and Rufus, as he was coming out of the country and passing by, to bear his (Jesus Christ's) cross.

John 19:17: And *he (Jesus Christ), bearing his cross*, went out to a place called the Place of a Skull, which is called in Hebrew, Golgotha . . .

27. Luke 23:43 and John 20:17 – Ascended or not?

Luke 23:43: And Jesus said to him, "Assuredly, I say to you, *today* you will be with me in Paradise."

(Stated to one of the other two crucified on the evening of his own crucifixion, predicting ascension *that very same day*)

John 20:17: Jesus said to her, "Do not cling to me, *for I have not yet ascended* to my Father." (Stated to Mary Magdalene *two days* after the crucifixion)

28. **Luke 23:46 vs. John 19:30 – Were the last words of Jesus "Father, into Your hands I commit my spirit" or were they "It is finished"?**

Luke 23:46: And when Jesus had cried out with a loud voice, he said, "Father, *'into Your hands I commit my spirit.'"* Having said this, he breathed his last.

John 19:30: So when Jesus had received the sour wine, he said, *"It is finished!"* And bowing his head, he gave up his spirit.

29. **John 1:18, 1 John 4:12, 1 Timothy 6:16 (God *cannot be seen*) vs. Genesis 12:7, 17:1, 18:1, 26:2, 32:30; Exodus 3:16, 6:2–3, 24:9, 33:11, 33:23, Numbers 14:14, Amos 9:1 (God *seen*).**

For example, John 1:18 and 1 John 4:12 both read: No one has seen God at *any* time.

Genesis 12:7: Then the Lord *appeared to Abram* and said . . .

Genesis 32:30: So Jacob called the name of the place Peniel: "For I have *seen God face to face*, and my life is preserved."

Exodus 6:2–3: And God spoke to Moses and said to him: "I am the LORD. *I appeared* to Abraham, to Isaac, and to Jacob, *as God Almighty*, but by My name

271

LORD. . .

30. John 5:31 and John 8:14 – Was Jesus' record true or not?

John 5:31: If I (Jesus) bear witness of myself, my witness *is not* true.

John 8:14: Jesus answered and said to them, "Even if I bear witness of myself, my witness *is* true, for I know where I came from and where I am going . . ."

31. Acts 9:7 and Acts 22:9 – Fellow travelers heard a voice or not?

Acts 9:7: And the men who journeyed with him stood speechless, *hearing a voice* but seeing no one.

Acts 22:9: And those who were with me indeed saw the light and were afraid, but they *did not hear the voice* of him who spoke to me.

32. Acts 9:7 and Acts 26:14 – Paul's companions fell to the ground or remained standing?

Acts 9:7: And the men who journeyed with him *stood speechless*, hearing a voice but seeing no one.

Acts 26:14: And when *we all had fallen to the ground*, I heard a voice speaking to me and saying in the Hebrew language, "Saul, Saul, why are you persecuting me? It is hard for you to kick against the goads."[278(EN)]

33. Matthew 1:6–16 and Luke 3:23–31—twenty-six or forty-one generations in the lineage between David and Joseph?

These two lineages simply don't gibe. No two

names correspond *in sequence* except for the last, Joseph, who by no stretch of the imagination was the true father of Jesus. Furthermore, God's name is left out, which is significant. After all, if Jesus were the "Son of God," would God have left His name out of the lineage, not once but twice?

The mismatch in the list of names is as follows (from the New King James Version):

MATTHEW 1:6-16		**LUKE 3:23-31**
	DAVID	DAVID
1)	SOLOMON	NATHAN
2)	REHOBOAM	MATTATHAH
3)	ABIJAH	MENAN
4)	ASA	MELEA
5)	JEHOSHAPHAT	ELIAKIM
6)	JORAM	JONAN
7)	UZZIAH	JOSEPH
8)	JOTHAM	JUDAH
9)	AHAZ	SIMEON
10)	HEZEKIAH	LEVI
11)	MANASSEH	MATTHAT
12)	AMON	JORIM
13)	JOSIAH	ELIEZER
14)	JECHONIAH	JOSE
15)	SHEALTIEL	ER
16)	ZERUBBABEL	ELMODAM
17)	ABIUD	COSAM
18)	ELIAKIM	ADDI
19)	AZOR	MELCHI
20)	ZADOK	NERI
21)	ACHIM	SHEALTIEL

22)	ELIUD	ZERUBBABEL
23)	ELEAZAR	RHESA
24)	MATTHAN	JOANNAS
25)	JACOB	JUDAH
26)	JOSEPH (husband to Mary)	JOSEPH (no relation to Mary)
27)		SEMEI
28)		MATTATHIAH
29)		MAATH
30)		NAGGAI
31)		ESLI
32)		NAHUM
33)		AMOS
34)		MATTATHIAH
35)		JOSEPH (no relation to Mary)
36)		JANNA
37)		MELCHI
38)		LEVI
39)		MATTHAT
40)		HELI
41)		JOSEPH(husband to Mary)

Christian apologists defend this imbalance with the claim that one lineage is that of Jesus through his mother, and the other is that of Jesus through his mother's husband, Joseph. However, many consider this defense just one more of the unacceptable "believe what I say, not what you see with your own two eyes" claims, for the Bible clearly defines each lineage as the bloodline through the Virgin Mary's husband, Joseph.

4—Inconsistencies Within the New Testament: Part 2

The best, when corrupted, becomes the worst.

—Latin Proverb (*Corruptiooptimipessima*)[279]

Despite all the evidence to the contrary, many Christians believe that the New Testament is the unadulterated word of God. Even Paul refuted this claim in 1 Corinthians 7:12: "But to the rest I, not the Lord, say . . ."—indicating that what follows was from him, and not from God. So if nothing else, this section of the Bible, by Paul's own admission, is not the word of God. 1 Corinthians 1:16 points out that Paul could not remember if he baptized anybody other than Crispus, Gaius, and the household of Stephanas: "Besides, I do not know whether I baptized any other." Now, does this sound like God talking? Would God say, "Paul baptized Crispus, Gaius, and the household of Stephanas, and there may have been others. But that was a long time ago, and, well, you know, so much has happened since then. It's all kind of fuzzy to Me right now"?

1 Corinthians 7:25–26 records Paul as having written, "Now concerning virgins: I have no commandment from the Lord; yet I give judgment as one whom the Lord in His mercy has made trustworthy. *I suppose* therefore that this is good because of the present distress . . ." (italics mine). 2 Corinthians

11:17 reads, "What I speak, I speak not according to the Lord, but as it were, foolishly . . ." Again, does anybody believe that God talks like this? Paul admitted that he answered without guidance from God and without divine authority, and that he personally believed himself to be divinely trustworthy in one case but speaking foolishly in the other. Paul justified his presumption of authority with the words, "according to my judgment—and I think I also have the Spirit of God" (1 Corinthians 7:40). The problem is that a whole lot of people have claimed the "Spirit of God," while all the time doing some very strange and ungodly things. So should Paul's confidence be admired or condemned? However we answer this question, the point is that whereas human confidence wavers at times, such is not the case with the all-knowing, all-powerful Creator. God would never say, "I suppose . . ." as Paul does.

Whereas one man may have assumed "perfect understanding of all things," lifted pen and authored a gospel because "it seemed good to me" (Luke 1:3), lots of people have written on religion assuming "perfect understanding" and because it seemed good to them. But such lofty sentiments do not a scripture make.

The fallback position of the Bible defendant is to assert that the New Testament is not the literal word of God, but the *inspired* word of God. Such an assertion takes support from 2 Timothy 3:16, which states the obvious: "All scripture is given by inspiration of God . . ." That is not to say that something becomes scripture just by naming it as such. Just because an ecumenical council canonized four gospels, to the exclusion (and destruction) of the other thousand or so gospels, that does not make any one of them scripture. The proof is not in the opinion of men, even if unanimous, but in the divinity of origin, as indicated by the internal and external evidence. Those books which fail the tests of divine origin and/or inspiration can be assumed to either have been impure from the outset, or corrupted. It is simply not in God's perfect nature to reveal or to inspire errors.

Isaiah 40:8 helps to define one measure by which authenticity of revelation may be determined: "The grass withers, the flower fades, but the word of our God stands forever." We need not question the source of Isaiah 40:8, for the truth of the statement is self-evident, timeless and undeniable—the word (that is, the teachings) of God *does* stand forever. The point, however, is that not all *books* "stand forever," as is obvious from the lengthy list of corruptions in the previous chapter. And if "the word of our God stands forever" means it doesn't get lost, where is the original gospel of Jesus, if not lost? There is not a true biblical scholar alive who would dispute the fact that not even a single page of the original gospel of Jesus is known to exist. Scholars aside, we can realize this conclusion on our own by recognizing that Jesus spoke Aramaic, not Greek.[280],[281] The oldest known manuscripts canonized as "gospel truth" date from the fourth century CE, and are predominantly written in a language Jesus never spoke—*Koiné* Greek!

Largely written by unknown authors, with unknown motivations and peppered with easily identifiable and ungodly mistakes, the void left by the loss of the original gospel of Jesus is readily apparent and poorly compensated.

The mistakes and inconsistencies encountered in even the oldest surviving manuscripts are so numerous as to have prompted C. J. Cadoux, professor of church history at Oxford, to write,

In the four Gospels, therefore, the main documents to which we must go if we are to fill-out at all that bare sketch which we can put together from other sources, we find material of widely differing quality as regards credibility. So far-reaching is the element of uncertainty that it is tempting to "down tools" at the outset, and to declare the task hopeless. The historical inconsistencies and improbabilities in parts of the Gospels form some of the arguments advanced in favor of the Christ-myth theory. These are, however, entirely outweighed—as we have shown—by other considerations. Still, the discrepancies and uncertainties that remain are serious—and consequently many moderns, who have no doubt whatever of Jesus' real existence, regard as hopeless any attempt to dissolve out the historically-true from the legendary or mythical matter which the Gospels contain, and to reconstruct the story of Jesus' mission out of the more historical residue.[282]

Cadoux is not alone in his opinion. Any serious seeker quickly recognizes the frustration that exists among Christian theologians, largely owing to the lack of original scripture, identifiable authors, and definitive guidance.

For example, in the words of Robert W. Funk, the

founding scholar of the *Jesus Seminar*,

> To add to the problem, no two copies of
> any of the books of the New Testament
> are exactly alike, since they were all
> handmade. It has been estimated that
> there are over seventy thousand
> meaningful variants in the Greek
> manuscripts of the New Testament itself.
> That mountain of variants has been
> reduced to a manageable number by
> modern critical editions that sort,
> evaluate, and choose among the myriad of
> possibilities. The critical editions of the
> Greek New Testament used by scholars
> are in fact the creations of textual critics
> and editors. They are not identical with
> any surviving ancient manuscript. They
> are a composite of many variant
> versions.[283]

Professor Dummelow of Cambridge attributes the lack of ethics in scriptural recordkeeping to how so many variants of the text came into being:

> A copyist would sometimes put in not
> what was in the text, but what he thought
> ought to be in it. He would trust a fickle
> memory, or he would even make the text
> accord with the views of the school to
> which he belonged. Besides this, an

enormous number of copies are preserved. In addition to the versions and quotations from the early Christian Fathers, nearly four thousand Greek MSS [manuscripts][284(EN)] of the New Testament are known to exist. As a result the variety of readings is considerable.[285]

Lest the above be taken as personal opinion, this quote is taken from a work derived from the combined scholarship of forty-two Christian scholars of international repute. We might fairly question why such a group of distinguished scholars would criticize their own book of guidance, if not out of dedication to truth.

Other noted scholars offer their explanations for the widely varying biblical texts:

The speeches in the Fourth Gospel (even apart from the early messianic claim) are so different from those in the Synoptics, and so like the comments of the Fourth Evangelist himself, that both cannot be equally reliable as records of what Jesus said: Literary veracity in ancient times did not forbid, as it does now, the assignment of fictitious speeches to historical characters: the best ancient historians made a practice of composing and assigning such speeches in this way.[286]

Rev. J.R. Findlay notes: "None of the evangelic writings thus produced, not even those now in the New Testament, claimed on their appearance to have canonical authority; all alike were the offspring of the desire to present what was known or believed about Christ with the aim of satisfying the religious needs of the communities for which they were severally written."[287]

Findlay's remarks on the apocryphal gospels could equally apply to the canonical gospels:

> The desire would naturally arise for a presentation of the evangelic facts which would be in harmony with prevailing thought and feeling. If this desire was to be satisfied, some manipulation of the generally accepted tradition was necessary, but that did not seem a serious matter in an age which had little conscience for the obligation of depicting things as they actually were. Thus Gospels were produced which clearly reflected the conceptions of the practical needs of the community for which they were written. In them the traditional material was used, but there was no hesitation in altering it or in making additions to it or in leaving out what did not suit the writer's purpose.[288]

Or, in plain language, "For the early Christians who passed along the stories we now have in the Gospels, it was sometimes legitimate and necessary to change a historical fact in order to make a theological point."[289]

The fact that gospel authors modified the text to suit their purpose is so well known among scholars, it has spawned a particular methodology of gospel analysis known as redaction criticism. The work of redaction critics is to guess each author's intentions, theological stance, and evangelical purpose through analysis of the gospel form and editorial modifications—including insertions, deletions, reinterpretations, and rearrangements—made to the sources from which each gospel was derived.[290]

Whether we agree with the argument that the New Testament is an unreliable source of truth, the silence of church authorities in the face of such criticism can be assumed to imply assent. But whatever the reason for the vast variability of the scriptural accounts, the fact remains that they *do* differ, and the lack of uniformity remains a malignant difficulty which grossly disfigures the claim of inerrancy.

With all the inconsistencies, we have to wonder why conflicting books were canonized together. The simple answer is that these are the Christian writings which best served the purpose of the early church.

And isn't that a scary thought?

But it does lead to the question of how the canon of the New Testament was derived, so let us turn to that subject next.

5—Problems with the New Testament Canon

I raped history, but at least I gave her children.
—Alexandre Dumas[291]

According to *Harper's Bible Dictionary*, "The NT canon also has an uneven and complex history. . . . no canonical lists appear before around AD 150 . . ."[292] John Reumann, in his *Variety and Unity in New Testament Thought*, comments, "The canon as a collection becomes more problematical when one sees how varied are the writings that have been included (and how some of those left out are by no means intrinsically inferior in style or later in date) or how opinions differed over some of these writings in the patristic centuries."[293]

Graham Stanton adds, "The early church retained four gospels in spite of regular embarrassment over the differences . . ."[294]

Nonetheless, the *New Catholic Encyclopedia* claims, "All the books in the canon are inspired, but it is debated whether or not there is or could be any inspired book that, because of its loss, is not in the canon. The Church has not settled the question. The more general opinion is that some inspired books probably have been lost."[295]

Why this lurking suspicion that some of the books have been lost? Biblical evidence—1 Cor 5:9 and 2 Cor 2:3–9; 7:8–12 describe two of Paul's letters that have vanished.[296] Paul also speaks of the "epistle from Laodicea" in Col 4:16—where is that? Furthermore, between 1 Chronicles 29:29, 2 Chronicles 9:29, and 2 Chronicles 12:15, a total of six lost books are disclosed in the Old Testament.[297] So material most certainly has been lost. How much has been inappropriately *added* is yet another disputed issue.

Aside from those books which were lost, five (2 Peter, 2 John, 3 John, James, and Jude) suffered reversals in acceptance because of their doubtful attribution. In addition, canonicity was claimed for other books that have since sunk into the obscurity of the Apocrypha, and the legitimacy of Hebrews and Apocalypse has remained a subject of debate to this day.[298] Even following the "final stabilization" of the Bible in the fifth century, the above five books, as well as Hebrews and Apocalypse, remained controversial.[299] This controversy proved so problematic that an end was sought. Consequently, after well over a thousand years of indecision and debate, dogmatic definition of the biblical canon was laid down at the Council of Trent on April 8, 1564, in the decree, *De CanonicisScripturis.*[300]

Now, to be fair, we find mention of the twenty-seven books of our New Testament as early as 367 CE, in an annual pastoral letter penned by Athanasius, bishop of Alexandria. In this letter, Athanasius defined these twenty-seven books, and these books only, as scripture.[301] Unfortunately, neither Athanasius nor anyone else succeeded in establishing a universally accepted canon. The Syrian church excluded five books from its twenty-two-book New Testament canon, whereas the Ethiopian church added four more, for a total of thirty-one.[302] Factoring in the Old Testament books, the traditional Catholic Bible (Douay-Rheims) as well as more modern translations—the New American Bible and Revised Standard Version (Catholic Edition)—lists seventy-three books, seven more than the

Protestant Bible and seven less than the Orthodox version. So to this day, the world of Christianity remains divided over what constitutes the New Testament.

Nonetheless, we focus our discussion on the Catholic Church for reason of its prominence in history, and return to the Council of Trent, the year 1564, and the cementing of New Testament canon. We might wonder on what authority such canonization was made, almost sixteen centuries following the ministry of Jesus. The Catholic Church takes the stand that "The decree of Trent, repeated by Vatican I on April 24, 1870, is the infallible decision of the magisterium. In the decree, certain doubtfully authentic deuterocanonical sections are also included with the books (*cum omnibus suispartibus*): Mk 16.9–20; Lk 22.19b–20, 43–44; and Jn 7.53–8.11."[303]

Of note are the back-to-back claims of magisterial infallibility and doubtful authenticity, which suggests that claims to infallibility are little more than papal propaganda.

This is, after all, the same church that posthumously anathematized Pope Honorius I at the Third Council of Constantinople (the Sixth Ecumenical Council) in 680 CE. Now, Pope Honorius ruled the Vatican for thirteen years (625–638 CE), and was sanctioned by the synod of Constantinople in the year of his death as "truly agreeing with the apostolic preaching."[304] Yet forty-four years later, the same church that had previously sanctioned Honorius declared him anathema because he "did not, as became the apostolic authority, extinguish the flame of heretical teaching in its first beginning, but fostered it by his negligence," and "allowed the immaculate rule of apostolic tradition, which he received from his predecessors, to be tarnished."[305]

Whoa, Nelly. Now which one is it? Did Pope Honorius

"truly [agree] with the apostolic preaching," or did he tarnish the apostolic tradition?

In 682 Pope St. Leo II, with the support of The Trullan Synod as well as the seventh and eighth ecumenical councils, formalized the Sixth Ecumenical Council's condemnation.[306],[307],[308] So here we have two opposing popes, and we have to wonder which one of them, if either, were infallible. *Someone* has to be wrong—either Pope Honorius deserved to be anathematized according to the rules of the church, or Pope St. Leo II anathematized an innocent man. So someone has to be wrong, but according to the doctrine of papal infallibility, the church wants us to believe both were right!

Skimming the chronicles of papal history, similar accounts raise more than a few speculatively arched eyebrows. Pope Pius IX defined the doctrine of papal infallibility at the First Vatican Council, which convened from 1869 to 1870. So in other words, the doctrine evaded recognition for over fifteen centuries. This delay in recognition is understandable, however, given the history of the papacy. The seventh century witnessed the colorful intrigue surrounding Pope Honorius I, as described above. The tenth century introduced John XII, whose crimes against humanity and religion were of such breadth, depth, and depravity as to have prompted one author to declare him a Christian Caligula, adding,

> The charge was specifically made against
> him that he turned the Lateran into a
> brothel; that he and his gang violated
> female pilgrims in the very basilica of
> St. Peter; that the offerings of the humble
> laid upon the altar were snatched up as

casual booty. He was inordinately fond of gambling, at which he invoked the names of those discredited gods now universally regarded as demons. His sexual hunger was insatiable—a minor crime in Roman eyes. What was far worse was that the casual occupants of his bed were rewarded not with casual gifts of gold but of land. One of his mistresses was able to establish herself as a feudal lord "for he was so blindly in love with her that he made her governor of cities—and even gave to her the golden crosses and cups of St. Peter himself."[309]

Benedict IX assumed the chair of St. Peter in 1032, only to sell the papacy to his godfather, Giovanni Gratiano, for the impressive sum of 1,500 pounds of gold.[310] Similar debacles surfaced with subsequent popes, such as when the chair of St. Peter became uncomfortably overloaded by the fifteenth-century trinity of popes Benedict XIII, Gregory XII and John XXIII[311(EN)] (himself an ex-pirate, as if the situation demanded even more intrigue), all occupying the office of the papacy at the same time.[312]

Perhaps the most noteworthy peculiarity is that of the thirteenth-century Pope Celestine V, about whom the *New Catholic Encyclopedia* notes, "Celestine's reign was marked by an unfortunate subservience to Charles II and by administrative incompetence. . . . Realizing his incompetence, Celestine issued a constitution (December 10) declaring a pope's right to resign, and on December 13 freely resigned."[313] A more interesting twist to the tale would be hard to find—a pope who recognized his own incompetence and resigned! The Catholics claim a pope can't do anything wrong, but Celestine, so it would seem, couldn't do anything right. Infallible but incompetent—a truly peculiar proposition.

More recently, in 1962 Pope John XXIII convened the Vatican II Council, which ultimately issued the *Nostra Aetate*, proclaimed by his successor Pope Paul VI on October 28, 1965. The *Nostra Aetate* is a document that exonerated the Jews of the alleged crime of having crucified Jesus Christ. Not only that, but the document asserts that "Indeed, the Church believes that by His cross Christ, Our Peace, reconciled Jews and Gentiles, making both one in Himself."[314] A collective "Now, wait a minute" was voiced around the world, and has echoed through the canyons of Christian consciousness ever since.

Whether Jesus Christ ever was in fact crucified holds no relevance to this subject. What *is* relevant is the observation that a view held and supported by every pope since the inception of the Roman Catholic Church was opposed by one pope and his council in the twentieth century, and then endorsed by all who followed. So, were all preceding popes wrong not to have recognized the proposed innocence of the Jews, or did Pope John XXIII, Pope Paul VI, and Popes John Paul I and II all endorse politically correct ideologies from the dark side of reality?

The Jews, most certainly, rejoice in their exoneration, for the practical implication is an end to nearly two millennia of Catholic-sanctioned anti-Semitism. Pope John Paul II called for the church to do *tshuva* (Hebrew for repentance) for its protracted history of anti-Semitism, and for all Catholics to henceforth refrain from harassment and discrimination against the Jews on the basis of their being wrongly considered accursed and condemned for two millennia. However, just as the other "infallible" popes of history clearly did not agree, neither do all members of the present day orthodoxy, for,

> During the Vatican Council debate on the declaration dealing with the Jews, the Holy Synod of the Coptic Orthodox Church communicated to Rome its forthright understanding that "the Holy Bible gives a clear testimony that Jews have crucified Lord Jesus Christ and bore the responsibility of His Crucifixion." The communication recalled that "the Jews repeatedly said to Pontius Pilate: 'Crucify him, crucify him (Luke 23:21).' 'His blood be on us and our children (Matthew 27:25).'" The Coptic Orthodox Church then provided documentation for the view that the Jews stand "condemned" according to the New Testament. "Said St. Peter the Apostle: 'but ye denied the Holy One and the Just and desired a murderer (Barabbas) to be granted unto you; and killed the Prince of Life (Acts 3:14–15).'" Furthermore, the condemnation rests upon all Jews in their collective existence whether in ancient days or in this time. "This condemnation does not include a specific group and not others; for St. Peter addressed the Jews

'of every nation under Heaven (Acts 2).'"[315]

But is any of this mind-changing and prevarication so surprising? After all, Christians are asked to believe that Jesus' pious companions and followers couldn't agree upon the canon of Christian scripture a month, a year, or two years following the ministry of Jesus, but somehow some extraordinarily enlightened clergy distilled the truth of Christology from the scriptures fifteen centuries later.

Perhaps we should be concerned over trusting the progressive clergy who ushered so many religious innovations down the aisles of traditional worship. Innovations such as the cross, the crucifix, paintings, religious icons, and stained-glass depictions of Jesus and the saints. Of course, many Christians love these innovations and defend them on the basis of their inspiring and evocative nature, and because they serve as religious reminders. That may be so. But what human judgment outweighs the commandments of God on the scales of opinion? What "person of God" would ever say, "Well, yeah, God forbids it, but I think it's okay"? The supreme arrogance is to believe that somehow God failed to consider all the angles, and we as human beings have the right to veto His decree based upon our own caprice.

For example, the most familiar symbols of Christianity are the cross and the crucifix. A person might assume that wearing, display, and reverence of these items dates from the time of Jesus.

Nothing could be further from the truth.

In fact, adoption of the cross and crucifix into Christian worship was innovated centuries after the ministry of Jesus.

Representation of the bare cross came first, during the period of Constantine in the fourth century.[316] The earliest crucifixion scenes date from the fifth century, while the image of Christ crucified on the cross date from the sixth century; not until the thirteenth century did the crucifix appear on the altar table.[317] The *New Catholic Encyclopedia* comments, "The representation of Christ's redemptive death on Golgotha does not occur in the symbolic art of the first Christian centuries. The early Christians, influenced by the Old Testament prohibition of graven images, were reluctant to depict even the instrument of the Lord's Passion."[318]

Rarely are two sentences so rich in information. To learn that Christians of the first centuries honored Old Testament prohibitions makes one wonder what happened between then and now. Early Christians avoided graven images out of respect for God's laws. Only when softened up by four hundred years of "progressive" attitudes did artists begin to challenge the boundaries of their religion.

Further innovations such as the commissioning of statues, paintings, frescoes, and stained glass windows subsequently became commonplace. These being the fruits of those who claimed to follow in the name of Jesus—turning Jesus the iconoclast into Jesus the icon—the religious purist can hardly be blamed for pointing out the differences between the teachings of Jesus and the practice of Christianity. Some applaud the movement away from harsh and restrictive Old Testament laws. Others shudder over the ramifications of following a path other than that which God prescribes.

Men and women of God will seek scriptural clarification to secure their beliefs. Men and women of institutions will seek the reassurances of clergy, which by this point should be considered suspect, if not unreliable. Or, dare we say, completely corrupt?

6—Old Testament Meets New Testament Meets Holy Qur'an

It is as dangerous to believe too much as to believe too little.

—Denis Diderot[319]

Despite Old and New Testament corruptions, despite all the additions, omissions and alterations, despite the forgery of entire books and the doctrinally motivated modifications of pre-existing texts, despite the fact that the authors of the New Testament gospels and half of Paul's letters are anonymous, despite not knowing who wrote what, and precisely when, where or why, the argument can nonetheless be made that the word of God is still to be found in the Bible. *This* may be true! The problem is, a lot of questionable teachings are encountered as well. How, then, do we distinguish the word of God from the word of man?

Some claim we can, others claim we can't—only God can.

And this is one explanation for the growing interest in the Islamic religion within Western nations—so much so, Islam is today the fastest-growing religion in the world.[320]

The Islamic proposal is that those whose hearts and minds are open to evidence will recognize both the Godly *and* the human elements of the Bible. The Godly elements serve as a scriptural skeleton of laws, morals, and codes of conduct while the human elements drive the sincere to search for God's final revelation. Muslims propose the Holy Qur'an as the final revelation that fills out the framework of truths scattered throughout the Old and New Testaments.

As the translation of the Holy Qur'an reads, "It is He Who sent down to you (step by step), in truth, the Book, confirming what went before it; and He sent down the Law (of Moses) and the Gospel (of Jesus) before this, as a guide to humankind, and He sent down the Criterion (of judgment between right and wrong)" (TMQ 3:3).

Many infer from the above passage that the Qur'an endorses the Jewish and Christian bibles (the Old and New Testaments) as scripture. Not true. The Qur'an teaches that God did indeed send down the Law (of Moses) and the Gospel (of Jesus) and that, to this day, some of that truth remains within the books of the Christians and Jews. However, just where the Law (of Moses), the Gospel (of Jesus), and the truths therein are to be found—in which passages, and whether in books of the Bible, the Apocrypha, or elsewhere—the Qur'an does not specify.

Perspective is an issue here. We might read "the Law (of Moses) and the Gospel (of Jesus)" and reflexively equate this reference to the Old and New Testaments. However, the preceding analysis should convince even the most committed devotee that wherever the scriptures of Moses and Jesus are, they are not preserved in the Bible in the unadulterated purity in which they were revealed. Hence the need for a final revelation to confirm the truth of "what went before," to refute the scriptural corruptions of men, and to function as a "criterion (of judgment between right and wrong)." Hence, also, the need for a revelation bearing the welcome announcement,

O People of the Book! There has come to

you Our Messenger, revealing to you
much that you used to hide in the Book,
and passing over much (that is now
unnecessary): There has come to you
from Allah a (new) light and a
perspicuous Book, wherewith Allah
guides all who seek His good pleasure to
ways of peace and safety, and leads them
out of darkness, by His Will, unto the
light—guides them to a Path that is
Straight (TMQ 5:15–16).

The unfortunate corruption of Old and New Testaments
has hampered our ability to distinguish true revelation from
man-made insertions. Some scriptural misunderstandings are of
a relatively minor nature, others catastrophic. For example,
"born-again" Christians believe, as recorded in the King James
Version, "Unless one is born again, he cannot see the kingdom
of God" (John 3:3), and "You must be born again" (John 3:7).
This modern sect depends upon an ideology which hinges on the
phrase "bornagain"—a phrase that is, in fact, a mistranslation of
the Greek *gennaoanothen*, which means "generated" or
"begotten" from above.[321] According to the true translation,
*all*humankind is *gennaoanothen*, whether we want it or not, for
where is the person who is "generated from below"? Some
modern bibles are more faithful to the true translation, others are
not, and we can only imagine the soul-sucking pressures that led
to changing two words in order to sell a few more million
copies. For example, the New International Version goes
halfway and translates *gennaoanothen* as "born from above."
Consequently, there are literally millions of souls who have

departed this worldly life with their hopes for salvation pinned on a key phrase, which in fact is nonexistent in the meaning of the Greek.

A plethora of such misunderstandings have blossomed from the fertile field of the last twelve verses of the Gospel of Mark, as previously discussed. One author writes, "How did Mark end his Gospel? Unfortunately, we do not know; the most that can be said is that four different endings are current among the manuscripts but probably none of them represents what Mark originally intended."[322]

That's "the most that can be said"?

Hardly.

These last twelve verses (Mark 16:9–20) have long been in dispute, and for good reason. The two most ancient manuscripts (Vatican MS. No. 1209 and the SinaiticSyriac Codex) end at Mark 16:8. Mark 16:9–20 is not found in any known papyri prior to the sixth century CE, and even then, in a Syriac version of 616 CE, these twelve verses exist only as a marginal note (as can be confirmed in the marginal references of Nestle, *NovumTestamentumGraece*). To Clement of Alexandria and Origen, these verses didn't exist.[323] Eusebius and Jerome testify that this ending to Mark was not to be found in virtually any of the Greek manuscripts of which they were aware.[324] Professor Metzger elaborates, "Not a few manuscripts that contain the passage have scribal notes stating that older Greek copies lack it, and in other witnesses the passage is marked with asterisks or obeli, the conventional signs used by copyists to indicate a spurious addition to a document. . . . It is obvious that the expanded form of the long ending has no claim to be original . . . It probably is the work of a second or third century scribe . . ."[325]

As the 1977 RSV acknowledges in a footnote to Mark 16:8, "Some of the most ancient authorities bring the book to a close at the end of verse 8."[326] *TheInterpreter's Bible* comments, "Attempts have been made to recover the 'lost ending' of Mark in the remaining sections of Matthew or Luke, or even John or Acts; but none of these has been generally approved, and it is doubtful if Luke's and Matthew's copies of Mark went beyond 16:8. The problem is a fascinating one for research; but it is probably insoluble at present."[327]

Hope is offered that "further discoveries of early MSS [manuscripts] may help toward a solution."[328] In the meantime debate rages, and these verses, though most likely penned by the second-century presbyter Ariston,[329] are retained by the Catholic Vulgate and many Protestant bibles. Consequently, those who trust their bibles to convey only "gospel truth" continue to accept the teachings these verses convey. What's the harm? Just this—these last twelve verses of "Mark" support evangelism, baptism, exorcism, speaking in tongues, and testing faith by handling rattlesnakes. More than half the fatalities by rattlesnake bite in the United States are purportedly from snake-handling cults, not because more people are bitten, but because they consider it an act of faith to neither report nor treat the bites.

Should modern bibles honor the most ancient textual sources and eliminate Mark 16:9–20, Jehovah's Witnesses would be one step closer to sleeping late Saturday mornings (as would their unfortunate neighbors), Pentecostals could untie their twisted tongues for noble and intelligible speech, and all Christians would have one less reason to agonize over the fate of the unbaptized deceased.

So all in all, what do we have? We have an inerrant Creator and a very, very, *very* errant Old and New Testament.

How do we rectify these two? Either by closing our eyes to the textual deficiencies, or by acknowledging these deficiencies and trying to make sense of them. And at this, Jewish and Christian apologetics have failed miserably.

Enter the Muslim point of view.

Muslims assert that whenever the recorded "word of God" was corrupted by the hand of man, God, in His mercy, renewed His message through a new, clarifying revelation. In this manner the Old Testament, once corrupted, was replaced by the New Testament, and the New Testament by the Holy Qur'an. Muslims contend that throughout this repeating cycle of divine revelation–human corruption–clarifying revelation, the one constant Allah did not permit to be lost in the muddle was His message of divine unity. This creed is the keystone of true faith, and as such, Allah preserved His creed throughout time and throughout revelation. And if this present book has not proven any other point, it has shown that whether we speak of divine unity in the commandments of the Old Testament, in the teachings of Jesus Christ, or in the message of the Holy Qur'an, we speak of the same eternal creed: God is One, without partner or co-sharer in divinity.

Let us remember that each doctrinal element of Trinitarian creed is either based on non-biblical evidence, or on the manipulation and/or misunderstanding of ambiguous, questionable or isolated New Testament verses. In every case these verses lack support from the other books or epistles, as discussed above, and in some cases are flatly contradicted by the recorded teachings of Jesus.

Now, we can reasonably expect God would not hide the most critical elements of true belief, since the point of revelation is to *reveal*. After all, as most teachers know, the bulk of teaching is repetition. Hence, the ingredients of true faith can be expected to have been conveyed in clear and unambiguous terms, over and over again. With regard to the Bible, this is precisely the case. The most repeated, consistent, and verifiable teachings of the Old and New Testaments convey the oneness of God and the mandate to obey Him, which incidentally includes the directive to accept the final messenger and revelation.

Now, many well-read Christians will be quick to point out that the Bible ends with a strong warning in the book of Revelation. Never mind that "Hebrews was for long under suspicion in the West, and Revelation was usually excluded in the fourth and fifth centuries where the school of Antioch held sway."[330] No, never mind that, but just consider this: the last verses of the Bible (Revelation 22:18–19) warn against anyone adding or taking away from "this book"—a warning that should prompt the question, "Umm, which book?" The Bible is a collection of books. That's how it got the name—from the Latin *biblia*, literally meaning "the books." Hence "bibliography" for a list of books, "bibliophile" for a lover of books, the French *biblioteque* for "library"—the list goes on and on. As F. F. Arbuthnot notes,

> Another short journey takes us back to the fourteenth century, when people began to say "The Bible." The simple fact that we call this collection of books "The Bible," as if it were one book and not a collection of books, is a very important fact—a fact that has been fruitful of misunderstanding. We naturally think of one book as having one author, or one

directing genius. . . .

Prior to the fourteenth century it was
not called "The Bible." It was not thought
of as one book. In Greek it was not *Ton
Biblion,* but *Ta Biblia*—the books. And
prior to the fifth century these were not
called books at all, but writings—Hebrew
and Christian writings.[331]

We should also note that the books of the Bible are *not*
compiled in chronological order. The book of Revelation was
not the last book written. However, strategic placement at the
end of the Bible gives this false impression. In fact, James, the
First, Second, and Third Epistles of John, the Gospel of John,
Jude, First and Second Timothy, Titus, and 2 Peter are all
thought to have been written between five to sixty-five years
after the book of Revelation.[332] A difference of five seconds,
much less five to sixty-five years, would violate the "thou shalt
not add to" clause, *if* the above verses of Revelation were meant
to apply to the Bible as a whole. But they do not, and cannot.

The oldest known New Testament manuscript, the
fourth-century *Codex Sinaiticus,* contains both The Shepherd of
Hermas and the Epistle of Barnabas—two books which were
recognized by many early Christians as books of the New
Testament.[333] However, these two books subsequently were
removed and placed in the Apocrypha. The Protestant Bible
eliminated seven more books, as well as portions of others, to
include Esdras I and II, Tobit, Judith, the additions to the book
of Esther, the Wisdom of Solomon, Ecclesiasticus, Baruch, the
Letter of Jeremiah, the Prayer of Azariah and the Song of the

Three Young Men, Susanna, Bel and the Dragon, the Prayer of Manasseh, Maccabees I and II. These omissions would violate the "thou shalt not take away" clause in each and every instance, had the teachings of Revelation applied to the Bible as a whole.

Hence, the "book" the last line of Revelation refers to can be none other than itself, the *book* of Revelation, and the book of Revelation alone. Otherwise, the principal violators of the warning regarding deletions and insertions are the Christian clergy themselves, for quite a lot has both been added to and removed from the *biblia*, or collection of books as a whole.

Such arguments are not foreign to Christian clergy, but are largely hidden from the lay public. Few scholars step out of the doctrines in which they are entrenched, and few laity possess sufficient interest and motivation to wage the intellectual battle necessary to confront Christian authorities with the baselessness (and in many cases frank falsehood) of their beliefs. All the same, more forthright Christian sources admit some amazing things. For example, as previously mentioned, no Christian scholar of significant worth considers Greek to have been the original language of Jesus. Nonetheless, many speak of the "original Greek," knowing that, in time, public imitation will follow. However, if asked directly, most clergy are honest enough to admit that Jesus spoke Aramaic and ancient Hebrew, but not the *Koiné* Greek in which the New Testament manuscripts are recorded.[334] Reverend J. R. Dummelow of Queen's College fame (Cambridge, England), is just one of many who readily volunteer such information.[335]

Running countercurrent to the overwhelming flow of evidence and scholarly opinion, a handful of fringe theologians have recently struggled to suggest that Jesus did in fact speak *Koiné* Greek. There was a time when it was easier to pass off such glib answers to a gullible public, but that time is long past. The burden of Christianity, then, is to accept untenable tenets of faith, despite evidence that assaults every wall of the infirm castle of Trinitarian belief, right down to the very foundation: which is to say, the New Testament.

The challenge of Islam is to accept Moses and Jesus as human prophets (but nothing more), to understand the infidelity of those who molded Judaism and Christianity to their present forms, to recognize Muhammad as the final prophet predicted in both Old and New Testaments, and to revere the revelation he transmitted. Muslims claim this revelation is consistent with previous scripture, congruent with human nature, and in conformity with the realities of worldly existence. They claim this revelation withstands the highest levels of critical analysis, being Godly in content, design, and complete perfection. They claim this revelation to be the Holy Qur'an.

Conclusion

Be sure that you go to the author to get at his meaning,
not to find yours.

—John Ruskin, *Sesame and Lilies*

What conclusions does the evidence given in this book suggest?

We began by proposing that the name *Allah* is consistent with Old and New Testaments, as well as the Holy Qur'an, and showed that these three scriptures share the royal plural as well. Analysis of the doctrinal differences between Christianity and Islam reveal much of Christian canon to have been derived more from non-biblical sources than from the teachings of Jesus himself. Shockingly, much of Christian canon, and the Pauline teachings from which they were derived, actually contradict Jesus' teachings.

When we search the Bible for clarification, we find both Old and New Testaments corrupted. And if we can't trust part of these books, which parts *can* we trust?

Nonetheless, we discover continuity of creed between Old and New Testaments, and are not surprised. From a gut level, we expect God's reality to be eternal. So when we find both Moses and Jesus teaching of God as one God, and of a final prophet to follow, perhaps we should pay attention.

Another critical point is that Moses, Jesus and

Muhammad's teachings are remarkably consistent. In fact, they agree more often than not. Of course, Muhammad's teachings sharply conflict with Paul's, but then again, so do those of Moses and Jesus. And this is just one more issue upon which the three prophets, and the revelations they conveyed, concur: all three contradict Paul's teachings!

So if we cannot trust the Old and New Testaments for spiritual guidance, why should we trust the Holy Qur'an? And does Muhammad live up to his claim of prophethood? These questions cannot be answered in a sentence, paragraph, or even a chapter. They demanded a book—specifically, a sequel to this present volume—which I titled *God'ed*. I invite you to read it.

> *Absurdity supported by power will never*
> *be able to stand its ground against the*
> *efforts of reason.*
>
> —Joseph Priestley

Appendix: *Hadith* Methodology

The Qur'an commands believers to obey Allah's messenger and follow his example. For this reason, early Muslims preserved Muhammad's teachings and example in the volumes of traditions known as *hadith*. No detail was too small, and from that day to this, the devout have modeled their lives after that of the prophet. From the *hadith* record we not only know how often Muhammad brushed his teeth (never less than five times a day), but in what *order* he brushed them (laterally, beginning on the right). We know how he ate, drank and slept, his dress, manners and comportment, down to the finest detail. Most importantly, we know how he lived the religion he conveyed, and from this many social and legal precedents were established.

Not surprisingly, after his death impious "followers" attempted to modify the religion closer to their hearts' desires through falsifying *hadith*. Contrary to what we might at first expect, this strengthened, rather than weakened, the *hadith* records. Just as counterfeit money forces governments to higher standards of production and authentication, false *hadith* forced the Muslims to deeper levels of *hadith* analysis. In the same manner that experts can differentiate valid currency from fake, Muslim scholars can distinguish valid *hadith* from those that are weak or fabricated.

The process of *hadith* authentication became the gold standard of historical recordkeeping during its time, and for

305

centuries to follow. Certainly, it remained unrivaled in the West. To this day we don't really know what life was like in England and Europe at the turn of the first millennium, due to the dearth of reliable records and verifiable information. But through the *hadith* records, we know the most intimate details about Muhammad and his life in early seventh-century Arabia.

The following is a brief overview of the exacting standards of *hadith* authentication: Individual *hadith* are classified into one of two broad categories—*Sahih* (authentic) and *Daif* (weak). *Sahih hadith* are further subdivided into four subcategories, all of which are accepted, whereas weak *hadith* are subdivided into over thirty subcategories, all of which are rejected. In order for a *hadith* to be accepted, the *sanad* (chain of transmission) must be an unbroken chain of narrators all the way back to the Prophet. Each narrator in this chain must have been a fair and honest person, known for a strong memory and accurate records. The text of the *hadith* itself must not have any internal defects, and must not conflict with other accepted *hadith* or with the Qur'an. *Each* of the above requirements has a multitude of disqualifiers, totaling twenty-five categories of disqualification. For example, a narrator would have been disqualified if mentally imbalanced, non-Muslim (and therefore more liable to subvert the religion), immature, an innovator, a liar (or even accused of being a liar), known to have committed great sins or to have persisted in the commission of minor sins, or one who failed to exemplify praiseworthy values.

Accuracy was nullified by absentmindedness, such as relating the same story on two or more occasions using different wording, even if it did not change the meaning. Records reconstructed after being lost in a natural disaster such as a fire are not accepted, and a narrator whose story conflicted with a *hadith* of higher authentication found his *entire collection* of *hadith* disqualified. Even simple internal defects disqualify a *hadith*. For example, if a teacher relates a *hadith*, and explains a word without the student understanding that the explanation is not part of the *hadith*, and the student subsequently relates the *hadith* complete with the explanation, the student's narration of the *hadith* is disqualified. Even such a simple error as transposing two names in the chain of transmission (and certainly losing one name in the chain) brings disqualification, even though the body of the text remains unchanged.

Hadith are further subdivided by the *sanad*(chain of narration) into *Mutawatir* and *Ahad* modes of transmission. A *Mutawatirhadith* is one related by a sufficiently large number of narrators (a minimum of four, but usually ten or more) to prevent the creation of a lie, *from the beginning to the end of the chain of narrators.* Why would it be considered impossible for the narrators to have plotted a lie? For practical reasons, such as the narrators never having known each other, having been geographically isolated from one another, or because the narrators were all known to have possessed impeccable characters, for any one of whom lying would have been inconsistent with the witness of their lives.

Any *hadith* passed down through the ages by a chain of narration less than *Mutawatir* is classified as *Ahad*, which itself bears three subcategories. A *hadith* related by a thousand reliable witnesses at each chain of the *sanad* of narration, with the exception of one stage which has less than four narrators, automatically is demoted to the *Ahad* class.

The two classifications—one by authenticity and the other by mode of transmission—are largely complementary, for a *Sahih* (authentic) *hadith* with a *Mutawatir* chain of transmission certainly deserves more respect than a *Daif* (weak) *hadith* with an *Ahadsanad*. Fabricated *hadith*, it would seem, have little chance of slipping through either one of these filters of authentication, but to slip past both would border on the impossible.

Bibliography

Achtemeier, Paul J. (General Editor). *Harper's Bible Dictionary*. 1985. New York: Harper and Row.

Aland, Kurt and Barbara Aland. 1995. *The Text of the New Testament: An Introduction to the Critical Editions and to the Theory and Practice of Modern Textual Criticism*. William B. Eerdmans Publishing Co.

Aland, Kurt, Matthew Black, Carlo M. Martini, Bruce M. Metzger & Allen Wikgren (Editors). 1968. *The Greek New Testament*. Second Edition. United Bible Societies.

Arberry, A. J. 1996. *The Koran Interpreted*. A Touchstone Book: Simon & Schuster.

Arbuthnot, F. F. 1885. *The Construction of the Bible and the Korân*. London: Watts & Co.

Ayto, John. *Dictionary of Word Origins*. 1991. New York: Arcade Publishing, Inc.

Baigent, Michael and Richard Leigh. 1993. *The Dead Sea Scrolls Deception*. Simon & Schuster.

BeDuhn, Jason David. 2003. *Truth in Translation*. University Press of America, Inc.

The Bible, Revised Standard Version. 1977. New York: American Bible Society.

Burman, Edward. 1984. *The Inquisition: The Hammer of Heresy*. New York: Dorset Press.

Butler, Trent C. (General Editor). 1991.*Holman Bible Dictionary*. Nashville: Holman Bible Publishers.

Buttrick, George Arthur (Ed.). 1962 (1996 Print). *The Interpreter's Dictionary of the Bible*. Nashville: Abingdon Press.

Buzzard, Anthony. 2007. *Jesus Was Not a Trinitarian*.

Restoration Fellowship.
    Cadoux, Cecil John. 1948. *The Life of Jesus. Middlesex*: Penguin Books.
    Carmichael, Joel, M.A. 1962. *The Death of Jesus*. New York: The Macmillan Company.
    Carroll, Lewis. 1905. *Alice's Adventures in Wonderland.*
    Catholic Encyclopedia. CD-ROM; 1914 edition
    Chamberlin, E. R. 1993. *The Bad Popes.* Barnes & Noble, Inc.
    Chapman, Dom John. 1907. *The Condemnation of Pope Honorius.*London: Catholic Truth Society.
    Cohen, J.M. and M.J. 1996. *The Penguin Dictionary of Twentieth-Century Quotations.* Penguin Books.
    Conybeare, Fred. C., M.A. 1898. *The Key of Truth.* Oxford: Clarendon Press.
    Cross, F. L. and E. A. Livingstone (editors). 1974. *The Oxford Dictionary of the Christian Church.* London: OxfordUniversity Press.
    Dawud, Abdul-Ahad (Formerly known as Reverend David Benjamin Keldani, Bishop of Uramiah). 1992. *Muhammad in the Bible.* Jeddah: Abul-Qasim Publishing House.
    Douglas, J. D. (general editor). *The New International Dictionary of the Christian Church.* 1978. Grand Rapids, MI: Zondervan Publishing House.
    Dow, Lorenzo. *Reflections on the Love of God.*
    Dummelow, Rev. J. R. (editor). 1908. *A Commentary on the Holy Bible.* New York: Macmillan Publishing Co., Inc.
    Easton, M. G., M.A., D.D. 1897. *Easton's Bible Dictionary.* Nashville: Thomas Nelson Publishers.
    Ehrman, Bart D. 2009. *Jesus, Interrupted.* HarperOne.
    Ehrman, Bart D. 2005. *Lost Christianities.*

OxfordUniversity Press.

Ehrman, Bart D. 2003. Lost Scriptures: Books that Did Not Make It into the New Testament. OxfordUniversity Press.

Ehrman, Bart D. 2005. *Misquoting Jesus*. HarperCollins.

Ehrman, Bart D. The New Testament: A Historical Introduction to the Early Christian Writings. 2004. OxfordUniversity Press.

Ehrman, Bart D. 1993. The Orthodox Corruption of Scripture: The Effect of Early Christological Controversies on the Text of the New Testament. OxfordUniversity Press.

Eisenman, Robert and Michael Wise. 1993. *The Dead Sea Scrolls Uncovered*. Penguin Books.

Encyclopaedia Britannica. 1994–1998. CD-ROM.

EncyclopaediaJudaica. 1971. Jerusalem: Keter Publishing House Ltd.

Findlay, Rev. Adam Fyfe, M.A., D.D. 1929. *The History of Christianity in the Light of Modern Knowledge*. London: Blackie & Son, Ltd.

Funk, Robert Walter. 1996. *Honest to Jesus, Jesus for a New Millennium*. Polebridge Press.

Funk, Robert W., Roy W. Hoover, and the Jesus Seminar. 1993. *The Five Gospels: The Search for the Authentic Words of Jesus*. HarperCollins Publishers.

Gehman, Henry Snyder (editor). 1970. *The New Westminster Dictionary of the Bible*. The Westminster Press.

Gibbon, Edward, Esq. 1854. *The History of the Decline and Fall of the Roman Empire*. London: Henry G. Bohn.

Gilbert, Arthur. 1968.*The Vatican Council and The Jews*. New York: The World Publishing Company.

Goodspeed, Edgar J. 1946. *How to Read the Bible*. The John C. Winston Company.

Guillaume, Alfred. 1990. *Islam*. Penguin Books.
Guinness Book of Knowledge. 1997. Guinness Publishing.
Gwatkin, H.M. 1898. *The Arian Controversy*. London: Longmans, Green, and Co.
Hart, Michael H. 1998. *The 100: A Ranking of the Most Influential Persons in History*. Citadel Press.
Hastings, James (editor). 1913. *The Encyclopedia of Religion and Ethics*. Charles Scribner's Sons.
Hastings, James (editor); Revised edition by Frederick C. Grant and H. H. Rowley. 1963. *Dictionary of The Bible*. Second Edition. Charles Scribner's Sons.
The Holy Bible, New King James Version. 1982. Thomas Nelson Publishers.
The Holy Bible, New Revised Standard Version. Grand Rapids, MI: Zondervan Publishing House.
Huxley, Thomas H. 1870.*Discourse Touching The Method of Using One's Reason Rightly and of Seeking Scientific Truth*.
IbnHisham. *As-Seerah An-Nabawiyyah*.
The Interpreter's Bible. 1957. Nashville: Abingdon Press.
Kee, Howard Clark (Notes and References by). 1993. *The Cambridge Annotated Study Bible, New Revised Standard Version*. CambridgeUniversity Press.
Kelly, J. N. D. 1978. *Early Christian Doctrines*. San Francisco: Harper & Brothers Publishers.
Kittel, Gerhard and Gerhard Friedrich (editors). 1985. *Theological Dictionary of the New Testament*. Translated by Geoffrey W. Bromiley. William B. Eerdmans Publishing Co., Paternoster Press Ltd.

Küng,Hans. 2007. *Islam, Past, Present and Future*. One World Publications.

Lea, Henry Charles. 1958. *A History of the Inquisition of the Middle Ages*. New York: Russell & Russell.

Lehmann, Johannes. 1972. *The Jesus Report*. Translated by Michael Heron. London: Souvenir Press.

Lejeune, Anthony. 1998. *The Concise Dictionary of Foreign Quotations*. Stacey London.

London *Daily News*. June 25, 1984.

McBrien, Richard P. (General Editor). 1995. *HarperCollins Encyclopedia of Catholicism*. New York: HarperCollins Publishers.

McManners, John (Editor). 1990. *The Oxford Illustrated History of Christianity*. Oxford University Press.

Meagher, Paul Kevin OP, S.T.M., Thomas C. O'Brien, Sister Consuelo Maria Aherne, SSJ (editors). 1979. *Encyclopedic Dictionary of Religion*. Philadelphia: Corpus Publications.

Metzger, Bruce M. 1963. "Explicit References in the Works of Origen to Variant Readings in New Testament Manuscripts," in J. N. Birdsall and R. W. Thomson (ed.), *Biblical And Patristic Studies In Memory Of Robert Pierce Casey*. Herder: Frieburg.

Metzger, Bruce M. 2005. *A Textual Commentary on the Greek New Testament*. Deutsche Bibelgesellschaft, D–Stuttgart.

Metzger, Bruce M. and Ehrman, Bart D. 2005. *The Text of the New Testament: Its Transmission, Corruption, and Restoration*. Oxford University Press.

Michener, James A. May, 1955. "Islam: The Misunderstood Religion," in *Reader's Digest* [American Edition].

Motley, John Lothrop. 1884. *The Rise of the Dutch Republic: A History*. London: Bickers & Son.
Musnad Ahmad.
Myers, Jacob M. 1966. *Invitation to the Old Testament*. New York: Doubleday & Company.
New Catholic Encyclopedia. 1967. Washington, D.C.: The Catholic University of America.
The New International Encyclopaedia. 1917. 2nd Ed. New York: Dodd, Mead and Company.
Nostra Aetate. 28 October 1965. Item #4. Official publication of the Vatican website: www.vatican.va.
Nydell, Margaret K. 2006. *Understanding Arabs*. Intercultural Press.
Ostrogorsky, George.1969.*History of the Byzantine State*.(Translated from the German by Joan Hussey).New Brunswick: Rutgers University Press.
Parke, David B. 1957. *The Epic of Unitarianism*. Boston: Starr King Press.
Powell, J. Enoch. 1994.*The Evolution of the Gospel*. Yale University Press.
Reumann, John. 1991. *Variety and Unity in New Testament Thought*. Oxford University Press.
Roth, Cecil B. Litt., M.A., D. Phil. and Geoffrey Wigoder, D. Phil. (editors-in-chief). 1975. *The New Standard Jewish Encyclopedia*. W. H. Allen.
Sahih Al-Bukhari
Sale, George. 1734. *The Koran*. London: C. Ackers.
Scofield, C. I., D.D. (Editor). 1970. *The New Scofield Reference Bible*. New York: Oxford University Press.
Shakespeare, William. *The Merchant of Venice*.
Shaw, George Bernard. 1944. *Everybody's Political*

What's What?
Stanton, Graham N. 1989. *The Gospels and Jesus.* Oxford University Press.
Strong's Exhaustive Concordance of the Bible. 1980. World Bible Publishers.
Toland, John. 1718. *Tetradymus; bound with, Nazarenus: or, Jewish, Gentile and Mahometan Christianity.* London.
Tugwell, Simon OP. 1989. *The Apostolic Fathers.* Harrisburg, Pennsylvania: Morehouse Publishing.
Twain, Mark. *Following the Equator.* "Pudd'nhead Wilson's New Calendar."
Wakefield, Gilbert, B.A. *An Enquiry into the Opinions of the Christian Writers of the Three First Centuries Concerning the Person of Jesus Christ.* 1824. Editor's dedication.
Wallace, Robert, F.G.S. 1850. *Antitrinitarian Biography.* London: E.T. Whitfield.
Weiss, Johannes. 1909. *Paul and Jesus.* (Translated by Rev. H. J. Chaytor). London and New York: Harper and Brothers.
Wells, H. G. 1921. *The Outline of History.* Fourth Edition. Volume 2. Section XXXI – "Muhammad and Islam." New York: The Review of Reviews Company.
Werblowsky, R. J. Zwi and Geoffrey Wigoder (editors in chief). 1997. *The Oxford Dictionary of the Jewish Religion.* Oxford University Press.
Wrede, William. 1962. *Paul.* Translated by Edward Lummis. Lexington, Kentucky: American Theological Library Association Committee on Reprinting.
Zahrnt, Heinz. 1817. *The Historical Jesus.* (Translated from the German by J. S. Bowden). New York: Harper & Row.

Endnotes

[1] Funk, Robert W., Roy W. Hoover, and the Jesus Seminar. 1993. *The Five Gospels: The Search for the Authentic Words of Jesus*. HarperCollins Publishers. p. 9.

[2] Guillaume, Alfred. 1990. *Islam*. Penguin Books. pp. 73–74.

[3] Arberry, A. J. 1996. *The Koran Interpreted*. A Touchstone book: Simon & Schuster. Preface, p. 24.

[4] McManners, John (Editor). 1990. *The Oxford Illustrated History of Christianity*. OxfordUniversity Press. p. 22.

[5] Achtemeier, Paul J. (General Editor). *Harper's Bible Dictionary*. 1985. New York: Harper and Row. p. 163.

[6] The abbreviation CE, meaning either "Common Era" or "Christian Era," has largely replaced AD in modern scholastic literature, for AD (*Anno Domini*, "the year of our lord") fails to accommodate non-Christian faiths.

[7] Meagher, Paul Kevin OP, S.T.M., Thomas C. O'Brien, Sister Consuelo Maria Aherne, SSJ (editors). 1979. *Encyclopedic Dictionary of Religion*. Philadelphia: Corpus Publications. Vol 1. p. 741.

[8] Meagher, Paul Kevin et al. Vol 1, p. 741.

[9] Since the mid-nineteenth century, some have regarded Unitarianism as synonymous with Universalism, despite separate and distinct theologies. The union of the Universalist Church of America with the American Unitarian Association in 1961, to form the Unitarian Universalist Association, has done little to alleviate this misunderstanding. However, while most Universalists may be Unitarians, the opposite is certainly not the case, for the Universalist concept of salvation of all souls is

contrary to the creed of Unitarian Christianity, which teaches salvation conditional upon correct belief and practice, according to the teachings of Jesus. Perhaps for this reason, in combination with the diversity of Universalist beliefs, the Universalist church has failed to formulate a statement of creed accepted by all affiliates. Furthermore, Universalist theology is more heavily based upon philosophy than scripture, which explains the disunity. For the purposes of this work, "Unitarian Christianity" refers to the classic Unitarian theology which was founded upon scripture and united in affirming divine unity. Universalism is by no means to be inferred in the mention of Unitarianism herein, and will not be discussed any further in this work.

[10]*Encyclopaedia Britannica*. 1994–1998. CD-ROM.

[11]Ehrman, Bart D. 2003. *Lost Christianities*. Oxford University Press. p. 260 – endnote #1 to Chapter 1.

[12]Nydell, Margaret K. 2006. *Understanding Arabs*. Intercultural Press. p. 83.

[13] Meagher, Paul Kevin et al. Vol 2, p. 1842.

[14]Ibid.

[15] Parke, David B. 1957. *The Epic of Unitarianism*. Boston: Starr King Press. p. 35.

[16] Sale, George. 1734. *The Koran*. London: C. Ackers. Preface, A2.

[17] Lord George Carey's cover endorsement of Hans Küng's book, *Islam, Past, Present and Future*. One World Publications. 2007.

[18]Küng, Hans. 2007. *Islam, Past, Present and Future*. One World Publications. p. 172.

[19]*Guinness Book of Knowledge*. 1997. Guinness Publishing. p.

194.

[20]Michener, James A. May, 1955. "Islam: The Misunderstood Religion," in *Reader's Digest* [American Edition]. p. 73.

[21]*Encyclopaedia Britannica,* CD-ROM.

[22] Huxley, Thomas H. 1870. *Discourse Touching The Method of Using One's Reason Rightly and of Seeking Scientific Truth.*

[23] Meagher, Paul Kevin et al. Vol 2, p. 1843.

[24]*New Catholic Encyclopedia.* 1967. Vol 7. Washington, D.C.: The Catholic University of America. p. 680.

[25]Islam teaches that as God never changed, neither did His creed. Not so His laws, which God periodically modified according to changes in the human condition.

[26]IbnHisham. *As-SeerahAn-Nabawiyyah.*

[27]Ibid.

[28]*Musnad Ahmad.*

[29]IbnHisham. *As-SeerahAn-Nabawiyyah.*

[30]*Sahih Al-Bukhari.*

[31]*EncyclopaediaJudaica.* 1971. Vol 2. Jerusalem: Keter Publishing House Ltd. p. 54.

[32]Ibid.

[33]Douglas, J. D. (general editor). *The New International Dictionary of the Christian Church.* 1978. Grand Rapids, MI: Zondervan Publishing House. p. 27.

[34]*Encyclopaedia Britannica.* CD-ROM.

[35]Ayto, John. *Dictionary of Word Origins.* 1991. New York: Arcade Publishing, Inc. p. 258.

[36]Achtemeier, Paul J. pp. 684–686.

[37]Werblowsky, R. J. Zwi and Geoffrey Wigoder (editors in

chief). 1997. *The Oxford Dictionary of the Jewish Religion.* Oxford University Press.p. 277.

[38]*Encyclopaedia Britannica.* CD-ROM. (Under "Elohim").

[39]Hastings, James (editor). 1913. *The Encyclopedia of Religion and Ethics.* Vol. VI. Charles Scribner's & Sons. p. 248.

[40]Achtemeier, Paul J. p. 684.

[41]Ibid.

[42]Ibid.

[43]*EncyclopaediaJudaica.* Vol 7, p. 679.

[44]Douglas, J. D. p. 27.

[45]*Encyclopaedia Britannica.* CD-ROM. (under "Elohim").

[46]Achtemeier, Paul J. p. 686.

[47] Meagher, Paul Kevin et al. Vol 1, p. 1187.

[48]Kittel, Gerhard and Gerhard Friedrich (editors). 1985. *Theological Dictionary of the New Testament.* Translated by Geoffrey W. Bromiley. William B. Eerdmans Publishing Co., Paternoster Press Ltd. p. 325.

[49]Dawud, Abdul-Ahad (Formerly known as Reverend David Benjamin Keldani, Bishop of Uramiah). 1992. *Muhammad in the Bible.* Jeddah: Abul-Qasim Publishing House. p. 14.

[50] Carroll, Lewis. *Alice's Adventures in Wonderland.* Ch. 12.

[51]Those who associate the burning of heretics with the punitive arm of the Roman Catholic Church may be interested to learn that the practice was not unknown to the Protestant church as well. Michael Servetus was condemned to this horrific fate by none other than John Calvin, one of the founders of Protestantism. Despite the fact that Servetus, a Spaniard, possessed a letter of safe conduct, he was executed in Geneva

for the alleged crime of being an Anabaptist and a Unitarian.

[52] Wallace, Robert, F.G.S. 1850. *Antitrinitarian Biography*. Vol. III. London: E.T. Whitfield. p. 180.

[53]Ibid., p. 190.

[54]Ibid., p. 191.

[55] Parke, David B. pp. 31, 33.

[56] Motley, John Lothrop. 1884. *The Rise of the Dutch Republic: A History*. Volume II. London: Bickers & Son. pp. 155–156.

[57] Wells, H. G. 1921. *The Outline of History*. Volume II. The Macmillan Company. p. 209.

[58]Sabellianism was an early Christian heresy that conceived God in unity, but triune operationally, being manifest as Creator in the Father, Redeemer in the Son, and Sanctifier in the Holy Spirit. Sabellianism was denounced by Arius and the Trinitarian church alike.

[59]Gwatkin, H.M. 1898. *The Arian Controversy*. London: Longmans, Green, and Co. pp. 32–33.

[60]Ibid., p. 34.

[61]Ibid., p. 35.

[62]Ibid., p. 35.

[63]Ibid., p. 35.

[64]Toland, John. 1718. *Tetradymus; bound with, Nazarenus: or, Jewish, Gentile and Mahometan Christianity*. London. pp. 75–76.

[65] Wells, H. G. 1921. *The Outline of History*. Volume II. The Macmillan Company. p. 91.

[66]Kittel, Gerhard and Gerhard Friedrich. p. 1323.

[67]Ibid., p. 1322.

[68] Hastings, James (editor); revised edition by Frederick C. Grant and H. H. Rowley. 1963. *Dictionary of The Bible*. Second Edition. Charles Scribner's Sons. p. 646.

[69] For example, kings were either directly or indirectly referred to as "the anointed of God" in 1 Samuel 2:10, 12:3, 12:5, 16:6, 23:5, 24:7, 24:11, 26:9, 26:11, 26:16, 26:23; 2 Samuel 1:14, 1:16, 19:22, 22:51, 23.1; Lamentations 4:20; Psalms 2:2; 28:8, 84:9, 132:17.

[70] Kittel, Gerhard and Gerhard Friedrich. p. 1323.

[71] Ibid.,p. 1323.

[72] Stanton, Graham N. 1989. *The Gospels and Jesus*. Oxford University Press. p. 221.

[73] Gibbon, Edward, Esq. 1854. *The History of the Decline and Fall of the Roman Empire*. Vol. 4. London: Henry G. Bohn. Chapter XXXVII, p. 146.

[74] Once again, the reader is referred to Bart D. Ehrman's indispensable books, *Misquoting Jesus* and *Lost Christianities*.

[75] Kittel, Gerhard and Gerhard Friedrich. p. 607.

[76] Ibid.

[77] Ibid.

[78] Meagher, Paul Kevin et al. Vol 3, p. 2821.

[79] Werblowsky, R. J. Zwi and Geoffrey Wigoder. p. 540.

[80] *EncyclopaediaJudaica*. Vol 11, p. 1026.

[81] Werblowsky, R. J. Zwi and Geoffrey Wigoder. p. 540.

[82] Roth, Cecil B. Litt., M.A., D. Phil, and Geoffrey Wigoder, D. Phil. (editors-in-chief). 1975. *The New Standard Jewish Encyclopedia*. W. H. Allen. p. 1550.

[83] Werblowsky, R. J. Zwi and Geoffrey Wigoder. p. 540.

[84] Hastings, James. *Dictionary of The Bible.* p. 292.

[85] Myers, Jacob M. 1966. *Invitation to the Old Testament.* New York: Doubleday & Company. p. 26.

[86]*New Catholic Encyclopedia.* Vol 7, p. 690.

[87]Werblowsky, R. J. Zwi and Geoffrey Wigoder. p. 653.

[88] Hastings, James. *Dictionary of the Bible.* p. 143.

[89] Stanton, Graham N. pp. 224–225.

[90] Carmichael, Joel, M.A. 1962. *The Death of Jesus.* New York: The Macmillan Company. pp. 253–4.

[91]Achtemeier, Paul J. p. 981.

[92]*New Catholic Encyclopedia.* Vol 13, p. 431.The reader is reminded that the Aramaic, ancient Hebrew, and not-so-original "original Greek" from which the Bible is translated all lack capitalization. Hence, capitals such as the H in "Himself" and "His," and the capital S in "Son" in quotes to follow, reflect the lofty status to which Trinitarians elevate Jesus Christ in their doctrine. Similarly, capitalization in Bible translation is more a result of religious conviction than scholastic accuracy, conceived more out of doctrine than faithfulness to biblical narratives. For a blatant example of such textual manipulation, we can compare Matthew 21:9 with Psalm 118:26. Psalm 118:26 writes of an uncapitalized (dare we say nonspecific?) "he": "Blessed *is* he who comes in the name of the LORD!" However, when Matthew 21:9 quotes Psalm 118:26, referring to Jesus as the "he" who "comes in the name of the LORD," the Bible translators conveniently converted the lowercase "he" of Psalm 118:26 to a capitalized "He" in an effort to make Jesus appear divine. Lest a person make excuses, this is not a typographical error; Matthew 23:39 duplicates this exaggeration. The problem is, this textual manipulation is blatant. Genetic

analysis of the stains on the fabric of religious history is simply not necessary, for the verdict is obvious—someone has defiled the text. And lest a person defend the Bible on the basis of this being a very small corruption, any group who takes the Bible for a book of guidance finds themselves painted into a corner by the biblical caution that, "he who is unjust in what is least is unjust also in much" (Luke 16:10). How, then, does this quote apply to the Bible scribes and translators? For if they, having been unjust in what is least, means they are, according to their own scripture, "unjust also in much," how can we trust the rest of their work?

[93]Achtemeier, Paul J. pp. 979–980.

[94] Hastings, James. *Dictionary of The Bible.* p. 143.

[95] For discussion of John 10:36—the one and only Bible verse where Jesus Christ might have called himself a *metaphorical* son of God (but then again, most likely didn't)—see the next chapter.

[96]Kittel, Gerhard and Gerhard Friedrich. p. 763.

[97]Ibid.

[98]Kittel, Gerhard and Gerhard Friedrich. p. 765.

[99]Ibid.,p. 767.

[100] Carmichael, Joel. pp. 255–6.

[101] Stanton, Graham N. p. 225.

[102]*New Catholic Encyclopedia.* Vol 13, p. 426.

[103]The problem with blind indoctrination is that it doesn't work when a person knows better. A hypochondriac might believe that a placebo is medicine, if convincingly presented as such. Through blind faith in the doctor, a hypochondriac's imagined symptoms may be overcome by conviction that the prescribed

sugar pills are "just what the doctor ordered." On the other hand, if the hypochondriac believes the placebo is fake medicine, it won't work. Unitarians argue that the "Trinity" is a great doctrinal placebo swallowed by most of the world of Christianity. Believers embrace the doctrine trusting to the authority of their church, not realizing they are being fed a manmade doctrine lacking divine authority or scriptural substantiation.

[104]This statement may come as a shock, for Christians commonly believe that Paul attributed divine sonship to Jesus. It is possible he did, but given the fact that none of the Jews stoned him to death for blasphemy, most likely he did not. The confusion lies in differentiating Paul's teachings from those of Pauline theologians. The two do not necessarily agree. Whereas Paul appears to have spoken of Jesus Christ as a "son of God" in the metaphorical sense, typical of the idiom of his age, centuries later the designers of Pauline theology appear to have bent his words into a more literal interpretation. Hence, it appears that it wasn't Paul who conceived Jesus a literal "son of God," but rather those who designed a theology in his name. In the end, it's a fine point and one that doesn't matter much, for the teachings of Jesus and those of Paul were largely at variance with one another (as discussed in following chapters). A person simply has to choose sides between the two.

[105]*New Catholic Encyclopedia*. Vol 13, p. 426.

[106]*Encyclopaedia Britannica*. CD-ROM. (Under "Inquisition").

[107]Burman, Edward. 1984. *The Inquisition, The Hammer of Heresy*. New York: Dorset Press. p. 62.

[108]*New Catholic Encyclopedia*. Vol 13, p. 430.

[109]Ibid., p. 429.See Matthew 8:28–29 and Luke 8:26–28.

[110]*New Catholic Encyclopedia.* Vol 13, p. 429.Compare Matthew 27:54 and Mark 15:39 with Luke 23:47.

[111] Shaw, George Bernard. 1944. *Everybody's Political What's What?* Ch. 30.

[112]And they've proven pretty fruity, all right. There has to be some reason why hundreds of Roman Catholic priests have contracted and died of AIDS, as reported in *The Kansas City Star* (Jan 30, 2000). According to the front-page article, priests are dying of AIDS at a rate between four and eleven times that of the general U.S. population. Deceptive and falsified death certificates disrupt analysis, but "many priests and medical experts now agree that at least 300 priests have died." As per the article, some put the number closer to 1,000. Ruling out mosquito bites, a person has to conclude that a strong current of hypocrisy is coursing through the Roman Catholic clergy. In addition, *Time Magazine*'s April 1, 2002 article, entitled "Can the Church be Saved?" reports that approximately 5% of Catholic clergy are pedophiles. And yet, this is the quality of men who are chosen to be trusted leaders of congregations, counselors of faith, and absolvers of sins.

[113]*New Catholic Encyclopedia.* Vol 13, p. 431.

[114]*Catholic Encyclopedia.* CD-ROM. 1914 edition, under "Council of Chalcedon".

[115] Lehmann, Johannes. 1972. *The Jesus Report.* Translated by Michael Heron. London: Souvenir Press. pp. 138–9.

[116]Gehman, Henry Snyder (editor). *The New Westminster Dictionary of the Bible.* 1970. The Westminster Press. p. 958.

[117]McBrien, Richard P. (General Editor). 1995. *HarperCollins Encyclopedia of Catholicism.* New York: HarperCollins Publishers. p. 1270.

[118] Buzzard, Anthony. 2007. *Jesus Was Not a Trinitarian.* Restoration Fellowship. p. 27.

[119]Cross, F. L. and E. A. Livingstone (editors). 1974. *The Oxford Dictionary of the Christian Church.* London: Oxford University Press. p. 1393.

[120]Küng, Hans. 2007. *Islam, Past, Present and Future.* One World Publications. p. 509.

[121]Achtemeier, Paul J. p. 1099.

[122]One might wonder why, since Tertullian had such formative influence on the Trinity, the church never canonized him, as it did other church fathers. Why is there no "Saint Tertullian?" The answer is that Tertullian changed his views later in life, became a Montanist, and died upon beliefs the church considered heretical. Theological instability being a poor qualification for sainthood, the church nonetheless considered him qualified to propound the theology upon which it would be founded.

[123]Küng, Hans. 2007. *Islam, Past, Present and Future.* One World Publications. p. 504.

[124]*New Catholic Encyclopedia.* Vol 10, p. 437.

[125]Ibid., p. 433.

[126]McManners, John. p. 72.

[127]Ostrogorsky, George.1969.*History of the Byzantine State.*(Translated from the German by Joan Hussey).New Brunswick: Rutgers University Press.p. 47–48.

[128]Ibid.

[129]Ibid., p. 49.

[130]Ibid.,p. 53.

[131]*New Catholic Encyclopedia.* Vol 14, p. 295.

[132]Ibid., p. 295.

[133]Ibid., p. 299.

[134]For details concerning the creeds of the Ante-Nicene Fathers and the evolution of the Trinity, see *The Mysteries of Jesus*, by RuqaiyyahWarisMaqsood; Sakina Books, Oxford, pp. 194–200.

[135]*New Catholic Encyclopedia.* Vol 14, p. 306.

[136]Jesus Christ was one more prophet in the long line of prophets sent to the astray Israelites. As he so clearly affirmed, "I was not sent *except* to the lost sheep of the house of Israel." (Matthew 15:24) When Jesus sent the disciples out in the path of God, he instructed them, "Do not go into the way of the Gentiles, and do not enter a city of the Samaritans. But go rather to the lost sheep of the house of Israel." (Matthew 10:5–6) Throughout his ministry, Jesus was never recorded as having converted a Gentile, and in fact is recorded as having initially rebuked a Gentile for seeking his favors, likening her to a dog (Matthew 15:22–28 and Mark 7:25–30). Jesus was himself a Jew, his disciples were Jews, and both he and they directed their ministries to the Jews. One wonders what this means to us now, for most of those who have taken Jesus as their "personal savior" are Gentiles, and not of the "lost sheep of the house of Israel" to whom he was sent.

[137] Lehmann, Johannes. pp. 125–6.

[138]Ehrman, Bart D. *The New Testament: A Historical Introduction to the Early Christian Writings.* 2004. Oxford University Press. p. 3.

[139]Eisenman, Robert and Michael Wise. *The Dead Sea Scrolls Uncovered.* 1993. Penguin Books. pp. 163, 184, 212–8.

[140]Ibid., p. 234.

[141]Ibid., p. 234.

[142] Lehmann, Johannes. p. 128.

[143]Ibid.,p. 134.

[144]Ehrman, Bart D. *Lost Christianities*. pp. 97–98.

[145]Ibid., p. 184.

[146] Carmichael, Joel. p. 270.

[147]Wrede, William. 1962. *Paul*. Translated by Edward Lummis. Lexington, Kentucky: American Theological Library Association Committee on Reprinting. p. 163.

[148] Weiss, Johannes. 1909. *Paul and Jesus*. (Translated by Rev. H. J. Chaytor). London and New York: Harper and Brothers. p. 130.

[149]Baigent, Michael and Richard Leigh. 1993. *The Dead Sea Scrolls Deception*. Simon & Schuster. pp. 181–187.

[150] Hart, Michael H. *The 100, A Ranking of the Most Influential Persons in History*. p. 39 of the 1978 edition by Hart Publishing Co.; p. 9 of the 1998 edition by Citadel Press. Go figure.

[151] Lehmann, Johannes. p. 137.

[152]Küng, Hans. 2007. *Islam, Past, Present and Future*. One World Publications. p. 492.

[153]*The Interpreter's Bible*. 1957. Volume XII. Nashville: Abingdon Press. pp. 293–294.

[154]Scofield, C. I., D.D. (Editor). 1970. *The New Scofield Reference Bible*. New York: Oxford University Press. p. 1346 (footnote to the verse of 1 John 5:7).

[155] Aland, Kurt and Barbara Aland. 1995. *The Text of the New Testament: An Introduction to the Critical Editions and to the Theory and Practice of Modern Textual Criticism*. William B.

Eerdmans Publishing Co. p. 311.

[156] Metzger, Bruce M. 2005. *A Textual Commentary on the Greek New Testament.* Deutsche Bibelgesellschaft, D—Stuttgart. P. 647.

[157] Metzger, Bruce M. and Ehrman, Bart D. 2005. *The Text of the New Testament: Its Transmission, Corruption, and Restoration.* Oxford University Press. p. 148.

[158] Those seeking a most eloquent exposé on how this was done, and the evidence in support of this conclusion, are referred to Metzger, Bruce M. and Ehrman, Bart D. *The Text of the New Testament: Its Transmission, Corruption, and Restoration.* pp. 146–149, and to Metzger, Bruce M. *A Textual Commentary on the Greek New Testament.* pp. 647–649.

[159] Gibbon, Edward, Esq. Vol. 4, Chapter XXXVII, pp. 146–7.

[160] Ehrman, Bart D. 2005. *Misquoting Jesus.* HarperCollins. pp. 81–83.

[161] *New Catholic Encyclopedia.* Vol 14, p. 306.

[162] Ibid.

[163] Funk, Robert W., Roy W. Hoover, and the Jesus Seminar. *The Five Gospels: The Search for the Authentic Words of Jesus.* Pp. 36-37, 127, 270.

[164] *Strong's Exhaustive Concordance of the Bible.* 1980. World Bible Publishers.

[165] Ibid.

[166] Analogies such as the egg and the triple point of water deserve rebuttal nonetheless. At the most basic level many refuse to demote the majesty of God to comparison with anything of creation, but especially to anything as low on the list as the product of a squawking hen's filthy cloacal tract. Furthermore,

nothing known to man does exist in a triune state, for the triune state is not defined just as three elements making one whole, but of three elements being consubstantial, coeternal, and coequal. Water at the triple point may be consubstantial—all of equivalent molecular structure. However, the intermolecular bonds differ and the three states of steam, water, and ice are not coequal. Nobody can make tea with ice or sorbet with steam. Similarly, the three parts of an egg are neither consubstantial, coeternal, nor coequal. You can't make an omelet with eggshells, or a meringue with yolks, and anyone putting the "coeternal" theory to the test will likely find the hypothesis stinks after a while.

[167]Perhaps it's worth suggesting that these would have been extremely bold verses, had Muhammad been a false prophet. Had evidence for the Trinity in fact existed in the Bible, the claim of the Holy Qur'an as revelation would have been too easily refuted. Additionally, such emphatic denial of the Trinity would have been an utterly peculiar manner of trying to draw Christians into the fold of Islam. On one hand, the Qur'an acknowledges the virgin birth and prophethood of Jesus, much to the alienation of Judaism. On the other hand, the Qur'an denies the Trinity, much to the offense of Christianity. The Holy Qur'an condemns paganism in even stronger terms. If the Holy Qur'an was one man's attempt to gather a following, it certainly lacked tactical appeal to Jews, Christians, and pagans. And in the Arabia of the time of Muhammad, there wasn't much else.

[168]See also Matthew 24:36, Luke 23:46, John 8:42, John 14:24, John 17:6–8, etc.

[169] Carmichael, Joel. p. 203.

[170] Man: see Acts 2:22, 7:56, 13:38, 17:31; God's servant: see

Acts 3:13, 3:26, 4:27, 4:30.

[171]In the past, some theologians attempted to validate the Incarnation on the basis of John 1:14 and Colossians 2:9. However, in the face of modern textual criticism these verses have fallen from favor, and for good reason. John 1:14 speaks of "the Word," which by no means implies divinity, and "the only begotten of the Father," which by no means is an accurate translation. Both of these subjects were discussed (and discredited) in previous chapters. As for Colossians, problems transcend the incomprehensible wording, beginning with the simple fact that Colossians is now thought to have been forged. For details, see Bart D. Ehrman's *LostChristianities*, p. 235.

[172] Gibbon, Edward, Esq. Vol. 5, Chapter XLVII, p. 207.

[173] Metzger, Bruce M. and Ehrman, Bart D. *The Text of the New Testament: Its Transmission, Corruption, and Restoration.* p. 286.

[174]Ehrman, Bart D. *Misquoting Jesus.* p. 157.

[175]Ibid.

[176]For further clarification, see Metzger, Bruce M. *A Textual Commentary on the Greek New Testament.* pp. 573–4.

[177]Ehrman, Bart D. *Misquoting Jesus.* p. 113.

[178] London *Daily News.* June 25, 1984.

[179]The exercise is only valid when comparing practicing Muslims with practicing Christians. Unfortunately, the majority of those who claim the title of Islam in Western nations are either not practicing, or poor examples of Islamic virtues. Hence, to be fair, a person has to search out the best examples of Islamic piety in order to appreciate the comparison.

[180] Gibbon, Edward, Esq. Vol. 5, Chapter L, p. 442.

[181] Carmichael, Joel. p. 223.

[182]For a brief discussion of *hadith* methodology, see Appendix. For more in-depth study, the reader is referred to *Hadith Literature: Its Origins, Development and Special Features*, by Muhammad Zubayr Siddiqi (Islamic Texts Society, London, 1993), and *Studies in Hadith Methodology and Literature*, by Muhammad Mustafa Azami (American Trust Publications, Indianapolis, 1977).

[183] Funk, Robert Walter. 1996. *Honest to Jesus: Jesus for a New Millennium*. Polebridge Press. p. 8.

[184] Aland, Kurt, Matthew Black, Carlo M. Martini, Bruce M. Metzger & Allen Wikgren (Editors). 1968. *The Greek New Testament*. Second Edition. United Bible Societies. pp. x–xi.

[185] Metzger, Bruce M. *A Textual Commentary on the Greek New Testament*. Introduction, p. 14.

[186]Whereas *hadith* are preserved word-for-word, "There are more differences in our [biblical] manuscripts than there are words in the New Testament." Ehrman, Bart D. *The New Testament: A Historical Introduction to the Early Christian Writings*. pp. 252–253.

[187] See *New Catholic Encyclopedia*, Vol 2, p. 395, where Mark 16:9–20 is listed amongst the "doubtfully authentic deuterocanonical sections" included in the Bible canon by the decree of Trent. Alsosee footnote to these verses in the NRSV.

[188]Ehrman, Bart D. *Misquoting Jesus*. pp. 66–67.

[189]*Strong's Exhaustive Concordance of the Bible*.

[190]Ibid.

[191] Carmichael, Joel. pp. 202–206.

[192]*New Catholic Encyclopedia*. Vol 4, p. 486.

[193]Ehrman, Bart D. *Misquoting Jesus* and *Lost Christianities*.

[194]Zahrnt, Heinz. 1817. *The Historical Jesus*. (Translated from the German by J. S. Bowden). New York: Harper and Row. p. 42.

[195]*New Catholic Encyclopedia*. Vol 13, p. 428.

[196]Ehrman, Bart D. *Misquoting Jesus* and *Lost Christianities*.

[197]Kittel, Gerhard and Gerhard Friedrich. pp. 876–877.

[198]BeDuhn, Jason David. 2003. *Truth in Translation*. University Press of America, Inc. pp. 158-159, 162

[199]Ibid.,p. 886.

[200]*New Catholic Encyclopedia*. Vol 10, p. 989.

[201]Kittel, Gerhard and Gerhard Friedrich. p. 782.

[202]Achtemeier, Paul J. p. 749.

[203]*New Catholic Encyclopedia*. Vol 10, p. 989.

[204]Kittel, Gerhard and Gerhard Friedrich. p. 783.

[205] Hastings, James. *Dictionary of the Bible*. p. 183.

[206]Kittel, Gerhard and Gerhard Friedrich. p. 43.

[207]*New Catholic Encyclopedia*. Vol 10, pp. 990.

[208]Ibid., pp. 989.

[209]See 1 Samuel 10:10, 1 Samuel 11:6, Isaiah 63:11, Luke 1:15, 1:35, 1:41, 1:67, 2:25–26, 3:22, John 20:21–22.

[210]Kittel, Gerhard and Gerhard Friedrich. p. 892.

[211] Carmichael, Joel. p. 216.

[212]McManners, John. p. 50.

[213]Ehrman, Bart D. *Lost Christianities*. p. 2.

[214] Gibbon, Edward, Esq. Vol. 6, Chapter LIV, p. 242.

[215] Lea, Henry Charles. 1958. *A History of the Inquisition of the*

Middle Ages. New York: Russell & Russell. Vol. I, p. 101.

[216]Conybeare, Fred. C., M.A. 1898. *The Key of Truth.* Oxford: Clarendon Press. Preface, p. xi.

[217] Lea, Henry Charles. Vol. I, p. 154.

[218]Ibid., p. 306.

[219]Ehrman, Bart D. 2003. *Lost Scriptures: Books that Did Not Make It into the New Testament.* Oxford University Press. p. 2.

[220]*New Catholic Encyclopedia.* Vol 8, p. 338.

[221]Kittel, Gerhard and Gerhard Friedrich. p. 54.

[222]*New Catholic Encyclopedia.* Vol 8, p. 339.

[223]Ibid., p. 339.

[224] Twain, Mark. *Following the Equator.* Ch. 12. "Pudd'nhead Wilson's New Calendar."

[225] Shakespeare, William. *The Merchant of Venice.* Act I, Scene 3.

[226] Dow, Lorenzo. *Reflections on the Love of God.*

[227]BeDuhn. p. 161.

[228]Buttrick, George Arthur (Ed.). 1962 (1996 Print). *The Interpreter's Dictionary of the Bible.* Volume 4. Nashville: Abingdon Press. pp. 594–595 (Under Text, NT).

[229]Ehrman, Bart D. *Misquoting Jesus.* p. 88.

[230]Ibid.,*Lost Christianities.* p. 78.

[231]Ibid.,*Misquoting Jesus.* p. 89.

[232]Ibid.,*The New Testament: A Historical Introduction to the Early Christian Writings.* p. 12.

[233]Ibid.,*Lost Christianities.* p. 49.

[234] Metzger, Bruce M. *A Textual Commentary on the Greek New*

Testament. Introduction, p. 1.

[235] Funk, Robert W., Roy W. Hoover, and the Jesus Seminar. *The Five Gospels: The Search for the Authentic Words of Jesus.* p. 6.

[236]Ibid., p. 6.

[237]Ehrman, Bart D. *Lost Christianities*and *Misquoting Jesus.*

[238] Metzger, Bruce M. and Ehrman, Bart D. *The Text of the New Testament: Its Transmission, Corruption, and Restoration.* p. 275.

[239]Ehrman, Bart D. *Lost Christianities.* pp. 49, 217, 219–220.

[240]Ibid.,p. 219.

[241] Metzger, Bruce M. and Ehrman, Bart D. *The Text of the New Testament: Its Transmission, Corruption, and Restoration.* p. 265. See also Ehrman, *Orthodox Corruption of Scripture.*

[242]Ehrman, Bart D. 1993. *The Orthodox Corruption of Scripture.* Oxford University Press. p. xii.

[243]Ehrman, Bart D. *Lost Christianities.* p. 220.

[244] Metzger, Bruce M. *A Textual Commentary on the Greek New Testament.* Introduction, p. 3.

[245]Ibid., p. 10.

[246] Metzger, Bruce M. and Ehrman, Bart D. *The Text of the New Testament: Its Transmission, Corruption, and Restoration.* p. 343.

[247] Funk, Robert W., Roy W. Hoover, and the Jesus Seminar. *The Five Gospels: The Search for the Authentic Words of Jesus,* p. 5.

[248] Powell, J. Enoch. 1994.*The Evolution of the Gospel.* YaleUniversity Press. p. xx.

[249]Ibid., p. xxi.

[250]Ehrman, Bart D.*Misquoting Jesus*. pp. 62–69.

[251]Ibid., p. 68.

[252]Ehrman, Bart D. *Lost Christianities*. pp. 9–11, 30, 235–6.

[253]Ibid., p. 235.

[254]Ehrman, Bart D. *Lost Christianities*. p. 3, 235. Also, see Ehrman, Bart D. *The New Testament: A Historical Introduction to the Early Christian Writings*. p. 49.

[255]Ehrman, Bart D. *Lost Christianities*. p. 235.

[256] Stanton, Graham N. p. 19.

[257] Funk, Robert W., Roy W. Hoover, and the Jesus Seminar. *The Five Gospels: The Search for the Authentic Words of Jesus*. p. 20.

[258]Ehrman, Bart D. 2009. *Jesus, Interrupted*. HarperOne. p. 5.

[259]Ehrman, Bart D. *Jesus, Interrupted*. p. 112.

[260]Kee, Howard Clark (Notes and References by). 1993. *The Cambridge Annotated Study Bible, New Revised Standard Version*. Cambridge University Press. Introduction to gospel of "John."

[261] Butler, Trent C. (General Editor). *Holman Bible Dictionary*. Nashville: Holman Bible Publishers. Under "John, the Gospel of."

[262] Easton, M. G., M.A., D.D. *Easton's Bible Dictionary*. Nashville: Thomas Nelson Publishers. Under "John the Apostle."

[263]Goodspeed, Edgar J. 1946. *How to Read the Bible*. The John C. Winston Company. p. 227.

[264]Stanton, Graham N. pp. 134–135.

[265]Ehrman, Bart D. *Lost Christianities*. p. 236.

[266]Ibid., p. 235.

[267] Metzger, Bruce M. *A Textual Commentary on the Greek New Testament*. Introduction, p. 14.

[268]Ibid., p. 11.

[269] Metzger, Bruce M. and Ehrman, Bart D. *The Text of the New Testament: Its Transmission, Corruption, and Restoration*. p. 316.

[270]Ibid., p. 343.

[271]Metzger, Bruce M. 1963. "Explicit References in the Works of Origen to Variant Readings in New Testament Manuscripts," in J. N. Birdsall and R. W. Thomson (ed.), *Biblical And Patristic Studies In Memory Of Robert Pierce Casey*. Herder: Frieburg. pp. 78–79.

[272]Ehrman, Bart D. *Lost Christianities*. p. 217, 221–227.

[273] Metzger, Bruce M. *A Textual Commentary on the Greek New Testament*. p. 388.

[274] Funk, Robert W., Roy W. Hoover, and the Jesus Seminar. *The Five Gospels: The Search for the Authentic Words of Jesus*. p. 10.

[275] Funk, Robert W., Roy W. Hoover, and the Jesus Seminar. *The Five Gospels: The Search for the Authentic Words of Jesus*. p. 21.

[276] Funk, Robert W., Roy W. Hoover, and the Jesus Seminar. *The Five Gospels: The Search for the Authentic Words of Jesus*. p. 22.

[277] Quoted from: Cohen, J.M. and M.J. 1996. *The Penguin Dictionary of Twentieth-Century Quotations*. Penguin Books. p. 273.

[278]Paul's alleged vision (as discussed in #31 and #32 above) is a keystone upon which Trinitarian ideology depends, for if Paul's testimony were discredited, from which other Bible author would Trinitarian ideology take origin? The fact that the three accounts of Paul's vision differ is cause for concern. Could these inconsistencies be the earmarks of falsehood?Furthermore, we shouldn't forget the differences among all four gospels concerning the events following the alleged crucifixion, as described in the chapter, "Divinity of Jesus? The 'Evidence.'"

[279] Quoted from: Lejeune, Anthony. 1998. *The Concise Dictionary of Foreign Quotations*. Stacey London. p. 7.

[280]Ehrman, Bart D. *Lost Christianities*. p. 102.

[281] Funk, Robert W., Roy W. Hoover, and the Jesus Seminar. *The Five Gospels: The Search for the Authentic Words of Jesus*. p. 27.

[282]Cadoux, Cecil John. 1948. *The Life of Jesus*. Middlesex: Penguin Books. p. 16–17.

[283] Funk, Robert Walter. 1996. *Honest to Jesus, Jesus for a New Millennium*. Polebridge Press. pp. 94–95.

[284] This quote is a century old. To the present date, we have discovered 5,700 Greek manuscripts.

[285]Dummelow, Rev. J. R. (editor). 1908. *A Commentary on the Holy Bible*. New York: Macmillan Publishing Co., Inc. Introduction, p. xvi.

[286]Cadoux, Cecil John. p. 16.

[287] Findlay, Rev. Adam Fyfe, M.A., D.D. 1929. *The History of Christianity in the Light of Modern Knowledge*. London: Blackie & Son, Ltd. p. 318.

[288]Ibid., p. 320.

[289]Ehrman, Bart D. *The New Testament: A Historical Introduction to the Early Christian Writings.* p. 57.

[290] For more information, see Stanton, Graham N. 1989. *The Gospels and Jesus.* Oxford University Press. pp. 24–26.

[291] Quoted from: Lejeune, Anthony. 1998. *The Concise Dictionary of Foreign Quotations.* Stacey London. p. 72.

[292]Achtemeier, Paul J. p. 111.

[293]Reumann, John. 1991. *Variety and Unity in New Testament Thought.* Oxford University Press. p. 281.

[294] Stanton, Graham. p. 135.

[295]*New Catholic Encyclopedia.* Vol 2, p. 386.

[296]Ibid., p. 386.

[297]Ibid., p. 386.

[298]Ibid., p. 391.

[299]Ibid., p. 395.

[300]Ibid., p. 395.

[301]Ehrman, Bart D. *Lost Christianities.* p. 54, and *Misquoting Jesus.* p.36.

[302]Ehrman, Bart D. *Lost Christianities.* p. 231.

[303]*New Catholic Encyclopedia.* Vol 2, p. 395.

[304] Chapman, Dom John. 1907. *The Condemnation of Pope Honorius.* London: Catholic Truth Society. p. 25.

[305]Ibid., pp. 114–115.

[306]Ibid., p. 115.

[307]*Encyclopaedia Britannica.* CD-ROM.

[308]*New Catholic Encyclopedia.* Vol 7, pp. 123–125.

[309] Chamberlin, E. R. 1993. *The Bad Popes.* Barnes & Noble,

Inc., p. 43–44. The subquoteis attributed to Liudprand of Cremona, *Liber de Rebus GestisOttonis*, translated by F. A. Wright. London, 1930. Chapter x.

[310]Ibid., p. 70–71.

[311]BaldassareCossa (1360–1419), not to be confused with the twentieth-century Pope John XXIII. In his *History of the Decline and Fall of the Roman Empire,* Gibbon accused the fifteenth-century Pope John XXIII of "piracy, murder, sodomy, rape and incest." He was deposed in 1415 and his title invalidated, so the next Pope John, namely that of the twentieth century, became the true Pope John XXIII in the eyes of the church.

[312] Chamberlin, E. R. p. 158.

[313]*New Catholic Encyclopedia.* Vol 3, p. 365.

[314]*Nostra Aetate.* 28 October 1965. Item #4. Official publication of the Vatican website: www.vatican.va.

[315] Gilbert, Arthur. 1968. *The Vatican Council and The Jews.* New York: The World Publishing Company. p. 7.

[316]*New Catholic Encyclopedia.* Vol 4, p. 486.

[317]Ibid., pp. 485–6.

[318]Ibid., p. 486.

[319] Quoted from: Lejeune, Anthony. 1998. *The Concise Dictionary of Foreign Quotations.* Stacey London. p. 105.

[320]*Guinness Book of Knowledge.* p. 195.

[321]*Strong's Exhaustive Concordance of the Bible.*

[322] Metzger, Bruce M. and Ehrman, Bart D. *The Text of the New Testament: Its Transmission, Corruption, and Restoration.* p. 322.

[323] Metzger, Bruce M. *A Textual Commentary on the Greek New Testament*. p. 103.

[324] Ibid.,p. 103.

[325] Ibid.,pp. 103–4.

[326] The Bible, Revised Standard Version. 1977. New York: American Bible Society. Footnote at end of "Mark."

[327] *The Interpreter's Bible*. p. 915.

[328] Ibid.

[329] Ibid.

[330] Kelly, J. N. D. 1978. *Early Christian Doctrines*. San Francisco: Harper & Brothers Publishers. p. 60.

[331] Arbuthnot, F. F. 1885. *The Construction of the Bible and the Korân*. London: Watts & Co. pp. 8–9.

[332] Goodspeed, Edgar J. pp. 226–7.

[333] Ehrman, Bart D. *The New Testament: A Historical Introduction to the Early Christian Writings*. p. 14.

[334] Ibid.,p. 48.

[335] Dummelow, Rev. J. R. Introduction, p. xvi.